Praise for
Heartwood

"With poetic tenderness, depthful knowledge, and embodied presence, *Heartwood* will guide readers to their inherent belonging, interconnectedness, and relationship with the living earth. In a landscape of forgetting, this book offers a remembrance and a homecoming toward our own nature and interwoven humanity. There is so much to reckon with as we face layers of collapse; *Heartwood* provides a map, a prayer, and a path back toward kinship with trees, with the earth, with life itself."

—Lisa Olivera, author of *Already Enough*
and *When the Ache Remains*

"In this luminous love song to trees, Lindsay Branham transmutes science into poetry, converts the scholarly into the sacred, and engages language to point beyond itself to a place of profound silence our souls yearn for. Through Lindsay's fearless example, our own wounds become portals to a deeper intimacy with all that is. Bold and dignified, intelligent and sensual, this book helped me fall in love with the world again."

—Mirabai Starr, author of *Wild Mercy*
and *Ordinary Mysticism*

"A wonderfully perceptive and generative book, filled with invitations to open our bodies and imaginations to the many gifts offered by trees. A powerful reminder, too, of the healing powers of trees for individuals and communities."

—David George Haskell, biologist and two-time-
Pulitzer-finalist author of *Sounds Wild and Broken*,
The Songs of Trees, and *The Forest Unseen*

"In *Heartwood*, Lindsay has crafted a narrative that paints nature as the center point of our healing. Woven together with a beautiful prosaic touch, she has magically connected the dots between our liberation and the centuries-old knowledge rooted firmly in the mother of our existence: the trees."

—Joél Leon, author of the 2025 Gotham Book Prize–nominated *Everything and Nothing at Once*

"Lindsay's mesmerizing book is both a comfort and a call to action in a time of climate crisis. A map to guide us out of overwhelm and despair, and into a reciprocal relationship with the more-than-human world that is the missing piece in conversations about environmental activism."

—Ruby Warrington, author of *Sober Curious* and *Women Without Kids*

"With reverence and courage, this book draws us back into the circle of life, where trees stand not as resources but as relations. Interweaving the rigor of doctoral research with the depth of personal healing, the author's prose calls us home. With grounded, proven practices, she shows how the wisdom needed to restore balance in our lives and on Earth is already alive in the voices of the natural world."

—Wahinkpe Topa (Four Arrows), author of *Restoring the Kinship Worldview, Sitting Bull's Words: For a World in Crisis, Teaching Truly,* and *Last Song of the Whales*

"In a world full of distraction, cruelty, and pain, many of us are working to engage with the healing wisdom of Earth. With *Heartwood*, Lindsay Branham invites us to remember our deepest ties to the planet we call home, bringing us back to our bodies, asking us to recall our roots and the trees who long to guide us. Her instruction is both personal and researched, backed by scientific exploration and spiritual connection that is earthbound, practical, and holistic. Even in our most existential confusion, Branham offers reassurance."

—Jacqueline Suskin, author of *The Verse for Now*, *A Year in Practice*, *Every Day Is a Poem*, and *Help in the Dark Season*

"I have personally witnessed Lindsay Branham's loving kindness and vision for a transformed world. I very much believe that how you do anything is how you do everything, and I have no doubt that *Heartwood* is a gift to us all to widen our hearts with more love for this suffering world."

—Richard Rohr, *New York Times* bestselling author of *The Universal Christ* and *The Tears of Things*

"*Heartwood* is a radiant and deeply urgent book. Lindsay Branham reminds us that healing—of our bodies, our spirits, and our planet—is not found in separation but in relationship. Through sharing her personal story and combining it with her intellectual rigor, she guides us to see how trees can be not only our kin but also our guides back to belonging. For those ready to divorce themselves from the extractive, patriarchal, and capitalistic ways of living that have severed us from ourselves and Mother Nature—this book is the map for a new way forward."

—Anna Malaika Tubbs, *New York Times* bestselling author of *The Three Mothers* and *Erased: What American Patriarchy Has Hidden from Us*

"As the world literally and figuratively burns, Branham isn't panicked or frozen. She is giving us a vibrant, vision-changing way to survive what's coming. And it requires a rethinking of everything. She doesn't come with a sword but a gentle invitation to learn to hear the wisdom of trees. If we follow her lead, we just might make it."

—Jedidiah Jenkins, *New York Times* bestselling author of *Like Streams to the Ocean*, *To Shake the Sleeping Self*, and *Mother, Nature*

HEART WOOD

The Wisdom and Healing Kinship of Trees

LINDSAY BRANHAM

New York Boston

The information, advice, and practices herein are not intended to replace the services of trained health professionals, or be a substitute for medical advice. You are advised to consult with your health care professional with regard to matters relating to your health, and in particular regarding matters that may require diagnosis or medical attention.

Copyright © 2026 by Lindsay Branham

Cover design by Jim Datz. Cover image by Eugène Stanislas Bléry ("The Branches of an Oak Tree," ca. 1837) courtesy of the Metropolitan Museum of Art / Met Collection.
Cover copyright © 2026 by Hachette Book Group, Inc.

Hachette Book Group supports the right to free expression and the value of copyright. The purpose of copyright is to encourage writers and artists to produce the creative works that enrich our culture.

The scanning, uploading, and distribution of this book without permission is a theft of the author's intellectual property. If you would like permission to use material from the book (other than for review purposes), please contact permissions@hbgusa.com. Thank you for your support of the author's rights.

Balance
Hachette Book Group
1290 Avenue of the Americas
New York, NY 10104
GCP-Balance.com
@GCPBalance

First Edition: March 2026

Balance is an imprint of Grand Central Publishing. The Balance name and logo are registered trademarks of Hachette Book Group, Inc.

The publisher is not responsible for websites (or their content) that are not owned by the publisher.

The Hachette Speakers Bureau provides a wide range of authors for speaking events. To find out more, go to hachettespeakersbureau.com or email HachetteSpeakers@hbgusa.com.

Balance books may be purchased in bulk for business, educational, or promotional use. For information, please contact your local bookseller or the Hachette Book Group Special Markets Department at special.markets@hbgusa.com.

"Remember." Copyright © 1983 by Joy Harjo from *She Had Some Horses* by Joy Harjo. Used by permission of W. W. Norton & Company, Inc.

"The Facts of Life" from *Sorry for Your Troubles* by Pádraig Ó Tuama is © 2018 by Pádraig Ó Tuama. Published by Canterbury Press. Used with permission of the poet.

Alexis Pauline Gumbs, "Letting Go," in *Dub: Finding Ceremony*, pp. 246–252. Copyright © 2020, Duke University Press. All rights reserved. Republished by permission of the copyright holder and the Publisher. www.dukeupress.edu.

To Watch the Earth Die," from *The Verse for Now* by Jacqueline Suskin. Flower Press. Used with permission from the poet.

Print book interior design by Marie Mundaca

Library of Congress Cataloging-in-Publication Data has been applied for.

ISBNs: 9781538778562 (trade paperback), 9781538778579 (ebook)

Printed in the United States of America

LSC-C

Printing 1, 2025

For the trees

Every creature is a glittering, glistening mirror of Divinity.
—Hildegard von Bingen

Contents

Preface   *xv*
Introduction   *xvii*

I: THE SENSORY LIFE OF THE BODY

1. The Language of Trees   3
2. The Body Is a Place   19
3. Easing Into Consent   40

II: NEARNESS: REVERIES OF EROS

4. Erotic Ecology   59
5. Kinship: Secure Attachment to the Earth   81
6. Heart to Heartwood: Listening to the Soul of the Earth   101
7. Composting Grief   117

III: EMBODIED COSMOLOGY

8. Spirals of Belonging   139
9. Sacred Reciprocity   159
10. Cosmic Entanglement   177

IV: FERAL PRAYERS FOR LIBERATION

11. Spirit, Magic, and Ceremony   197

12. Intersectional Wild Weave of Justice   225

13. Queer Ecology and Making Vows   246

Conclusion: Death Doula to a Dying World   260

Epilogue   277

Acknowledgments   279

Notes   281

Index   295

List of Exercises

Noticing Sensation	15
Relationship with a Tree	16
Body Scan	37
Knowing Place	38
Inner Yes, Inner No	53
Seeking Permission	54
Welcoming Back Embodiment	77
Touching the Tree	79
Heartbeat Awareness	98
Family System of the Earth	99
Mindful Awareness to Sound	114
Listening to a Tree's Biophonies	115
Rhythmic Tapping	134
A Letter to Grief	135
Inner Belonging Through Toning	156
Kinship Origin Stories	157
Gratitude for Our Embodied Life	173
Offering the Gift	175
Earth to Sun Breath	192
Entanglement with the Living World	193
Trusting the Body	219
Ceremony Walk	221
Honoring Our Ancestors	242
What Does the Tree Need?	243
In Devotion to the Body	256
Taking a Vow	258
Practicing Equanimity	273
Closing Ceremony	274

Preface

There are mysteries and there are miracles. This was both.

In the mesmeric dawn of the Roaring Fork Valley, I awoke cradled by a familiar foe: physical pain. The last few years had been shot through with rivers of undiagnosable illness. I felt pinioned.

The urge to crawl beyond my form sent me walking into the forest. I always received far more than I sought from nature. The thigh-high August wildflowers erupted on the valley floor. The red mountains stretched languidly, their rocky spines a high alpine relevé.

I pushed through a riot of purple thistle and blue aster, the hues puncturing the golden ferns with oracular shine. The air was still—calm enough to hold a single candle flame alight.

I could go no farther; something primordial paused me in place.

The Aspen trees were all over me. I inhaled quick and deep, my fingers instinctively curling into little fists. Bracing against sensation was a fragile barrier to a world of contact.

The knots on their white bark stretched into wide, blinking eyes. They beheld me, diffusing the borders of bodily form.

In their presence, my discomfort waned. A world of care was everywhere I looked.

What is it to be relative to a tree? What is it to relate across skin and bark, feet and soil, breath and wind?

We're here, the trees seemed to say.

Listen, they cooed.

And then—

The wind came first, starting at my feet, kicking those golden ferns into a whip. It grew stronger—full as a harvest moon—a tide lifting us together in its froth, waxing until the tops of all the Aspens shivered at once. A geyser of ace-shaped leaves revolved like whirling mirrors, ecstatic in rhapsody. Their voice was the most beautiful sound I had ever heard.

The branches exhaled, blushing into an infinity loop. As the leaves spun out to emerge into whatever they would become, one gleamed in bodily ecstasy and whizzed off. As it floated through the air, I felt my own consciousness inside it. The next thing I knew, I could feel what it was like to *be* a tree, rooted in the Earth, surrounded by my kin, woven with communion.

Sturdy, sensual, symbiotic.

I'd forgotten—the felt sense of being a tree.

I'd forgotten—there is a language we both can speak.

I'd forgotten—trees are a refuge of "endless forms most beautiful."[1]

Introduction

Kinship with the Earth is our birthright. But we have forgotten who we are. We are not only of the Earth, we *are* the Earth. Our health, wellness, and continuity as a planetary ecosystem hinge on our entanglement with each other. Yet we are hurtling through a human-made climate crisis—we are not taking very good care of our kin.

This book is a journey into the idea that our relationship with trees could change the trajectory of climate collapse. The forest might just be the revelation.

Out of the intracellularly connected matrix of forested life, an invitation rises: *return home*. Return home to the body—return home to the body of the Earth.

Our sentinel elders can carry us through this struggle. Our generous teachers, who defy domination, upend individualism, and subvert scarcity, are waiting to help us remember—with wisdom and love—our connection to everything. Let us press our faces to the soil and listen:

What if we need each other to heal?
What if healing is a collective, embodied ecological process?
What if we are kin?

The steadfast companions capable of deliverance, of repairing our sacred relationship with the Earth, are speaking. We can learn to hear them. We can learn to see them, perhaps for the very first time. If we wake up, we will realize they've always been here. Our most ancient forms of life.

They are miracles on all sides.

They are the *trees*.

In some beautiful accident in the midst of my chronic illness, I stumbled upon a profound relationship with trees, which began in the Roaring Fork Valley of Colorado. Their luminous care and astonishing powers of healing are shared here as best as I could bring them into being from our remarkable conversations. They are the coauthors of *Heartwood*.

I started and finished this book during active wildfires. The twin nature of losing what we love and loving what can still live has been its own heat to share these words with you now. Recent wildfires in Western Colorado and Los Angeles swept through the lands I love. Policies under the new presidential administration threaten wild places and long federally protected lands with logging, mining, and oil and gas exploration. Climate science is being erased. National parks are under attack. Now is the time of the trees.

Five years ago, at the onset of an unexplainable chronic illness, while smoke strangled the sky and pain suffocated my body, I sensed an entanglement between myself and the Earth. Was I not deeply interwoven with every single molecule, cell, seed, and speck of soil? I now see that we will get through this together, or not at all. For imbalance is rippling beyond the human. For what happens to nature also happens to us.

Our one Earth is experiencing rampant ecological destruction. Our billions of living beings are facing unprecedented instances of chronic illness. This looks like dying coral reefs and soaring rates of heart disease, species extinction and widespread autoimmune illness, melting glaciers and rising depression, surging temperatures and crippling anxiety, structural racism and acidifying oceans, flash floods and dollars for bombs. Climate change is deeply entangled with health disparities, sociopolitical inequalities, economic gaps, and threats to all aspects of human well-being. These symptoms of the polycrisis point to a fundamental disconnection between humans and the Earth. I amplify Indigenous scholars and peoples who have long said that, in contrast, *right* relationship with nature is how we will heal both ourselves and the planet. Everything is connected.

Nature's remedy, balm, and healing elixir for the disconnection crisis is all around us. The wound is our separation from the Earth. The medicine is our homecoming.

Trees can walk us back into the wide field of loving belonging with the living world. With that return will come more life, because *aliveness* is the code of life within all that is living.

Trees are the oldest living organisms on Earth and outnumber humans 422 to one.[1] They are our family and our kin. They keep our atmosphere livable and our air breathable. They nourish our bodies, imbuing us with phytoncides that bolster our immune, hormonal, circulatory, and nervous systems. They soothe our blood pressure, ease our anxiety, and ground us in an ancient and staggeringly beautiful existence.

Trees stand as sovereign and grand individuals, yet through their communal entanglement in forests, they reassure our bodies that we are not alone. Trees are beings that catalyze and regulate connections to myriad other forms of life. They teach us how to be good neighbors and are physical invitations to come home. Even a tree's death does not end the networked nature of the forest, writes David Haskell in *The Songs of Trees*.[2] The knowledge carried in light and leaves dwells embedded in relationships. Trees embody a form of mutual aid in unending ecological creativity. Trees, indeed, teach us how to be both gracefully unique as well as essential participants in a community of life. They invite us into infinite sensuous relations with the living world. The false binary between individual and community dissolves in the forest. There is no need to assert one's exceptionalism because the *forest* is the miracle. How much would change if we could live in such continuous communal care like they do?

But now, even trees are at risk of extinction. Yes, trees are under threat of elimination. In the first Global Tree Assessment by the IUCN Red List, it was found that more than one-third of all tree species worldwide face extinction.[3] Another study in *Nature* warns that there has been a substantial underestimation of the extinction risk for trees.[4] And yet again, a recent study foretells that for the first time, due to climate change, forests are losing their ability to store carbon, and by the year 2070, instead of being carbon sinks, forests will instead become carbon producers.[5]

Without trees, there would be a significant reduction in oxygen and an increase in carbon dioxide in our atmosphere. We would not be able to breathe. Without trees, soil erosion would increase. We would not be able to eat. Without trees, precipitation patterns and water availability would be impacted. We would not be able to drink. Without trees, global temperatures would rise. We would not be able to survive.

Everything is connected. A tree's life is tied to our life. At every moment of the day, our tree kin are part of our lungs, just as forests are the lungs of the Earth. If all life is entangled in a kin-centric web, as Indigenous peoples teach, then taking care of this web of life is, in essence, how we take good care of ourselves. Our health is bound together.

In my PhD research, I discovered that a core reason why people might care about nature but do not act to protect the Earth is because they do not feel close to the living world. As an environmental psychologist, I have experienced how people can reconnect with the Earth through mind, body, and spirit. As an eco-doula, I have heard from countless individuals, in retreats and workshops across the world, that remembering their kinship with nature has transformed them. That this tether is a live wire of loving return into a way of being that enables fuller participation, love, pleasure, and kindness. As a scientist, I understand that individual actions alone will not subvert the damage of fossil fuels on the planet. I know that the systems of big banks that finance fossil fuel projects—those that profit from extraction and the relentless drive for imperial growth—are responsible for environmental destruction. Our recycling habits will not save the blue whale. However, my research underscores what Indigenous peoples have long taught and know: Kinship with the Earth is a powerful wellspring to sustain our compassionate action. An intimate, loving, embodied bond with nature is the very origin source for our protest, action, creativity, art, and endless forms of care on their behalf.

I carried the seed of this bond in me—we all do—but I did not awaken to an intimate eco-love affair with trees until sickness brought me to their feet. Our love has deeply held me since, through pain and grief, both my own and that for our wider ecological family. The relationship they offer is Earthy and as fertile and fecund as soil, yes, but is also emotional, embodied, and erotic. It is a relationship so deep, vast, and weird that it can reorient our capacity to dream together for new worlds, to meet the crisis of the moment we are in with expansive compassion and liberatory creativity. Trees embody the mystery. And it is mystery and moral imagination, more than rationality, that can help us move beyond the tired and violent patterns that have caused climate collapse to begin with.

I named this book *Heartwood* because the word is both structural, referring to the densest, innermost part of a tree, as well as relational, reminding us that our deepest connections are from the heart. In the Majjhima Nikāya of the Pali Canon, the Buddha is cited as saying that the heartwood, or the point of the spiritual life, is the "unshakable freedom of the heart." The heartwood points us to what is most precious: a return to sacred relationship with the Earth. In this kinship is a freedom that is for us and *for all*.

In times as dire as these, we need to lean on the sturdiness of our collective heartwood. And although the trees' heartwood has ceased to conduct water and nutrients, and the cells in it are no longer living, it is still vital to support their lives. The layer just outside of it continues to grow new cells, and the bark that protects it all, lets us know that the tree we can see with our eyes or touch with our hands is only a small part of what a tree is, of what a tree is connected to. The trees' heartwood exemplifies the blurriness between life and death. What is discarded is surprisingly what holds life together.

Heartwood traces my experience of how illness brought me into kinship with the trees and how this bond can be healing for ourselves and our planet. This book is filled with stories, conversations with the land from the Roaring Fork Valley in Colorado. We begin in part I, "The Sensory Life of the Body," where we will explore the sensuous language we can speak with the Earth. Our body is the gateway to presence. Here, we will practice our body's eighth sense, interoception; learn to talk to the trees, move at the pace of place; and inhabit the landscape of our bodies. In part II, "Nearness: Reveries of Eros," we will explore the intimate closeness of a relationship with trees and the good things that flow from it, like pleasure, healed attachment injuries, and unitive love. We widen in part III, "Embodied Cosmology," into sacred reciprocity and how we can truly belong to one another. And finally, in part IV, "Feral Prayers for Liberation," we explore the liminal and the magical, rooting this relationship with trees in intersectional justice and closing with an invitation to become death doulas for a dying world. Embodiment practices to develop interoceptive awareness, tree prompts to open to kinship with the forest, and reflection questions after each chapter will guide you to experience a sensory, intimate relationship with trees for yourself, unlearn separation from nature, and embark on your own healing pilgrimage. You are invited to become phenomenologically rerooted and rewilded. To practice the ecological creativity of belonging like a forest. To leaf, branch, and widen.

I am often asked if I have hope for the Earth. I will answer that question in the words of the Lady of Deep Ecology, Joanna Macy: "Active Hope is waking up to the beauty of life on whose behalf we can act. We belong to this world."[6] Do I experience beauty, and daily? Immensely so.

Perhaps, then, we need not hope. We need courage. We need intimacy with the Earth. We need appreciation for the myriad ways simply being a breathing, living being is an act of enormous miracle. From *this* place, active hope, right action in motion, will come.

After working on human and environmental crises for twenty years—mostly in the Democratic Republic of Congo, Central African Republic, South Sudan, India, and Myanmar—I still believe in change. And it is the everyday expressions of generosity that fill me with the belief, day in and day out, that our hearts are mostly good, and will be so if given the chance. We are in this for the long haul. And we shall keep on.

A few notes on language. The Earth is polymorphous, and as Potawatomi botanist Robin Wall Kimmerer writes, "There is no it for nature." She continues: "Living beings are referred to as subjects, never as objects."[7] Following her lead, in this book, I do not refer to the Earth with gendered pronouns or the disembodied *it*. Such "grammars of animacy" impact our perceptions, beliefs, and actions.[8] I have also avoided the affectionate term *Mother Earth* to be more inclusive, following a queer, feminist science framing. Instead, I use the pronouns they/them for the Earth and their creatures. I enjoy how this signals a multiplicitousness that upends the notion of the individual. I also capitalize *Earth* and the proper names of trees to practice the dignity of honoring their personhood.

The term *Indigenous* can be problematic in that it appears to generalize distinct populations whose experiences under imperialism have been vastly different. In line with a suggestion from scholar and researcher Linda Tuhiwai Smith, I have elected to use the phrase *Indigenous peoples* in this book to recognize the collective voices of colonized peoples and acknowledge that the world's Indigenous populations belong to a network of peoples.[9]

Last, when I use the word *healing*, I do not mean an end point or the cessation of all painful sensation. Instead, trees have shown me how healing is more of a spiralic experience than a linear compass. Forests have also taught me that healing is dependent on every other creature's wellness, too. To be close to trees is to heal because it helps me to fully live. Is that not what healing is? To have access to more life in our lives?

Upending the trope of the hero's journey, *Heartwood* is instead a rhizomatic refiguring of healing as a process of collective liberation, of healing as a forest. In so doing, healing becomes possible for all. Can healing be more about our kinship than an individual destination? Can healing be too thin a word to describe the sheer magnanimity of life compounding on life?

Throughout our journey to remembering what is held in root and soil, we will play with weirding and queering our notions of time, body, nature, and even knowledge itself out of the binaries and dualities that reproduce damaging ideological frameworks that oppress, extract, and harm bodies. We will plant our sacred relationships with trees into justice for the entire collective, stirring the cauldrons of an equanimous hope that transcends fears for our future peril. A radical revisioning of what is possible is very much at the heart of heartwood.

Although our kinship to trees offers tender emotional, psychological, and spiritual refuge, a relationship with them will not eradicate all suffering. I still live with symptoms. However, they are far reduced and bother me less. When I remember myself as a tree and touch the parts of me that have died or are dying, I know that they are forming my heartwood. I see how what hurts is essential compost for what else is on its way.

My hope for you, dear reader, is that you borrow the qualities of trees that can help you to be kinder, more loving, and more liberated. May you learn to lean on the dense inner column within you that helps a tree not bend or break. May you trust that the compounds of your tender places are also exactly what is needed to preserve your entire being. And may you, like trees, surrender to the alchemy of turning your own sapwood into heartwood to focus your resources, your gifts, and your magic into blessings for the Earth.

May you develop kinship with trees, heart to heartwood.

I was on my daily meandering walk through the forest when the movement of the wind through the Pine needles caught my attention. But it wasn't wind, and it was also too late. A four-hundred-pound bear waddled over the rocks in front of me. I froze. The bear descended into a bush, turned around, and locked eyes with me. Was I supposed to look big? Yell? Wave my arms and become a fool?

The bear was less than ten feet from where I stood. Instinct took over—not logic—and I broke into a run for my life.

As I ran, I listened for the bear through wheezing belly breaths. I remembered that you are not supposed to run from a bear when I was already running. My heart beat so loudly I couldn't hear beyond it. The explosion of cortisol shook my limbs, wobbly with each step on the winding path. Finally, a sudden curve spit me into a wide meadow absolutely crammed with daisies. I didn't hear any grunts, growls, or pounding of the dirt. Instead, the sound of the river flooded my body, a welcomed sign that marked the end of the trail. I was safe.

In the Rocky Mountains of Colorado, there are between eight and twelve thousand black bears. Despite their name, their fur can range from cinnamon to brown and even blond. They have a sense of smell seven times more acute than a bloodhound and live up to twenty-five years. Black bears maintain the balance of plant and animal populations, aiding in forest regeneration. They are considered an indicator species, meaning that their presence and health reflect the overall condition of the ecosystem. To see a healthy bear is to know that things are well.

The next morning, I sat down to meditate. When I closed my eyes, the bear was there. But this time, the bear's eyes, so close together on their big bushy face, looked different. Softer. More vulnerable. I wondered, *What did they see?* Instead of reading threat in the bear's face, I saw fear. Who was the real predator now?

Humans are the Earth's apex predators, and everything wild is at risk. But it does not have to be this way. The forest can help us remember a time when humans knew how to be in right relationship with the Earth. The trees can help us make that time today.

In climate collapse and in chronic illness, we must rediscover the sources of resilience that are standing all around us. The unfurling processual life of a tree can remind us how to be sturdy and good neighbors through mutual aid and collective care. The wild entanglement of a forest can invite us to offer our gifts back to the Earth with joy.

As the Earth bends under the weight of change, it is not too late to speak the language of the trees. It is not too late to hear their wisdom about how to coexist in mutual dignity. This mode of being is dripping from their leaves and bursting through their branches.

Now is the time of the trees. In their living sanctuary, may we find the eyes of the bears and earn their trust once again.

I
The Sensory Life of the Body

I

The Language of Trees

To be native to a place we must learn to speak its language.

—Robin Wall Kimmerer

I was lying on a tray about to be fed into an MRI scanner. I was alone in this tube, in a white room with a large screen of projected nature scenes on loop. I felt like bacteria in a dish of agar. No rotating nature photography could comfort me out of this mechanical world. I giggled a little bit, which shook the cradle I was in.

"Don't move your head," the attendant had said before escaping the radiation hot zone. The machine started to vibrate deafeningly with a pulsing, smacking sound. *This can't be right*, I thought. I moved my head. Oops. I could still make out the attendants through my peripheral vision, little beetles behind a glass wall. But my body was on a platter, sliding into the rotating circle like a fish. The attendant's voice grew louder, coming through the speakers.

"Hold still. Hold your breath."

How many other people were on a scanner somewhere at that very moment, waiting for information that could change their lives? I envisioned them—young and old—a sprawling net of animal life. As I lay there, contemplating their fates, I realized how much like a spider I felt—I was caught, suspended by threads I could not find, each tendril spun around my body forming a sarcophagus of liquid protein. A silken tomb. I vibrated in this shared net of vulnerability. The imagined maze hummed all around me. But arachnids have curious relationships with their webs.

Spiders possess what's called extended cognition. Their webs are not merely structures they build as homes, but extensions of their very bodies, woven from strands of their intelligence.[1] Their webs are their consciousness, their bodies repeating in patterns of silken threads, sometimes too thin and delicate to see. Spiders show us that intelligence is not centralized, but rather is extended beyond the body and aspects of the world. If spiders can manifest their cognition through such labyrinthine, embodied networks, might we, too, be bound together in ways we have yet to fully comprehend?

I envisioned myself spinning a silken web of my own, this time instead of to trap me, to free me. I felt it wrap around me in a cocoon, lift me from the room, the hospital, the city, arching across the sky in a kaleidoscope of colors. Even in pain, I sensed my animacy, and my body, couldn't be confined to the limits of my skin. Was "I" an imagined geodesic dome of continuous sentience? The raucous banging jolted me back into the tube. I was just a human. And I was scared.

A 3-tesla MRI machine generates a magnetic field roughly sixty thousand times more powerful than the Earth's. But I tried to forget about all that. I recalled that summer day in the Aspen grove. Ever since I'd gotten sick, *trees* had come into my life. Maybe—well, certainly—they were always there. But I was starting to see them. And I was starting to hear them.

What are trees? Trees offer shelter and care. Through a seamless exchange of breath, trees sustain our lives—what we inhale from them becomes the breath they use to renew us in turn. Trees share nutrients, including carbon and other sugars; they warn one another of danger; and they live in symbiosis with the seasonal cycles. Trees are intelligent, and they never forget their collective responsibility to keep the forest alive.

Trees are also pure *beingness*. Yes, they are a shape and form, but they are more than that. A tree is a candle flame. A ribbon. A tree is an album. Like an arrangement, trees are a cosmos and a bouquet in their ever-unfurling, processual lives. Trees are an idea unto themselves, offering blueprints of how to coexist with the entire living world. Trees are libraries, coffins, secrets, gifts, letters, tears, and gestures. If poetry is a refraction of the divine put into sensuous symbols, then trees are pure poetry.

I felt the faces of the Aspen, the Cottonwood, and the Redwood take shape in me. These were companions, not just dendrological wonders. And while I'd always appreciated nature, this was otherwise. As if the trees were reaching to speak to me, I turned my head just slightly in that MRI scanner. Could I hear them even from here?

My reverie was pierced by the harsh command of the operator's voice crackling through the MRI intercom. "Hold still. Hold your breath."

Was I forgetting my humanness to cope with my chronic health issues? Or was I remembering my place in the biodiversity, liveliness, and presence of the forest?

I was in that scanner because my body was in pain. A lot of it. Unrelenting migraine headaches; internal body tremors; intermittent heat on one side of my face; cognitive decline; eye, neck, and shooting nerve pain; severe fatigue; widespread inflammation; and skin rashes. My body felt awful to be inside of.

The banging stopped, and the MRI powered down. I was thrust back into the sterile room. Neon green trees emblazoned the TV screen. They looked sad and radioactive. We were both disfigured by forces beyond our power.

"Did I do it right?" I asked the attendant.

"Your doctor will contact you with the results. It should take three to seven business days," he said flatly.

I knew he couldn't give anything away, but I searched his face for clues. A little crease in the corner of his left eye. A bit of a frown, or was that a smile? Three to seven business days. As if illness adheres to the work week.

"Thank you," I said as I shimmied off the tray, making a point to make eye contact. I wanted to remember I wasn't just a specimen in a lab. I still had life in me.

Aliveness is a language. It's as old as all biological life. It's as ancient as our ever-expanding universe. It is the first word and will be the last one. It's a vocabulary of sensation beyond the lines that make the written word. Language is a world.

The Beech tree was originally called Boc by the Anglo-Saxons who migrated to modern-day England. *Boc* later became the present-day word for book. Before the printing press, people tore thin slices off the Beech tree and wrote on them, creating the very first "books." Trees gave humans a method to share our written language with each other. But what is *their* language?

Scientists are only just beginning to learn the language of trees. According to a recent study, trees emit ultrasonic airborne frequencies when they are stressed.[2] Trees also communicate through the air. They express themselves outwardly by releasing pheromones and detect the world inwardly through their leaves—a bona fide sense of smell. Even though we don't know exactly what their pheromones mean or how they communicate within their bodies, we do know they can feel what's going on around them and experience something analogous to pain. When a tree is cut, they send electrical signals like wounded human tissue does.

In a drought, scientists can detect the erratic sounds of trees. These unique vibrations are made by bubbles forming inside the drought-stressed trees.[3] And there's more. A recent study from the University of Utah published in the *New Phytologist* found that under heat stress, trembling Aspen trees can succumb to a process that even mimics a *heart attack*. The trees' inner hydraulic system falters as they yank and yank at dry soil. A slow embolism unfolds. Drought is causing these heart attacks in Aspen trees as young as three years old.[4] If we could hear their language, I think it might sound like screaming.

I thought of myself in that MRI scanner. The glowing ghosts of trees on the screen had emitted a sound. I tried to recall it. A high hum of cackling pixels. I didn't have to ask what they were saying. I already knew. Perhaps my body, and the trees, were protesting pain in our own way. Suddenly, I didn't feel so alone.

The language of trees begins with a sound but grows into a song. There is not one voice, but a symphony. Trees are a collective, and so to hear them, we have to be able to listen beyond the individual; we have to stretch toward the chorus instead of a singular note. In the forest, the trees speak of each other. No tree exists without their kin close by.

Western science used to argue that trees were competitors, in line with the Darwinian idea of survival of the fittest. But in recent decades, through the work of forest scientist Suzanne Simard and other researchers, they have found that trees are not rivals; they are in constant collaboration.[5] Their language is community. They seem to know that the entire life of the forest rests on the flourishing of each individual working in tandem with one another. This is not an abstracted intuition; it occurs by a precise accounting and redistribution of nutrients. Trees never forget their collective responsibility to each other.

How do they speak to one another? How do they communicate their care? How do they hear? Through tree language.

Perhaps our human yearning for connection is answered in their vocabulary. There's a fear, a promise, that somehow, we should be able to hear the trees. That we are missing a great song we used to know how to sing.

The author Paul Kingsnorth writes, "I wanted to be a tree, but I am not a tree. I wanted to sing to the forest, but no one ever taught me the words."[6] I, certainly, felt that same ache. I imagine many of us do. But trees *are* speaking. They are teaching us the words. To learn the language of trees, we must pay attention, from the ground of our shared soil. We must forget the written word. We must listen from the landscape of our bodies.

When I was very sick, I first started to learn the language of trees in the Rockies. A family of Aspens taught me by drawing me close.

The Rocky Mountains were formed by a series of orogenies, mountain-building events, that occurred 55 to 80 million years ago. Where there were once glaciers during the last ice age, now there are U-shaped valleys, carved out as the ice slowly advanced. This dramatic and rugged landscape was made by shifting tectonic plates, ice creep, and surge movement.

In this valley, the shimmering Maroon Creek canyon narrowed, leading toward a soaring cathedral of stone and ice, a 14,025-foot colossus that ascended with ease. This mountain kept watch over river, forest, people.

I had passed so many trees during my unhurried winter walks. It was slow going. But when I saw these three Aspens, perched on a slight bend overlooking Maroon Creek, I surrendered to the rhythm of the land. And stopped at their hearth.

The only sound was the river's defiant roar below them, refusing to freeze even in the heart of winter. A baby Aspen was to my right, hip-height; two adults faced me. The larger of the three seemed like the elder. Perhaps I was among three generations. Was I the fourth?

At that time, I'd spent about a year in what felt like a Tibetan bardo, a liminal state between birth, death, and rebirth. My chronic health journey was like living at the bottom of a well. I felt thrust into an underworld, a tangle of darkness and dampness where I choked on raw bits of matter and clawed for the sun. I could not break through back to the surface, no matter how hard I tried. So many seconds were excruciating. I felt I'd been consumed by sickness. Eaten by the guts of it. Relief from the torrent was always fleeting, and soon, the next wave would come. The sheer torque of pain and the accompanying fear and sorrow were unbearable at times. How would I survive this?

I smelled Pine, ice, and sun. My hands wrapped around the baby Aspen's branches, holding their twisted little hand. I rubbed the grains of white powder from their skin between my fingers. What were they saying? What could I hear? It was silent; I did not hear any words, except my own internal dialogue, on loop.

But in my own body, I felt a sensuous language. The sense of the tree seemed to fall from their hands into me. I felt a swelling vitality, such a contrast to my withering form. Our hand-to-hand contact held words. I could hear them. I could feel them.

Language is more than words, I thought. *It's embodied listening.*

I touched my face with that white powder, taking them onto my body, borrowing some of their ardor. A language of intrinsic homecoming and unwavering care floated into my body. Was I projecting qualities onto them or hearing them? It felt as if the knowing came from both beyond me and within me at once. *How generous*, I thought. *I can hear the trees.*

This family of Aspen trees reminded me of my first language. A language of the senses. This language is beyond words but not without them. This language makes sense of experience through sensations as they arise one by one. Joy Harjo, the first Indigenous US poet laureate, writes, "The land is the first thing we ever knew. It is the first language we learned."[7] I'd forgotten how to speak it in the disconnection of living in the overculture, a term coined by author Clarissa Pinkola Estés to describe the Western norms of capitalism, patriarchy, and imperialism. How hungry I felt for a different way of speaking, communicating, and knowing. How rapturous I felt for this sensory aliveness.

The phenomenal world offers us unending sensory contact. Moment to moment, we can hear the natural world through our sensing bodies. The Earth speaks through sensation. We "hear" this language in our inner soma. Buzzing, tingling, warmth, coolness, heaviness, lightness, zinging, cramping, tightness, butterflies, the beat of the heart, the wave of the breath—this sensational call and response is always occurring. Place your hand on a tree. Feel what's there. We do not speak the world, we feel it. And in that sensory interplay, a language is born.

Since we have two homes in this life—our physical body and the body of the Earth—and each only exists in relationship with the other, our mother tongue reflects this connection. This is an instinctual impulse, to experience the world through the sensing body. Our form is the linguistic portal to beyond-human kinship. Can we relearn the language of the land? A language that reflects our myriad web of relations?

When my mother was pregnant with me, she often walked along Maroon Creek in the Roaring Fork Valley. I like to imagine she passed by the particular Aspen family I met that day and who has been kin to me ever since. The science of epigenetics shows us that the environment a child experiences in utero, as well as the mother's own genetics, sheds important light on inadequacies of care and resulting trauma and harm.[8] Social conditions produce not only distinct meanings of health, risk, and disease, but also structure the very conditions of life.[9] If "embodied harm" encapsulates how environmental factors can cause changes in one's genes that create future risk, my experience points to embodied connection. I like to think I was better able to recognize my Aspen family because this was the ecological environment where my mother grew me.

The Aspens, and this particular valley, are quite literally in my bones. The language of trees is likewise intergenerational too.

Aspen trees taught me their language. Aspens in North America (*Populus tremuloides*) are known as trembling Aspens due to their shaking and quaking leaves. Their vibrating hands tell stories. They are graceful, white deciduous beings native to the western United States, Canada, and Mexico, and they live an average of 150 years. Their shape speaks in riddles. Aspens are generally found at higher elevations of five thousand to twelve thousand feet, and unlike most trees, they grow year-round. Their outer bark contains a thin green photosynthetic layer that allows the tree to make sugars and keep growing, even when other trees are dormant. Their life cycle communicates creative care.

When standing in an Aspen forest, it's clear to me that these trees each have a face. The poplar twiggall fly creates smooth, knot-like galls on the twigs of Aspens, which continue to expand for years, stretching into what look like eyes. Their faces are the dwelling place of their body's language.

By their nature, Aspens are not solitary. An Aspen forest lives and dies as one, and each tree is genetically identical; they very literally embody community.[10] In fact, Aspen trees only live between five and fifteen years when outside of their native habitat, severed from their community. Their world is their roots, soil, and the symbiotic organisms that are their family. Their lifespan and health are totally dependent on their connectedness to each other. Their entanglement speaks a language of exquisite belonging. Perhaps I was drawn to them because I ached to belong, too. Perhaps Aspens could teach me how.

There's no language like the sound of the quivering Aspen. It's like a hush from the hearth of the Earth. A soothing, familiar lull, for safety, sleep, surrender. The sound of the river and the sound of the Aspen's shuddering leaves layer into each other—every note deeper on an ascending spiral—a sound shot clear through the universe. I let myself go on this quest—where I become tree, then water, then tree, until there is no distinct difference anymore. The sound of the Aspen tree is unlike any other.

To speak the language of trees, our first language of the land, we begin in the body. In the middle of my health catastrophe, I set out to study the relationship between humans and the Earth in my PhD research. The experience with the Aspen family had opened a great well of questions in me. What had happened that day? What else was possible?

In my doctoral research, I found that interoceptive awareness, also called our "eighth sense," is our key to speaking the language of trees. Interoception is our body's inner radar and denotes how closely we can feel our inner bodily signals, like heart rate, respiration, hunger, fullness, temperature, and pain.[11] In my research, I discovered that interoception is also our doorway to the language of trees.

It works like this. Scientists theorize that interoceptive awareness, or body awareness, is essential to emotional regulation, and in my research, I found that it is also the foundation for creating a kinship with the Earth.[12] If we can accurately sense inwardly, we can connect outwardly. Through a series of studies, I pioneered the discovery that interoception is our doorway into animacy and kinship with the living world. Sensing and feeling, not cognition or information. If we can learn the language of the senses, my research suggests, we can speak the language of nature. We can speak *with nature*.

Every time our heart beats, it sends a signal to our brain. Our body responds, moment-to-moment, to our internal visceral organs. Why does that matter? Because the degree of how aware and accurate we are of our inner world predicts the degree of closeness we can feel to the outer world. To put this very simply, if I can hear my own heartbeat, I can learn to hear the heart of the Earth.

I find this intuitive, and follow the lead of Indigenous peoples who long knew the importance of interspecies communion, but as a scientist, I now have the data and discovery to support that gut instinct. The more attuned we are to our inner sensational language, the more heightened our capacity to emotionally regulate and connect to another, whether that is a human or a tree.

"The eyes, the skin, the tongue, ears, and nostrils—all are gates where our body receives the nourishment of otherness. The world and I reciprocate one another," writes David Abram in *The Spell of the Sensuous*.[13] Indeed, the body is the portal to hearing, sensing, and communicating with the Earth. We can only know what we can contact, through our direct, lived, embodied fleshy living. Our breathing bodies long to remember the language of the trees.

We are each born with this innate ability, just like we are born to learn the language of the land, despite mobility differences, illness, or otherwise. The language of trees is the language of the senses. To hear them, we must also feel and hear our bodies. I understand the gravity of this request to a person in pain. But the great paradox is that coming tenderly, lovingly close to the sensations of my lived experience—even, at points, nearly impossible to bear—is the exact pathway that engenders my capacity to hear the living world.

In the middle of waiting for a diagnosis, and during a particularly hard spell of pain, I will never forget what my dear friend Kerry asked me. "Can you bear this?"

I remember how the question felt. Not *What can stop the pain?* or, worse, *What is wrong with you?* But rather, a kind invitation to step into my own spine.

I did not want to feel pain, but I could bear it. *I could.*

Instead of suppressing, numbing, or avoiding sensation, if we can slow down, notice, and feel what is occurring inside the body, a doorway to a universal language can open up. Through growing our discernment in interpreting these signals, we can cultivate the ability to speak the language of trees. As poet and philosopher Gaston Bachelard writes, "The words of the world want to make sentences."[14]

By tuning in to our tendermost places, we develop an acuity and attunement to listen to the interiority of the trees. Hearing the Earth in their hurt and in their joy begins heart to heartwood. We can learn the language of the land yet. This mysterious material interflow will unfurl as we open. It's not too late. As I walk through the forest knowing that Aspen trees have heart attacks because of drought, I place my hands on an Aspen's body.

What is happening inside you?
Are you getting enough water?
Is your heart suffering?

The MRI results came back: NORMAL. I was equal parts relieved and filled with a deeper dread. My body certainly felt far from "normal," but perhaps it was exactly this abnormality that was my window to witness the Earth's ecosystems more clearly. Nothing, actually, was "normal." The Earth is disappearing under our watch.

In that moment, I knew that I could never become well alone. I wished a doctor could tell me how my brain was connected to the tree roots, and how, if trees are sick, if Aspen trees are having heart attacks, humans naturally would feel the effects of that. Our human bodies—including our beating hearts—are the living world. I wished medical care acknowledged our ecologically entwined life instead of splitting my body into parts. When I opened the results to my blood labs I should see fossil fuel levels instead of my personal C-reactive protein levels, a common measurement of inflammation. When I imagined a diagnosis tuned beyond the binary of normal/abnormal, I see an MRI result that says: ENTANGLED. WEIRD. ANIMAL. Treatment plan: TREES.

In the soft warmth of a Los Angeles spring evening, I walked outside, the air thick with night-blooming jasmine. The dripping white five-petaled blooms hung like lanterns in the night. The aroma swept over me. I realized I was the only one pausing on the street to smell them. I breathed in—for those bound by troubling sickness, confined to Western medicine's limited view of the body. I breathed in again—for the Earth—the weary, wonderful Earth.

I could sense I was created from a miracle and set into motion, just like the jasmine. I decided in that moment that if I had life, sense, and energy, so does a tree. I could intuit my healing was connected to theirs. I wanted to follow the patterns of nature. Leaf veins and lung bronchi, root tips and neural dendrites. Cell to cell, atom to atom, bacterial community to compost heap, dendrite to mycelium, synapse to rhizome. We live in a collective, chaotic spiral. I don't understand it, but it's home.

I looked around me. The moon poured its silvery liquid overhead, the Jacaranda tree wept their purple flowers at my feet, and the jasmine continued to give themself away. The Earth's bounty is enormous. The Aspen family, the infinite trees. It's all been given to us in good measure, pressed down, shaken together, and running over. The land is speaking, and we can learn their language. What delicious delights await us in these words beyond words beyond words?

Body Practice: Noticing Sensation

With all of the body practices, feel free to augment them for accessibility and access based on your body and your environment. These are suggestions, and there is no rule that they have to be followed precisely. The intention is to invite you into your body as you feel comfortable and to experience the landscape within. Each chapter will have one body practice and one tree practice. I recommend you do them together as they flow from the content of the chapter, but you can also do the ones that resonate more than others as you desire. With all the body practices, I recommend you try them at least twice a day for a week to fully notice their benefits. If possible, try them in nature. See if there is any difference in how you pay attention to your body among your Earth family. Enjoy and explore.

To begin learning the language of sensation, we will start very simply by tuning in and noticing the sensations that are here.

Wherever you are, find a comfortable position, whether sitting or lying down, where you can take about five uninterrupted minutes for this body scan.

The invitation of this practice is simply to notice physical sensation. This might be different from other mindfulness practices you have done. You do not need to shift your state, but just take note of it.

Begin by taking three deep breaths in through the nose and out through the mouth. Settle into your system.

Now, notice any temperature changes. Perhaps there are subtle shifts in the inhale or exhale. Is your breath quick? Easeful? Long and slow? What is the texture of the breath? What other sensations do you notice in your body? Is there tightness or ease anywhere? What does that feel like?

Now, turn your attention to what's *outside* of your body. What textures, sensations, or temperatures do you notice?

After a few minutes in this space of gentle observation, bring your awareness back into your body and let go of the practice. Feel free to reflect with this chapter's Growing Deeper questions, or simply take note of any expansion, lightness, or ease as a result of paying slightly closer attention to your body. If you do not notice any changes, that is fine, too. Body awareness takes time to develop, and you cannot do it wrong.

Tree Practice: Relationship with a Tree

For this practice, you are invited to create the very beginnings of a relationship with a tree that you will nurture as you experiment with the ideas and concepts throughout the book. In order to be consistent with the tree and encourage the relationship-building process, please choose a tree that is easy to access, perhaps close to home.

To find this tree, let yourself wander, and when you feel drawn to one, pause. Try not to overthink this, and just let your body lead you. Begin by introducing yourself to the tree in whatever way feels right, then listen back for the tree to introduce themself to you. You might take five minutes for this introduction. Then spend a few minutes in each other's presence, with the sole intention of beginning a relationship. See what happens with an open mind.

Over the course of this book and for at least a week, try to spend at least twenty minutes every day with this tree. During your time together, I suggest having the intention of getting to know one another. You do not need to do anything specific beyond making yourself available.

As you spend time with this tree day by day, invite your senses to be present, mindful, and available to this relationship's unfolding. Perhaps you get to know the tree and let the tree get to know you. Perhaps you share something with the tree and let the tree share something with you. Perhaps you spend time in stillness and mindfulness together. You might be surprised how you feel about this being after just a week of spending consistent time together. Think of it as building a sacred relationship with a tree.

Growing Deeper

1. Who is the tree you are building a relationship with? What has this process been like so far?

2. When I am with my tree, I sense _____ in my body.
3. Over the days spent with my tree, I noticed _____.
4. How have you experienced the language of the senses?
5. When you were with your tree, how did the language of trees begin to unfold?
6. Do you have experience practicing interoceptive awareness? What is one sensation that indicates you are tuning in to that eighth sense?

2

The Body Is a Place

The body is the zero point of the world . . . My body is like the City of the Sun. It has no place, but it is from it that all possible places, real or utopian, emerge and radiate.

—Michael Foucault

It was March 2020, before I got sick. I'd woken up in the middle of the night. I could hear footsteps racing up the stairs, followed by screaming on the landing and the sound of gunshots. My heart pounded and sweat pooled on my face. But I could not move. I thought I was dead when, suddenly, sensation returned to my limbs, I sprang out of bed and raced into the hallway, only to hear the stillness of night. That was my first sleep paralysis experience. I'd been awake within a nightmare.

The next week, I decided to leave Brooklyn, my home of eight years, and seek refuge in New Mexico. I felt connected to that land. My grandfather died in Albuquerque when he was twenty-seven, leaving behind my grandmother and my mother, who was only three years old at the time. In those days, they didn't let children into the hospital room. After getting a terminal cancer diagnosis while serving in the Korean War, he was flown back. There he was, taking his last breath. She told me she'd pressed her face to the glass of his Veteran Affairs hospital room to say goodbye. Years later, I still think of my mother's face, all squishy red cheeks on that cold, hard glass.

During lockdown in New Mexico, I volunteered for a COVID-19 hotline. I was desperate to be useful. The dissolution of felt, enfleshed, collective care hurt more than the social island I lived on. I'd patch into the system and get automatically connected to someone seeking stability in an impossibly unstable world. We were guided to create "islands of coherence" for callers. Yet no one—not the volunteer counselors, the supervisors, and certainly not me—had a sense of ground.

"This is Lindsay with the New York COVID support hotline. How can I help you?" I asked caller number four of the day.

"I'm immunocompromised, and I don't want to catch it through the window," a woman told me.

"How close is your window to the street, ma'am?" I asked.

"I'm on the second floor."

The phone line fell silent.

"I want to see the sun," she added, "but I'm scared to open the window. Everyone who dies looks like me."

I heard the subway rattling the windowpane. *Click-clack-click-clack.*

"I understand. I hear you. This is really scary."

She explained that she was hiding from the window on the other side of the room. I let the space breathe.

"Maybe—I could open it just a little?"

Rattling pops like the breaking of brittle dinosaur bones indicated she was creaking open the window.

The luminosity of the sun radiates at about 3.86×10^{26} watts every second. Since we are around 150 million kilometers from the sun, only a fraction of that light reaches the Earth. Yet it's enough. Every photosynthesizing plant, tree, and algae gets what they need to convert light into chemical energy. Magic. Sunlight takes around 8.5 minutes to reach us. We are fed constantly with waves of dispersions of solar fire.

This incandescent power had found her. Her breathing shifted from rapid and short to slow and deep. The place of her body had met the place of the sun. And in that warming, glowing orb, I sensed her relief. Together, we listened to the waterfalls of light.

The body is a place. A topography, geography, and landscape. We are watersheds, valleys, and great basins. We are plateaus, canyons, and ravines. The specificity, location, and dynamic life of the place of our bodies is the pathway to relationship with our Earth family. We can only know a place from a vantage point, a perspective, and a view. Our bodies are that horizon.

What is this place? A human body is made up of eighty-four minerals, twenty-three elements, and eight gallons of water spread across thirty-eight trillion cells. We are not just a discrete entity but rather are myriad and numerous. The body is comprised of endless relationships. Connections between our cells, bacteria in our gut, and infinitely layered exchanges with the rhythms of the world. Our bodies are in constant exchange with the Earth. We take in food, absorb light through our skin, drink and process water, host trillions of microorganisms, and respond hormonally to our environment. There is no such thing as a singular body. We are, in fact, legion.

I was recently on a plane, and from above, the American West looked like a giant copper wash. Out of the center of the wide-open high-desert expanse wound the Colorado River. From the air, the waterway looked like an aorta, the cane-shaped vessel that carries oxygen-rich blood through the human body. But from twenty-five thousand feet, it looked like the Earth's aorta, also snaking like the cane inside our breasts, this one channeling aquatic and riparian life through the patchwork below in their own nutrient transport system. I traced the scattered lines of the Earth's skin from above, as if we breathed through one heart, as if the contours of our bodies mirrored each other. Because they do. The precipice of my body was the map to hear the land and know the Earth in turn.

The body speaks the language of sensation, the language of trees, from a particular *place*. The territory of our flesh maps the topography of the land. In an interview for my PhD research, somatic ecologist, folk herbalist, and feminist scholar Tayla Shanaye explained that a relationship with the Earth starts in the body because "the body is a place." To relate to our bodies as landscapes invites a radical re-visioning to study, understand, and know that terrain. To speak and hear the language of that territory, too.

Our corporeal compass orients us to the Earth's contours. "I am a place, I am a location, I am an ecosystem, I am a sentient being," Tayla said.[1] Through our bodies, we are simultaneously present in a singular form and in manifold relations with the ground beneath our feet, the trees that breathe alongside us, and the multitudinous life all around us.

We could have been a viscous fluid or a puff of gas. But we enter this world sentient, in a form held up like a tent by poles of calcium and bone marrow. And like a spider, we do not end at our skin. Breath alone is proof. Oxygen exhaled by trees enters our lungs, and we have life. Our lungs and the tree's leaves breathe together. We survive in unison, shared chemicals, shared body, shared life. How do we define "my body" when that life is also careening veins through a leaf, is also a chemical compound moving through invisible space?

Our bodies are nature. In infinite relations. And trees are living landscapes of kinships. Trees do not belong to themselves alone. The tree is a geography of cellulose, lignin, and water. Their heartwood comprises their strong center, their roots enable their water uptake, and their sapwood carries that water to all their cells. The forest is their wider body, supported and nurtured by endless exchanges of sugar and nutrients handed off to one another like gifts beneath the Earth's surface.

What is the terrain of such places? I trace my fingers down the spine of my body. I trace my fingers down the trunk of a tree. How can I belong somewhere I don't embody? How can I love somewhere my body does not tread?

While colonialism and capitalism equate the body with an extractable resource for profit, the body belongs to the Earth. And it is the very intimacy with the place of our bodies that gives us the belonging to the wider world we crave.

When sickness made me hyperaware of the faulty and flickering nature of my body, increasing presence, openness, and receptivity became the way to both care for myself and the wider Earth. We are aware of and can tend to ourselves only in our relation to each other. But when that body is vulnerable to disease or is carrying illness, such a place needs gentle nourishment and protection alongside our collective kin. From such a cocoon, we can come to know and cherish the landscape of our breathing bodies. Just like how the canvas of light fed the woman on the call that day, our bodies need each other. I could not absolve her warranted fears of a dangerous sickness nor erase how systemic inequalities had made her more vulnerable. But for a moment, even a whisper of a second, the sun soothed her, as if the star could rock her body gently to the melody of a very old lullaby despite them.

We can become medicine to each other and to the Earth. Tree and human, human and sun. Such reverence will then lead us into connection with the body of the Earth on multiple scales. The microcosm of our bodies and the macrocosm of the cosmos. How we live *here* determines how we can participate *out there*.

The language of the land resides within. Right here. The trapdoor I seek is inside my belly breathing. My fluttering tears, my shaking limbs. I have no other language but the one I can feel. The geography of our bodies can decode the territory of the forest. We are not separate in our mutual decomposition nor our shared struggle for life. Trees and humans. Animate and animal. Unfathomable that our fingertips contain the same whorl pattern as a slice of tree rings. Sensory reconnection enables ecological protection.

To come home to sacred kinship with the Earth, to heal the human-nature relationship, we must care for the land of our bodies. We are one.

I was walking in a shimmering daze along the White River in midwinter. The landscape around me moved into the realm of the unreal. Zigzagging lines cut across my field of vision. Streaks of the brightest light, like a rippled mirror, floated through my sight in shreds. I saw only tatters of snow and sky. I couldn't distinguish depth of distance, and I stumbled, my feet no longer the correct amount of length from my hips. I couldn't be sure if what looked like a meteorite's blasting tail of fire, white-hot luminescence, was coming from outside of me or from within me. Everywhere were bits of deep black space and shining, gleaming brightness.

I squinted. The light dazzled, but it hurt my brain. What I saw made me dizzy. Size and distance confused me. Big black curtains of darkness haunted my peripheral vision. I could no longer see what was to either side of me. I knew this territory. Migraine aura.

Each step became a guess. Relief came from the contact of the soft pulse of snow with the bottom of my boot. In an instant, the senses I relied on had warped sideways and convoluted themselves into an undecipherable tangle hung upside down. I was filled with fear because I knew that after this, the pain would come.

Migraine headaches affect over 37 million people in the US and up to 148 million people worldwide. Western medicine is confounded by its pathology. The annual cost burden for migraines in the US alone is estimated to be over $56 billion.[2] Even the best migraine doctors don't quite know what's occurring inside the brains of migraineurs. Is it the hypothalamic-pituitary-adrenal axis gone awry? Calcitonin gene-related peptides flooding the brain? Serotonin deficiency? Serotonin dumping? Are people making it up?

Migraines affect women more than men, and there's a dizzying list of related symptoms beyond head pain.[3] Many of these are the same as a stroke: numbing on one side of the body, inability to speak, muscle weakness, confusion, visual disturbance. A migraine affects every part of the body because serotonin receptors are found in almost every tissue.

And that's all before the onset of head pain, which can last for up to forty-eight hours or longer. In the depths of this total oblivion, I've genuinely questioned how a migraine doesn't kill me. Like a dying star, the brain feels like it collapses inward and then explodes outward in bursts of shockwaves, erupting energy and pain throughout every cell. And lately, new studies indicate that the brains of migraineurs show signs of lesions, areas of damage.[4] Migraines are, in effect, somatic and electrical earthquakes. And they leave cracks in their wake.

Standing still in the snow, I thought about how to relate to an altered state while in one. I felt a sense of awe, even in the migraine's awfulness. I saw the world completely differently from that place. The mirage of certainty and the myth of permanence melted from my grasp as the land around me undulated. The hard snow path I was on became a river, and I was a trout. The ravishing light was so bright, clear, and eternal, it could eat me. I felt like I dissolved into the sound of birds growing louder around me. In surrender, there was less fear.

In one of the thousands of Reddit boards, blogs, and Facebook groups I'd joined to understand migraines, I'd read that super-fast breathing could flood the brain with oxygen and interrupt the neurological domino catastrophe well underway. I started to breathe in deep, circular breaths. The trees to either side of me moved in and out of my perception.

My friend Emerson, who also lives with migraines, calls these brain explosions by one letter alone: M. Just one shape makes the whole thing less catastrophic, simpler somehow, bound in between two pillars and that sloping V. M almost sounds like a beloved friend.

"Hi, it's M."

"Oh, hello, M, *again*."

"M, what a delight."

"M, what a disaster."

Fighting M straight on rarely worked. I would, *oh I would*, but I'd usually end up in more pain and more despair. But mindfully meeting the pain sideways, even when my mind felt so porous and weak, sometimes helped. I learned the hard way that there was a time to comfort myself in the grief of these experiences. And there was a time to gather up my grit and try to meet it gracefully. This time, a few rounds of fifteen quick pumping breaths was how I greeted my pain, and it tricked my brain like a trip wire. M was contained; M got sleepy; M went to bed.

The zigzagging lines started to recede, and the depth of field in my vision melted into coherence. I breathed out all the way and paused, finally able to see clearly where I was. I was in an Aspen graveyard.

Migraine headaches made me acutely aware that my body was a place. In the depths of one, I'd tunnel inward to survive, and so this place was the only one that existed. At least for those long, cold hours. But over time, my palace of pain became a portal to remembering my connection to everything else. My perceptual sensations, warped by the migraine, unspooled my experience of place far beyond my body.

Prior to this, during my fifteen years as a humanitarian filmmaker in conflict areas around the world—including a stint as a war journalist in the DR Congo—I had little intimacy with my body as a place. I *used* my body more like a machine, rather than relating to myself as a sacred being, and, for the most part, it did what I needed it to do. Once I got sick, my body was no longer metaphorical. I felt it every second because pain is loud.

We are also using the Earth, the Earth is sick, and their pain is loud, too. But it doesn't have to take chronic illness or environmental collapse to help us see that our connection to our bodies and the Earth has been severely damaged. We can open our eyes and hearts to witness the Earth's forms warping under the pressure of climate change. We can begin to tend to our kin now.

Much of Western extractive patterns of living are due to a great disconnection: between us and our bodies and our bodies and the Earth. To wayfind ourselves back into sacred kinship, we must know the map of our bodies first. We begin here. Soft, sweet body that carries me through this life. Terrified, painful body that keeps me awake at night. It took illness to bring me in touch with my body's territory as a portal to know, care, and love the Earth's terrain. But it does not have to be that way. We can decide to return to the Earth right now.

We've been very disembodied in the West, and there are reasons why. Scholars, writers, scientists, and artists have been exploring this very question for hundreds of years. There is no one lens through which we can understand the totality of this, but for the purposes of this book, an emerging consensus that explains our separation begins with worldview.

Indigenous scholar Wahinkpe Topa (Four Arrows) says there are really only two worldviews: one in which humans dominate nature and one in which humans are in deep kinship with nature.[5] Western disconnection from the living world could be reframed as ultimately a *disembodiment*, and we can trace backward to where this began. A foundational severing of self from the body occurred through certain philosophies that spread and gained cultural influence in the West, like Descartes's Cartesian dualism in the seventeenth century, which asserts that the mind is preeminent over the body, and the values of Judeo-Christianity, which purport a patriarchal deity and often teach that the body is profane. The myth of the Garden of Eden, in particular, inaugurated the illusion that humans and nature are separate, justifying dominion over both. Such stories were solidified into social and cultural norms over thousands of years, which still influence many today.

I was raised under evangelical Christian values, which included teachings on the impurity of the body and the "evil" intentions of the "flesh." Purity and the sacred were relegated to "God" alone (who was a man in the sky), the body was considered impure, everything outside of God was profane, and the value of women was measured in their submission to men. I deeply internalized these values and therefore didn't trust my body because I was too scared to know the land of it. After surviving sexual assault when I was sixteen, I was doubly rendered separate from a relationship with my senses.

Pleasure, certainly, was off-limits. I did not know my body held its own wisdom, or that what felt good might become its own map. Further, without a cosmology, or imagination, of the sacredness of the land of my body, I was not able to see the sacredness of the land.

We love a place because we know that place. When sickness struck me, I began to ask, what is the shape of me? What is my weather? What is the terrain of my body? And further, who, or where, is the divine in all this? And if god is nearly ubiquitously portrayed as a man, how can I possibly see myself, in a female body, reflected in the divine?

After the ideological mind-body split came the entwinement of colonialism, capitalism, and industrialization, which further severed people from the Earth and justified domination over the Earth. According to the Western code, people thought they could control nature, chop down this tree, build this dam. Look at what it's done. Settler colonialism and its tentacular extensions into contemporary capitalism sever our relations between humans and soil and even between minerals and our bones.[6] Combined with the Agricultural and Industrial Revolutions, it has become "normal" to dominate lands and peoples instead of live in harmony and equality with them. Objectifying living beings created further separation, for an object can be used, bought, and sold, including the human body. The modern Western culture, or overculture, is based on the dominion, ownership, and exploitation of the body and of natural resources and wild places.[7]

These disembodiments led to an epistemicide (silencing, annihilating, or killing a knowledge system, that of equality with nature), which then justified ecocide (destruction of the Earth). And the divine, as an animate force of the living world, was disappeared. The human body was no longer a landscape to be honored, revered, and likewise tended to, and neither was the Earth's body. Both became mere utilities, measured by their usefulness to capitalism.

If the Earth is merely an extractable good to be exploited, then the topography and terrain are flattened into profit. But the world's living systems are living, breathing, magnanimous beings, replete with unpredictable wildness and power. The myriad impacts of climate collapse flow from such original degradation of place. Everyone suffers under the Western code of living. Greed, growth, and progress are reflected back to us in the form of heat waves, extreme storms, and big floods. What happens to the Earth happens to us.

Today, in a postmodern, imperial world, "growth" and "progress" are possible only to the degree that we pillage the Earth. For example, as of the writing of this book, rampant scaling of AI technologies requires enormous power and freshwater usage to cool sprawling data centers, endless releases of new smartphones demand rare mineral mining, and access to travel to any corner of the globe at any moment involves untenable amounts of fossil fuels. In addition, consumption-driven deforestation to meet the demand of twenty-four of the developed countries threatens 7,600 forest-dependent species worldwide.[8] In effect, the myth of progress, convenience, and efficiency hinges on continued exploitation of the body of the Earth, even at the expense of both our lives. We've been sold a lie. *More* is not more.

But there's another way. *Kincentricity* is an older, wiser, harmonious worldview within Indigenous knowledge systems. It is a way of being that is still embodied by certain Indigenous communities who have managed to continue living within radical interspecies harmony. Indigenous anthropologist Enrique Salmón argues that Indigenous people have always viewed themselves and nature as part of an extended family, in a "kincentric ecology."[9] Like Four Arrows said, *we are kin*. Kincentricity emphasizes the relational entanglement of all of life, viewing each being as part of a larger kinship family. In this worldview, the place of the body is not severable from the land of the Earth. No being is more important than another.

Through kincentricity, many Indigenous communities understand the *land* as spiritual, emotional, and intellectual and experience land as connected to everything else.[10] Kincentricity prioritizes harmony and belonging with the Earth. For when all elements of the natural world are considered relatives, equally deserving of respect and care, then the whole biodiverse world is honored, stewarded, and conserved in myriad ways. To know, revere, and respect one's kincentric ecology, one must move slowly. Rapid speed is counter to a kincentric way of being.

As Indigenous scholar Gregory Cajete writes, the entire tree of knowledge is rooted in "the soil of direct physical and perceptual experiences of the Earth."[11] What do you see? What do you touch? What do you hear? In such a view, to exist, live, and breathe in a kincentric ecology can only be done at the pace of the rhythms of nature. This is a radical reorientation: from speed to soil. Life with the living world unfolds through the myriad relations within the funk of nature. Place is therefore a web of relations to be experienced through the sensing body, not a reducible singular site. And the body is likewise a flowing and complex geography and terrain. We are infinity interacting with infinity.

Indigenous peoples believe that the "spirit of the universe resided in the Earth and the things of the Earth, including human beings," according to Cajete.[12] This origin story creates a map and integrates, says Cajete, all their relationships with all aspects of the landscape. As Indigenous peoples show us, by recognizing the animacy and sacredness of every relationship, and therefore the places of our entanglement, we can slowly find our way back into right relationship with ourselves and the living world. The global community can learn from and value this ecological knowledge, recognize Indigenous peoples' right to self-determination, and involve them as leaders and equal partners in decision-making for climate restoration and healing.

Works by Indigenous scholars and poets like Robin Wall Kimmerer, Linda Hogan, Four Arrows, Gregory Cajete, and more, and by feminists and Black scholars like Donna Haraway, Bayo Akomolafe, Alexis Pauline Gumbs, Resmaa Menakem, Karen Barad, T. J. Demos, and so many more point to alternative fugitivities, a creative form of resistance concerned with new ways of seeing and being even in the face of oppressive systems.

These wisdom keepers offer countercultural ways of living in the Anthropocene that help us dream new myths under capitalism and the Western code, rooted in place-based imaginings that tie us in sacred responsibility to the Earth. A core invitation of many is this: Return to the place of your body and return to the terrain of the Earth. Shed harmful ideological dualities. Recognize that if the "colonial wound is embodied," an idea first put forth by anticolonial liberationist Frantz Fanon, then the body can become an essential discursive field of knowledge and being for repair.

The tangled global polycrisis illuminates the necessity of solutions not built on colonial logics or rhetoric. We need the language of the trees to help us repair. First, between us and our own bodies. How do we treat ourselves as simply a machine? How do we reject our somatic, fleshy, sensorial corporeality? How can we return to intimacy with our bodies? And then, second, with the land of the Earth. How do we treat the Earth as a machine? How do we reject the animate, intelligent lives of our Earthly family? How can we return to sacred relationship with the forest?

In both instances, we can begin by fostering openhearted awareness toward ourselves and the Earth in an experiential flow. We are surrounded by infinite, animate, sacred friendship. Both within ourselves and beyond the human.

Every living tree is a *subject* to honor and experience, not an object to exploit. Like the aorta I saw from the air, we can move beyond the Cartesian dualism split and directly experience the entire phenomenal world of wonder. We can feel spirit in nature. What happens to my body if I allow my imagination to stretch rhizomatically? To feel the Earth's aorta from within my own heart?

Feminist scholar Donna Haraway calls this reimagination a process of "making kin" with the more-than-human world. Kinship is a living organism that can contain both our embodied wounds as well as become a launch point toward possibilities for mutual flourishing. Kinship is not time-bound in linearity. To make kin is to become free.

Like the undulating snow river during a migraine, we can become very curious about our embodied experiences and come closer to them instead of creating more distance, split, and disconnection. We can let go of dualisms, literalism, and reification and embrace the unknown and surprising journey of exploration. We can venture like children through the valleys of our body and the place of the sun.

The geography of felt, subjective experience awaits us. Shimmering sensation, the language of trees, will bring us into radical intimacy with self and the teeming, greening Earth. The body is our living instrument of experiential miracle. And our humanness can only be experienced through what is indeed beyond the human. Psychologist James Hillman, who guided the C. G. Jung institute in Switzerland, writes, "the deepest subjectivity is not personal."[13] Rather, it is biological, cosmic, universal—rocks, animals, plants, trees, rivers, oceans. An ever-evolving, ever-unfurling, ever-unfolding processual life awaits us through our bodies and the forest alike.

The geography of pain had led me to this territory, where theory became flesh. I stood in the center of an avalanche track.

An Aspen graveyard stretched before me. Nature's disaster splayed around me in every direction. The snow had given way beneath the cornices and tumbled down the mountainside. The path must've been ferocious. And here, on the valley floor, lay hundreds of felled Aspen trees, sloping toward the opposite valley wall. The avalanche had been a few years ago, but the cemetery was fresh.

Tangled masses of trees, all topsy-turvy, made abstract shapes, their roots thrust up toward the sky. Tall and bright Aspens created a periphery to the graveyard. There was a clear demarcation where the ruin ended and life resumed. What must that have been like, I wondered, to have witnessed their family die in front of them, with no way to help? This was a place of tree bodies, dead and alive. I was on hallowed ground.

Yet in the midst of the body count sprang countless little bright Aspen shoots, rising from one common underground root. Aspens take advantage of disaster. The forest floor had been tossed around, creating room for new Aspen trees to penetrate up through the soil's surface. The tragedy had created a stage for abundant renewal. What a perplexing place. I noticed the way the new shoots wound up through the soil, so close to the other babies. I saw how the untouched trees were regal as they oversaw the metamorphosis of their kin. I could nearly taste the newness pressing up through the churned-up soil. I could feel how life made use of its own ruin.

My migraine had all but vanished into the land. I felt met, somehow, by this place. Where my own brain felt like a graveyard, here the Aspens showed me that death and life are indiscriminately linked, that each stage feeds the next.

Perhaps my brain wasn't dying after all. Perhaps I was becoming more intimate with my own landscape. Each migraine carved a canyon into my own being, inviting me into such deep kinship because I was the closest one to care. Just like these living Aspens had not abandoned their slain ones but had stayed steady in their duty to renew the forest, I wanted to likewise be such a loyal companion to myself. I wanted to trust that a forest was growing through me, out of me, and all around me, too.

Even without diagnoses or a path to recovery, my migraines brought me into an embodied ecological locality. I was forced to take good care of my body's land because it needed my attention. And as I did so, the Earth became more accessible. The intimacy I learned here translated into a capacity to engage subjectively with my more-than-human kin. If someone in pain can be seduced by the Earth, anyone can be.

To heal the place of my body, I knew I would have to fully inhabit the structure of it. The blood, baseness, fecundity, process, and mystery of its undulations. Healing and harm both happen in the landscape of sensation.

In the quest to re-vision my body's relationship to self, tree, and Earth, I sensed that journey would require attention, animacy, and sacredness. Even to the terrain of my migraine.

I felt the primordial experience of my body as a radiant circuit, filled with receptive waterways to explore the trees from—touch, sight, hearing, taste, smell, and interoception. I was not other. As I deepened into experiencing sensation, to learning the language of trees, the phenomenon of a privatized body began to widen into an embodied ecology. I started to sense the topography I was a part of. The Aspen graveyard, the new shoots rising. Were they not also part of my geology?

With the advent of technology and the ease of travel, place-based rooting and living can feel incompatible with modern life. And for half of the world's population that lives in urban centers, what does returning to the Earth even look like? But the Earth is everywhere, not just in preserved wild places.

To transcend the disembodiments that have wrought nearly irreparable damage to our Earth, we can each begin in earnest with the landscapes within our tender care. Even when that topography is a body in pain.

I imagined a fishing line dropping from my sparky, unpredictable brain to the forest. What was the terrain of my body now? Aren't I also vein, bark, trunk, and mycelium? Aren't I also care, creativity, and solidarity? The body speaks. Subtle at first, then louder and louder. I turned inward to decipher the hieroglyphics, and I turned outward to make sense of it.

The Roaring Fork Valley is the place I've chosen to know deeply, or perhaps these trees chose me. It's as if there's an echolocation underway for me here. The land found me, and I am in their sonar grasp. I cannot escape the sound waves that bounce from the trees, to the great blue heron, to all those red rocks, and straight into the place of me. Even in a migraine, even among an Aspen graveyard. I can only know myself by experiencing this particular valley, mountain, and forest.

This land draws me nearer, closer, just as I am drawn closer to my own body. We are in an ongoing conversation. It will never stop.

Urban or rural, highland or lowland, woodland or wetlands—choose your place, too. Let your body become intimate with place, as place is already drawing you near.

I was on retreat in the Redwoods at the midpoint of my Buddhist eco-chaplaincy training, a sixteen-month program to learn the spiritual tools to support others affected by climate collapse. At that time, I was in the height of my illness, and I didn't know if I'd be able to make this portion of the program. Without the ability to control my environment, I feared I'd have a migraine every day. But it was day 4, and no headaches—at least not yet.

That day, we'd been given the assignment to simply *listen to the forest*. I stood in a small glen in the Santa Cruz Mountains, surrounded by a grove of Redwood elders.

A delicate plume of sun wove like a single tear onto the forest floor through the Redwood canopy overhead. A leaf chased the sun, floating in zigzag patterns, carried side to side by the air. When the leaf finally landed, I felt a pang in my chest.

I remembered my favorite author Annie Dillard's words from *Pilgrim at Tinker Creek*: "The answer must be, I think, that beauty and grace are performed whether or not we will or sense them. The least we can do is try to be there."[14]

Here I was. I realized I couldn't really listen to the forest without first introducing myself. So, I did. I announced myself, out loud, to the family of beings around me.

Moments later, a Redwood in the distance moved their branches just so. I narrowed my eyes to make sure I saw what I thought I saw. Oh yes, a branch, heavy with needles, all flat and fan-like, was, without a doubt, waving at me. I felt their greeting in the place of my body. I felt the land of my body meeting the place of the sun. My heart swelled in appreciation for the gift. Tears sprang to my eyes. Not because I was sad, but because, in this forest of kinship relations, I was home.

Body Practice: Body Scan

Wherever you are, find a comfortable position—whether sitting or lying down—where you can take about five uninterrupted minutes for this practice. Begin by spending a few moments grounding yourself into your environment. What do you notice?

To begin the body scan practice, lightly move your awareness through your physical body. Breathe easefully. You can start by placing your awareness on the top of your head and slowly moving it down your entire body, all the way to your toes.

Notice what is there. Is there any tension in your body today? Are your shoulders tight and up by your ears? Is your face scrunched? Is your belly tense? What do you sense?

Now that you have noticed, what is your instinct? To avoid, distract, or repress? To overly fixate and start worrying? To shift it somehow?

Place your awareness in one of the areas where you feel tension. Breathe into that place. There is no need to avoid, pretend, or wish this tension away. It can be habitual to ignore uncomfortable sensations or, rather, to hyperfixate on them. What is your impulse?

Perhaps, as you place your awareness on a place of tension, it becomes more easeful, because it is being witnessed. Whatever occurs is perfectly fine.

Do you notice any subtle shifts within you by slowing down and placing your awareness in areas of tension?

If at any point this practice feels like too much, please stop and try it again in your nature place. You might feel the same or different when surrounded by living beings.

Once you have completed the body scan, just notice the overall sense of your body. Even small shifts are shifts nonetheless.

I understand this can seem rudimentary or elementary, depending on the intensity of pain you might be experiencing. However, in my absolute worst 10/10 migraines, placing caring attention on my pain would often soften it. It can be habitual to brace *against* what hurts, which seems to amplify it. Conversely, gentle loving attention can absolve the acute sensation into a wider field of awareness. This, in turn, can feel analgesic.

Tree Practice: Knowing Place

In chapter 1, you chose a tree to build a relationship with. This practice takes that knowing a little deeper. Where is this tree? What kind of topography and ecologies is this tree living within? Look up information on the kind of tree you've chosen to build a relationship with and learn about their particularities. Find out what weather they prefer, how long their lives usually are, what their contribution to their ecosystem is. Take a few minutes to research whatever catches your interest, with the intention of getting to know the tree. Then, with curiosity and this new knowledge in mind, spend time with your tree and place. Now that you have a broader understanding of who this tree is in their community, how does that shift the way you see, view, or feel about the tree as you deepen a sense of place?

Growing Deeper

1. The body scan felt _____.
2. When I consider the invitation to become intimate with the landscape of my body, I feel _____.
3. When I consider that my body and the body of the Earth are one, I feel _____.
4. What worldview, 1) kincentricity, or 2) dominance over nature, influences your life the most? How does it feel to recognize that influence?
5. How did knowing more about your tree affect your relationship with them?

3

Easing Into Consent

The language of trees might incline us to patience. To love. It might incline us to gratitude.

—Ross Gay

Once they're gone, they're gone. They bloom for just one day a year in the Rocky Mountains, or a few days at most. I rounded the bend and there they stood—a wild mountain rose. As if conjured from thin air, I was blindsided by their quiet presence. I held my breath, fearing even the smallest exhale might send the petals spiraling clear off the pistil. Dusty pink and milky white, if you held them up to the sun, they'd disappear. Each flower, five petals. As thin as dragonfly wings.

I leaned forward. The scent unfolded in stages. The top notes had a hint of clove, the heart notes a sweetness, and the bottom notes something woody like moss. The aroma then dispersed in a flash, swirling through a cloud of cabbage white butterflies. This perfume, unlike the deadened commercial roses in the grocery store, *was alive*. As I let it linger on my palate, I noticed my headache shift, as if a tiny balloon woven with these gentle petals was pulling the pain straight out of me.

As I hiked, I noticed more roses. I stopped every time I came upon a new bush, spellbound at their form and the undulating bouquet of smells. With each inhale, my headache progressively improved. Perhaps the wild mountain rose was a medicinal muse.

They continued their seduction. This time, I felt like they were asking to be my teacher. To learn from them, would I need to take them? It felt like stealing. They were so rare. *Maybe I'll decide on the hike back down*, I thought, putting the quandary aside. Just a moment later, I came across a flurry of petals resting serenely on the forest floor. I didn't have to pick them. Here they were. For the next forty-five minutes, I collected tiny petal after tiny petal, making sure to leave some before moving on. I didn't want to be greedy.

A man passed me, walking poles in hand, whom I'd gestured to about the wild roses earlier in the day. At that time, he didn't seem that interested.

"Thank you for telling me about the roses," he exclaimed, his countenance much brighter than at our first meeting. "I wouldn't have ever noticed them if you hadn't shown me."

Our eyes met. He looked different. I could see the rose had bewitched him, too. Ephemeral muse. Rose is creative, polymorphic, and fluid. No two relationships are alike.

When I got home, I prepared the petals, put them in a glass jar, filled it with alcohol, then sealed and stored it in a dark place. In four to six weeks, the tincture was ready, and we continued our lessons.

Consent is central to a relationship with the Earth; otherwise, it is bound to be extractive. Humans can't help themselves. Ekua Adisa, a medicine person who works with healing plants, said to me in an interview for my PhD research, "I'm not engaging outside of the consent of plants that aren't drawing me in." How do we know if a relationship is consensual? We use the terrain of our body to listen. We speak the language of trees. There must be an *invitation*, there must be *introductions*, and there must be a willingness and capacity to hear both *yes* and *no*. The wild rose introduced me to this slow, openhearted way of being.

Relationships between humans are built on implicit and explicit agreements, which form a skeleton of trust that holds the whole thing together. We often only think of consent in relation to sexuality, but we actually navigate consent, or lack thereof, continuously through our bodies in numberless ways every day. When we are overstretched or say yes when we mean no, our bodies tell us so. Tightness, constriction, and belly pain are sensations that our bodies use to communicate boundaries. Likewise, sensations like tingling, expansive warmth, and peacefulness are some of the ways our bodies tell us yes.

Before we can reach for the Earth's gifts, we must first learn to ask for permission. Consent is a central tenet in Indigenous knowledge systems and is considered a vital component of creating equal-status relationships.[1] Permission is foundational to a kincentricity with nature, according to Enrique Salmón, in the nonhierarchical loving and living systems of life.

And we can discover how to listen for and sense consent tenderly and inwardly. It's a way to display respect, reverence, and deep reciprocal care. For the Earth never agreed to have their soils plundered, their trees felled, and their waters polluted. And so seeking conscious consensual recognition with the living world can help us repair our relationship with them. Do we honor the Earth's agency? Fully?

In a world that has normalized extraction for profit, the proposition of seeking the Earth's permission is radical. In this way, consent is fundamentally a practice of justice because it attempts to rebalance exploitative power dynamics between humans and the living world. By pausing at the gate, we practice awaiting welcome by the Earth. In so doing, we begin to privilege not just our wants and needs, but the Earth's desires, too. We learn to develop the acuity to hear what those are at all.

There is a psychological theory called ecological dominance, which is defined as a preference to maintain an anthropocentric, hierarchical arrangement between humans and the natural environment. When humans maintain power over nature, disaster unfolds. Across five studies in two countries, scientists found that such an ecological dominance orientation is uniquely associated with adverse socially consequential attitudes like sexism, speciesism, and dehumanization.[2] In addition, an ecologically dominant orientation predicts less pro-environmental behavior. Ecological dominance is the extreme result of unequitable power between humans and nature and foretells the consequences for continuing down that path, both for people and the planet.

In contrast, in her book *Braiding Sweetgrass*, Robin Wall Kimmerer writes of an Indigenous canon of principles and practices that govern relationships with the living world called the Honorable Harvest. These guidelines create accountability to both the physical and the metaphysical worlds. In effect, the Honorable Harvest is a framework of consent. These tenets are not written down, but lived in daily life. She writes:

> Harvest in a way that minimizes harm.
> Use it respectfully. Never waste what you have taken.
> Share.
> Give thanks for what you have been given.
> Give a gift, in reciprocity for what you have taken.
> Sustain the ones who sustain you and the earth will last
>   forever.[3]

The wild mountain rose had communicated with me, through my body, to harvest in a way that minimized harm by collecting the already felled petals. The rose told me to leave some for others by inducing a feeling of tightness in my belly when I'd collected enough.

The Honorable Harvest is a sacred framework that has been offered generously in Kimmerer's book and is one we all can learn from. When we meet a tree, let us introduce ourselves. Let us share our relationship with trees with others. Let us live from the spirit of thankfulness.

The deer came out of nowhere. I was on a path in the woods when they suddenly leaped out of the brush. This happens, but usually they dart away faster than they appear. The deer was a warm ghost reminding me that I was in a wild place. They turned to face me.

The deer was on edge. Angling their body just slightly away from me, I sensed they were in a posture of defense. We held each other's gaze, and I knew there was just a split second for me to earn their trust.

I instinctively knelt on the ground. My body was lower and smaller than theirs now. I stayed completely still. My eyes drifted ever so quietly up at them. The deer studied me, leaning back on their hind legs. I felt their fear from fifty meters away. A shaky, erratic sense wavered between us. They looked skittish and unsure. I tried to pool a sense of steadiness in my body, knowing that the energy moving between us was imperceptible and, at the same time, completely transparent.

I felt I was already at the very closest edge of their safety radius. We were rings on the moons of a planet, orbiting around one another. One, maybe two minutes passed, which felt long and fat in my kneeling posture. Suddenly, the spell of fear broke. The wave between us collapsed into a still sea. The deer perked up their head and started to eat the berries on the closest bush. As I watched the elegant deer eating undefended, I immediately felt part of the forest instead of like a foreigner.

* * *

I recognized the sacredness of the deer because I felt respect for the creature. When we are face-to-face with divinity, it's natural to want to bow. To kneel, prostrate, and unwind our bodies onto the spine of the ground. This movement toward respect is our inner indication that our posture, our receptivity, is tuned to hear the sacred. By speaking the language of trees through sensation, we will hear the world around us. And if we move slowly enough to hear the subtle through the terrain of our bodies, we will be able to respect and honor the consent of the Earth.

Since the Earth has agency and intelligence and will, the Earth also has their own limits, and they are communicating them to us. The deer told me to stay back and moved at their own pace once they sensed I was not a threat. As our nervous systems found equanimity with each other, a tiny thread of trust was stitched into the fabric of our entangled bodies. But I would have missed this exchange had I been distracted from presence. "Why should we live with such hurry and waste of life? We are determined to be starved before we are hungry,"[4] writes Thoreau. *We need to slow down.*

On a macro level, we see the Earth's limits communicated loudly and plainly. Bleaching coral reefs, flash floods, melting glaciers, exploding wildfires, extreme heat waves. The Earth is saying, *No, that is enough. Stop.* Global warming caused by fossil fuel emissions has heated the planet to the point of breaching the 1.5°C threshold.[5] We've already crossed what climate scientists say is a critical juncture. To avoid permanent loss and damage would require rapid steep cuts of greenhouse gas emissions and a phase-out of fossil fuels, according to the United Nations. Instead, we are moving in the opposite direction—dismantling clean energy projects in the United States while advancing new fossil fuel infrastructure like the East African Oil Pipeline globally. We are not hearing the Earth's *no*.

But we can learn to. If we can begin to sense the Earth's *no* in small ways in our everyday lives, perhaps things could change.

I trust that these reciprocal bonds add up and could even impact social global patterns of rampant extraction, domination, and exploitation. If billions of people carry that *no* in our hearts, we will act, love, and respond in accordance with the measure of our love for nature, not our willful blindness and ignorance to what is unfolding right in front of our eyes.

The deer and I had moved in a delicate dance of yes and no, attuning to consent through our nervous systems. This body intelligence is a powerful tool of kinship relations.

The sympathetic nervous system carries the signals of fight, flight, freeze, or fawn and is implicated primarily in threat reduction and survival. Physiological indications that this system is online include increased heart rate, pupil dilation, sweat, and raised blood pressure. The parasympathetic nervous system, on the other hand, is predominant during "quiet" conditions and is responsible for resting and digesting.

The vagus nerve contains 75 percent of the parasympathetic nervous system's nerve fibers and is the longest cranial nerve in the whole body—running from the brain, through the throat, and down and around the intestines—carrying signals between the brain, heart, and gut. Activating the parasympathetic nervous system through meditation, walking, breathing, mindfulness, and time with the Earth lowers stress and anxiety and increases overall well-being. The term *vagal toning* refers to vocalization and singing techniques that vibrate the vagus nerve, setting off a waterfall of relaxation benefits.

Trees also have a nervous system. When scientists first studied the structure of the human brain's nerve cells, they noted their resemblance to trees. In fact, *dendrites*, the term used to describe projections from a nerve cell, comes from the Greek word *dendron*, meaning "tree." Our nervous system is built like a tree's root system; it is just that we have forgotten we are connected to everything in the forest.

Nature connection science has found that exposure to natural environments improves our parasympathetic nervous system functioning, indicated by reduced physiological arousal, and leads to a more emotionally regulated state.[6] Since emotions are features of the nervous system, caring for them is the primary way we can likewise tend to our emotions. Regulated emotions create the capacity to notice consent with ourselves and the Earth. Therefore, the nervous system, emotions, and relationships are all connected.

By expanding our nervous system flexibility, we can "widen our window of tolerance," a psychological term that defines the range of one's nervous system. Greater dexterity, versus rigidity, increases our capacity to digest life's experiences. To move with the waves, both their peaks and troughs alike.

However, this is not to say we should all just learn to "hold more." When sick, I did not find that invitation comforting. I found it enraging. At the same time, there is wisdom in growing the awareness of what those upper limits are, not necessarily to stretch them further, but to honor the holy range of what our bodies are telling us they can bear. When in chronic activation, that feeling of baseline regulation can disappear. A relationship with the Earth can help us rediscover it.

When we consider climate change, it's clear the Earth's window of tolerance has been surpassed. We could think of this as their "planetary boundaries," a concept first introduced in climate science to define the environmental limits in which humanity can safely operate.[7] In a novel study that quantified nations' responsibility for climate breakdown through their contributions to cumulative CO_2 emissions, it was found that the US was responsible for 40 percent of excess global emissions, and the Global North for 92 percent. By contrast, countries in the Global South were within their boundary fair shares, including India and China.[8] Yet the disproportionate burden of climate collapse falls on formerly colonized communities in the developing world.[9] The countries that are the most nature *disconnected*, as defined as a severed relationship with nature, are responsible for the most carbon emissions and resulting climate change, which disproportionately affects the nations that are more nature-connected. Thus, the ongoing reaches of coloniality continue.

Although the terms *Global North* and *Global South* are imperfect and have been rightly critiqued, they are a way to categorize countries that contribute more or less to climate change, based on economics. However, a new paradigm is needed altogether that is not mapped onto nation-states. A more accurate description would be that some elites are driving globalized extractive capitalism, which increases emissions, not necessarily the nations themselves. Not everyone in those countries is equally responsible, of course, or even has a choice.

Since our body is one with the Earth body, violating planetary boundaries harms us, too. Deforestation, polluted waters, and oceans filled with plastic affect our interconnected health, whether we realize it or not. Microplastics have been found in sperm; particulate matter from forest fires is damaging people's lungs; heavy metals from landslides and flooding can contaminate water sources. And on top of all of this, the Earth never said yes, never agreed to any of it. To hear the Earth's no more clearly, we have to begin to move slowly enough to register their language. *We must slow down.*

So, then, to seek consent is both a relational imperative and an act of climate justice. One must go slowly enough to hear a yes and also be willing to hear and respect a no. This is a direct contrast to both the pace and constant churn of capitalism. The imperial growth paradigm is driven by a relentless speed that does not match the slow, geological pace of the Earth. Consent, in contrast, is a delicious, *slow,* and deeply vibrational invitation. If you take one thing away from this book, I hope it is the deep need to slow down, *and then slow down more.*

As author and self-styled trans-public intellectual[10] Bayo Akomolafe says, "The times are urgent, *slow down.*"[11] If we do, we will be able to hear the language of trees. How can we kneel, like at the feet of the deer, and earn back the Earth's trust? How can we listen to the sublime subtlety of a yes, or a no, and act in kind?

One of the most potent tools for attuning to the sensual is to get into a regular habit of walking. Walking may be the single most important practice that changed my relationship with trees. Because I was able to move through the forest again and again, in our rhythmic encounters, I became more receptive and porous to their language. Walking is an easy pleasure and allows the body to move at a pace closer to place—unimpeded time, open awareness, and mindful attention. Rebecca Solnit calls walking an "indicator species" to signal an activity that exemplifies the health of an ecosystem. When you don't know where to start, or when you want to start again, go walking.

It's hard to accept that we've crossed so many of the Earth's boundaries. When we do slow down, we can feel shame about that. Things might look all right outside of our windows, but the Earth is suffering. The trees are struggling. Likewise, not listening to our own yeses and nos can create shame, too. It hurts that we have violated the planetary boundaries, and it hurts that we have violated our own or been violated in turn.

We do not need to be hypervigilant about this process, further stressing our nervous systems to "get it right." We simply need to be willing to listen, and we need to be *able* to listen. Body awareness can help us develop these capacities. By paying deep attention to our sensory life, we will be able to hear the Earth, too. We might need to back away, take less, or take nothing at all. We might need to give something in return. There are gifts that will come when we slow down. There might also be grief. Gifts and grief live side by side.

The whole world was in free fall. With the pandemic in full tilt, while living in New Mexico, my symptoms first began. I will never know what kicked the whole thing off. Was it the accumulation of all the psychological and physical impacts from years of humanitarian work? Gut parasites? Random chance? A roulette of fate? Did it matter? Chronic health symptoms are so confounding in their scale that the urge to trace them to their roots is irresistible.

I'd never consented to this, and I struggled to reconcile that fact. My own corporeality betrayed me in its most intimate places—inside my neurons, between my synapses, in the heart of my cells, deep within my nerves. And though I could *feel* the pain, I couldn't find it, locate it, excise it. I could kind of reduce it, subdue it, numb it, but remove it? No.

While the capitalist wellness industry complex propagates the myth of individual health, what about when the body goes rogue, autonomous, animal? No matter what biodynamic food, alkaline water, sunlight exposure, exercise, and supplements I ingested, my body threw fits, sneaking out sideways like a snake, refusing to be tamed.

On the outside I "looked" healthy—but inside, almost every hour of the day, I "managed" any number of pain symptoms. Before I got sick, I had been ableist without knowing it, taking my healthy, able body for granted. With that assumption blown to bits, I had to repair and reconcile the betrayal within me as part and parcel of repairing my relationship with the Earth. Our healing was connected.

New Mexico has been called "the land of enchantment" by many.[12] Austere, wide-open high deserts gave way to white sands and gorges, with mountains filled with Aspens, Junipers, and Pines, and exceedingly dry air thick with the scents of piñon and wild sage. Maybe since my grandfather died there, some piece of me was left in the burnt-orange Earth and phenomenal coral-colored expanse. Like a buried seed, a promise that would pull me back like gravity. It felt serendipitous and strange that all those years later, I found myself there during lockdown.

I was living in total isolation and with a body in pain. I had little else to do but go on long walks. One afternoon, I took to a hill in the Santa Fe National Forest and sat on a bench. Brain fog bewildered me. If I could have looked inside my mind, I swear it would have been all cobwebs of gossamer and silk. Everything was slow and muddled. I decomposed a bit under the density, robbed of my ability to directly participate in the world. I could not grip my own thoughts. They slid away from my awareness before I could see them. In this state, it was as if there was a veil between me, sensation, and the Earth. I couldn't quite feel the world, but I wanted to be touched.

I could see the clouds hanging low, and though my sensory capacity was dulled, the scent of the Pine was nourishing. I started to sing. But I didn't usually sing, so this seemed odd. I let the intoning become a question: *Do I have permission to know you? Do I have permission to touch you?*

"The Earth is the first sacred text," says Franciscan mystic Richard Rohr, who'd long been a spiritual teacher of mine. For years that phrase had been beautiful to me, but I'd never really understood it. From where I was standing, nature's sacred essence seemed to billow up from the land, a dusty plume of smoke from the kiva hearth of the Earth. Blackened by centuries of truth turning over itself in the molten core of the planet, the invitation to read the Earth like a sacred text became plain. All I needed to do was open my eyes.

Stands of mountain Juniper, so twisted and creative, gripped the sides of the Earth like a prayer. Juniper can grow in both acidic and alkaline soils, their needles expanding in alternating whorls. I marveled at their exquisite adaptability. A nervous system in regality. Below them were sandstone and limestone, granite and basalt. A cliffside fell away into the ravine.

A hermit thrush began to sing then, too. Hidden in the dense understory, the angel poured out their song. Each note rose like a clear bead of water, cascading through the air. Ethereal, flute-like chords spun into a fervent foray of confluent vitality. I wanted to open my hands, lift them.

Do I have permission to know you? I asked again.

A yes grew slowly like a moon inside my belly, pressing against my skin from the inside. The numbing fog in my body dissolved from the heat of the sun. I read the text of the Earth by listening from within me. The *yes* seemed to bloom into smooth stones inside my inner landscape, steady enough to stand on. *Yes* had its own texture. *Yes* had its own voice. *Yes* was its own song.

I could tell it was good because little pieces of pain coalesced around that yes and fell away like pearls. Perhaps I did not need to read the Earth in the traditional way. These were not words on a page. This was an experiential unfurling. The reading was closer to dreaming. My body was being dreamed by the sacred text of the Earth, and I was learning to read it.

Seeking consent is simply being wakeful. We are invited to fully *be here*. The Earth, the wild rose, the deer, the singing thrush, are meant to be read, by the body, by sensation. By slowing down, we can be receptive to the unspooling miracle.

As my experience of chronic illness collided with a growing awareness of the cataclysm of climate change, I saw that we are all braided together in a planetary health and climate crisis. Therefore, healing would not be something I could do on my own. Healing is the *process* of entangling ourselves back into kinship with nature. Healing is not an outcome but an ontological endeavor. To *heal* has more to do with participating consentfully and respectfully in the multimodal, sporadic, and interspecies living world than it does with eliminating a particular symptom. Healing will invariably take us beyond the human.

Back in Colorado, I learned to move slowly through the forest because I didn't want to miss a thing. The sun just so, the grasshopper just there, the river rousing my ears with its hum. This, here, was the gift.

It'd been a year since I made the wild rose tincture, and I used it sparingly. I placed one drop on my tongue before going on a walk in the forest. The aroma had intensified during the steeping process. One droplet sent my body spinning into a sense of ephemeral beauty.

As I walked, I surveyed the field undulating into the distant Aspen forest that was cloaked in twilight. Perhaps the rose had magnified my senses as I often had walked this exact path. Yet at that moment, it's as if I were seeing them for the first time.

The leaves were backlit, glowing orbs in resonance. I looked from the tip of the leaf, its gold-rimmed face billowing, and from leaf to branch, svelte arms pointing to the sky. Fullness was at its peak. I was enswirled in a golden cave, each leaf like a single firefly, pulsing light. *To see an Aspen forest at this time of day*, I thought, *is to see the face of god*.

I could hardly believe I got to be part of this. "Beauty will save the world,"[13] Dostoyevsky said, but as I read the sacred text of the Aspen forest around me, I ask myself, *What if beauty is the world?*

Body Practice: Inner Yes, Inner No

You can complete this practice inside or outside, whenever you have a few moments to go within. To begin, take a seated position with your spine reaching tall. If that is not comfortable or possible for you, you can complete this practice lying down.

Begin tuning in to your breath by taking slow, deep breaths through the nose. Inhale slowly and evenly, breathing first into your belly, then ribs, then chest for a count of four. At the top, hold for a count of four. Then, slowly and evenly, exhale for a count of four, allowing your shoulders and body to let go and relax a bit as you do. At the bottom, hold for a count of four, finding stillness in the hold.

Repeat this box breath for at least ten cycles.

At the end of these cycles, ask your body, "What does a yes feel like?" Wait for a sensory response. This might feel like warmth, a rising energy, or a sense of lightness.

Once you've noticed a clear sensation, ask your body, "What does a *no* feel like?" Wait for a sensory response. This might feel like tightness or a dropping, heavy sensation.

If nothing happens, and you feel that you cannot sense a yes or a no, that's okay. Sometimes it takes practice to sense these subtle sensations. If you need more support, choose a person in your life who is loving and who you feel safe with. When you bring this person into your awareness, how does your body respond? What sensations are there? This might be what a yes feels like to you. Take a few moments to write down what you noticed about your yes and no as these appear in your body. Thank your body for their wisdom.

Tree Practice: Seeking Permission

To experiment with consent and accessing your body awareness intelligence, spend time with your tree or special place in nature and seek permission to *continue* building a relationship with them. Even though you already introduced yourself, take what you learned from the previous yes/no practice and sense into that when you are with the tree.

Ask for consent to be in a relationship with the tree in a way that feels natural and authentic to you. What do you sense in your body? Wait for a clear answer. If you feel a *yes*, lean into that relationship, but like a human one, next time you are with the tree, ask for permission again. Building consent is not a onetime gesture, but a practice to return to again and again. Consent occurs continuously.

If you feel a *no*, that is perfectly okay. Ask the tree if there is anything you can do to help them feel more comfortable. Ask what they need. Respect that no and try again another time.

Growing Deeper

1. A yes in my body feels like _____.
2. A no in my body feels like _____.
3. When I listened for a yes/no in my body, I learned that _____.
4. What is a relationship in your life that feels particularly consensual? What are the qualities of this bond?
5. When you sought permission from the tree or place, what did they say? How did you know this was their response?
6. What does reading the Earth like a sacred text mean to you? Have you ever had this experience? What was it like?

II
Nearness: Reveries of Eros

4

Erotic Ecology

But if I could breathe a rainbow, I would grow myself towards you. I would brighten what's between us, filter nourishing possibilities. I would swallow worlds of yes.
—Alexis Pauline Gumbs

As I got closer, I felt the pull. A vein—straight from their heartwood—to mine. It'd been eight months. Then, it was all green and celebration. Now, the land was white and hushed, not long after the first big snow. I'd dreamed of them, longing for their presence during our time apart. Haunted by their graceful shapes, the impression of our fleshy contact was a sensory bewitchment buried in me. And now, as my body rounded the second to last bend after walking three miles in the snow, I could quite clearly hear my Aspen family hollering: *Welcome home!* I was a fool and a forest.

I arrived to a dazzling sun spun overhead, full of marigolds and radiant flares. I was hot from the walk, each step a struggle uphill. I took a handful of snow and stuffed it into my mouth, all clean and cold and calm. I ripped off my coat, then my sweater.

Bare chested, I threw my jacket on the snow and lay down next to my Aspen family. I closed my eyes and felt the gentle melt of the top few inches cradle my body in a perfectly molded hug. I was a pearly tusk on opalescent ice.

My mind went silent, as if my thoughts had fallen out the back door of my spine. I was completely at ease swimming in an iridescent peacefulness. The more I gave the sensation my attention, the larger it became.

A quick burst of wind flew through the Aspens, dislodging the tiniest tuft of snow from its resting place. The sigh of the sky scattered it like dandelion seeds all over my naked skin. The sensation of ice prickled and pranced on my chest, suspending me between pleasure and pain. The shimmering nature of the embrace brightened my body. I felt what I was feeling.

Listen.

Inside the inside.

This is all there is.

I'd never experienced that before. A homecoming song sung straight into my cells. Prying open my neurons and breathing desire into them. In the moment, I could only respond with the impulse to move closer. In retrospect, I see this dynamic interplay as mutual attraction.

The Earth *wants* us. At every second of every day, the Earth is seducing us. Our bodies respond with arousal, affection, and yearning. I *want* to hold a stamen in my palm; I *desire* to watch the butterfly undulate; I *long* to drape my chest across a felled tree. The Earth is constantly inviting us into bodily, sensual, and primal contact. This is an elemental romance as verdant as spring and as ancient as stone. Gravity and beauty are the Earth's attraction spells in a never-ending mythic resonance.

Look around. What color, shape, texture, temperature alights your senses? What do you notice in your body? This is attraction, more, *desire*. The atoms in our bodies are quite literally pulling and being pulled by other particles. The whole universe is full of attraction—whirring and whizzing within the wide web of erotic longing. We do not need to fear it.

Our bodies act as living tuning forks—exquisitely sensitive instruments designed to resonate with the Earth's frequencies, allowing us to detect, respond to, and ultimately understand the natural world surrounding us. I'm thinking of eucalyptus arms and moss laps, tidal hips and night flower kisses. Let us feel the world through our sensuous terrain. The supple softness of a stream, ebbing and flowing, cresting and falling. The calcined granularity of grains of sand, the prickle of a thistle, the solidity and smoothness of a cave. Contact and caress. Touch and tenderness. Embrace and enfoldment.

The Greek word for "the beautiful" is *kalon*, related to the word *kalein*, which, as the poet and philosopher John O'Donohue points out in his book *Beauty*, means to "be called." The beautiful world calls out to us. They are intoning us to come ever nearer. They are incessant in their pursuit. Beauty is nature's attraction spell, and we can respond to their seduction. Being drawn into eros with the Earth opens an ecological field of pulsing, magnetic, sensuous passion.

The Queen Anne's lace barely brushed my ankles. By the end of summer, we will be nipple to petal. And then they will collapse and compost, gone to seed. Isn't that excessive? All that growth for just one season? But nature's opulence—a wonderful immediacy—is never wasted. The ephemerality is intrinsic to their design, a flash you have to be awake enough to catch. It teaches you to pay attention.

A few years ago, I was visiting the Mendocino coast in Northern California—a wild, ragged stretch of Earth interlaced with old-growth Redwood forests. I had wandered down a trail to a razor-thin slice of rock. Turquoise-colored sea bashed the sidewall; frothy milky ocean swirled in eddies too cantankerous to calm. Purple wild orchids bloomed in swarms, such delicate, salty petals peppered with yellow hearts. Called Fairy Slippers, these creatures felt impossibly exposed next to such a feral sea. Enormous bumblebees fell drunk out of the orchids, faces smeared with pollen, and stumbled off in zigzagging flight. I stood right there in the midst of it all and knew—I was not the one who had walked myself there. I had been summoned.

Heeding the Earth's invitation in this way was an erotic experience. Where we think we have our own individual affinities for specific places and landscapes, perhaps we are being courted in a flowing, polymorphous, biological labyrinth. Why do some people need to see the ocean? The ocean longs for them. Why do some delight to stand inside a forest? The trees beckon them. Why do some seek wild animals? These beings yearn for them. "What you seek is seeking you," says the thirteenth-century poet and mystic Jalāl al-Dīn Rūmī.[1] A mysterious, multidirectional flow of enticement and bewitchment is at work in what is called our erotic ecology. The river runs both ways.

In Greek myth, Eros was the name of the Greek god of desire. Eros, as a concept, is tempestuous, voluptuous, and resplendent. Out of necessity, eros will always spill over any definition. One facet of eros that is often overlooked is the connection between the erotic and the Earth. Eros primordial. Eros primeval. Eros animal.

Some scholars say the word *eros* has never had a satisfying etymology, as there are multiple Greek words that touch on love: *eros* (passionate love and intense attraction), *philia* (love in friendship), *agape* (unconditional and selfless love), *epithymia* (longing or craving), and *pothos* (nostalgic yearning beyond reach). Eros is larger than categories. I am intrigued that *pothos* (nostalgic yearning beyond reach) is a direct descendant of the derivative of the Proto-Indo-European word for "pray."[2] Eros, then, could be considered as a primal prayer of pining. I resonate with a sense of *pothos* in my relationship with the Earth. There is certainly a wistful echo of a union I am always seeking that rises in a scintillating flare and then slips through my fingers. The dazzling reverie etches inside me and brings me back again and again for more. Is it not the same in love?

This makes me think of the term *solastalgia*, which was coined by Australian philosopher Glenn Albrecht to capture the pain of environmental changes to places we love. When we come close to love, we invariably come close to grief. Maybe solastalgia is also telling us something about the loss of our erotic connection to the Earth. We miss our kin. We ache and yearn for the Earth. Even if we can't pinpoint what it is, we may have a feeling that something is missing in our lives. *Pothos* lives like a residue in our temples, a phantasmic afterglow that tremors in our reflection. That low murmur of a remembrance barely slipping out of sight ripples backward and forward and keeps grabbing our attention. You belong here. You are moss and whale. You are bluebird and bluebell. You are the red rock desert. Perhaps this tender ache in our hearts is a longing for our heartwood. A prayer for the trees. A blood memory that we are erotically connected to nature.

Yet there is no term that captures the grief of losing one's embodied capacities. There is no word for the pain of watching our own sacred forms warp under the pressure of illness. Chronic pain can certainly feel like the opposite of eros. Instead of vitality, the constancy of discomfort and the free fall into the unknown carves thirsty gorges into the geography of the body. Let me offer a word that might meet this experience: *corporealgia* (from Latin *corporeus* "of the body" + Greek *-algia* "pain, suffering"). The ache of loving and losing some of our body's robustness, facility, and capacity. Naming this experience somehow brings slightly more dignity to it.

The myth of Persephone became a strange solace in my *corporealgia*. She was an exemplar of one who had survived her own bardo. A woman who had gone straight into the heart of the underworld and lived. A complex story fitting for the messiness of a life lived with illness. According to the myth, Persephone was abducted against her will into the great darkness. Like me, she had no agency over the world she would inhabit. Me in my body's pain, her in the loss of all she loved and knew. The story goes that her mother grieved her absence, which led to the season of winter. Persephone's return to the world above became symbolically marked by spring. In her movements between the worlds of the living and the dead, Persephone personified the natural cycles of decay and rebirth. She shows me that growth, change, and even brand-new seasons are always possible. The underworld is not a final destination. It's a portal. How deliciously ensorcelled. I wanted to be inclined toward such ecological eros, too. Toward redemption not through being saved, but by being the one who participates in an entangled multispecies blooming, despite every reason to stay buried, quiet, and dark. I didn't want my suffering to go to waste. Instead, maybe my pain could be planted. What might it become?

Twenty-three vials of blood, all with my name on them. The vein on my right arm collapsed, so the left was the winner. There were bruises on the creases of both, echoes of river deltas winding up my arms, evidence of too many lab visits to count. This time, I was at UCLA's rheumatology department. One by one, I was collecting stamps on my medical passport. Soon, I would have visited every single department in the sprawling medical complex. Too bad they didn't have Monopoly at the UCLA Medical Center like they had at McDonald's when I was a kid. With every doctor visit, you win another game piece until you fill your board and win prizes, vacations, and cars.

I felt anything but sexy. But even still, I was curious about the characters in these scenes. Like who, really, was Dr. X with the elfin ears? Or what was *really* going on with that lab tech and the nurse? I passed the time, and the anxiety, by spinning yarns. I stayed mostly in the genre of romantasy. The sterility of those rooms and the theater of medicine made my brain go extracelestial.

The doctor finally came in, iPad in hand.

"I think you have an autoimmune disorder," he said.

One game piece.

"These labs should tell us which one," he added, motioning to the cornucopia of blood standing tall like pillars in the Parthenon. This did feel like a Greek tragedy.

Another game piece.

"What does autoimmune mean?" I asked.

"It means your body's immune system is mistakenly attacking healthy cells and tissues."

"Why would it do that?"

"We don't know."

I'd just won the board.

In the search for answers to my health, I somehow stopped reading medical journals and started reading feminist scholarship. I came across the writer, feminist, and activist Audre Lorde's seminal work "Uses of the Erotic," which became a profound treatise for me on how to fully live. Much more helpful than most of my doctor appointments.

The erotic, Lorde argues, "has been made into the confused, the trivial, the psychotic, the plasticized sensation."[3] Instead, Lorde implores, the erotic is actually the capacity to find a yes deep in the body, which will bring one's life into alignment with their desires. Like the yes that rose up from the land in New Mexico in my belly. Like the faintest whisper I felt even in the worst spells of my pain. Something still wanted to live. My life depended on it.

Identifying, sensing, and becoming aware of this life force, ensconced in the sensation and texture of yes, is not always easy. In pain, where sensations are often huge, all-consuming, and incessant, *where is the yes?* It's too loud to hear the subtle. But through sensory attunement and increasing my body awareness with the trees, I started to find it. My yes to what was life-making and life-giving. My yes to what was delicious and luminous. My yes to what was full of flavor and texture. There was always a glimmer, no matter how bad it got. Even in the darkest caves, there is light. Radioactive decays in rocks form mineral luminescence. Cosmic ray muons create illumination that fluxes based on the shape of the cave. I never want to lose sight of the visible light. As I slowly learned to shift the frequency of my awareness from focusing on what was the loudest to learn to listen for the cracks, my life force started to come back to me.

In the previous chapter on consent, I offered a body awareness practice to help you locate your yes and no as a precursor to relationship. If you struggled to locate a yes, this chapter will widen the inquiry. Body awareness may grow slowly, but stay with it. Psychologist William James first theorized in the late nineteenth century that sensations *are* emotions. And since emotions are how we feel close to both people and nature, continuing to know and hear our body is also our way to come ever closer to our living forest kin. Here, we expand the body awareness inquiry to welcome sensations of pleasure, too. A yes could quite simply be *what feels good right now.*

Experiences of pleasure increase the quality and longevity of our lives. Our brains have become sophisticated over millions of years to refine a complex reward circuitry. Somewhere in our bodies, we know that what feels good can save us. A study published by the American Psychological Association found that pleasure, measured as trait positive affect, is associated with lower levels of the cytokine interleuken-6 (IL-6),[4] which plays a significant role in regulating the inflammation pathways that are often discordant in those with autoimmune disorders. A 2023 scientific report in *Nature* found that the more awe people experienced during the COVID-19 pandemic, the fewer somatic health symptoms and the greater well-being they felt.[5] Really? Awe can attenuate pain?

I see it like this. When I am with my Aspen family, their presence initiates the piercingly tender clarity that I am very much not alone. Call it wonder. Call it awe. Call it joy. IL-6 recognizes this state of endearment and backs away. Discordance is no match for the audible oracle of the forest, whose trees are feeding and healing each other all day long.

So yes, pleasure is not just a state of enjoyment; *it is medicine.* Increasing our awe and joy wherever and however we can is indeed an act of resistance to the many ways toxic systems harm us. Pleasure is food for our bodies.

The Earth continuously replenishes our capacity for aliveness. Studies suggest that merely being around trees lowers our blood pressure and the stress-related hormones cortisol and adrenaline.[6] Studies on shinrin-yoku, the practice of forest bathing, indicate that spending time with trees can increase serotonin levels and vitamin D. When we breathe in phytoncides, the airborne chemicals that plants give off to protect themselves from insects,[7] the body responds by increasing the number and activity of a type of white blood cell called natural killer cells, which are critical for regulating a healthy immune system and have roles in underlying pathogenesis of a number of autoimmune and autoinflammatory diseases.[8] Natural killer cells also have both predisposing and protecting roles in these disorders.[9] With an autoimmune disease, the opposite is happening. Cells have gone rogue, attacking the body's own tissues, glands, and organs. In one study, a three-day, two-night forest bathing trip increased natural killer cells in participants for thirty days.[10] Trees have a way of attending to my autoimmune condition better than I could.

Medical science has identified more than one hundred autoimmune diseases, and 50 million people in the US have one or more; 75 percent of those people are women. A recent scientific review in *Neurology, Psychiatry, and Brain Research* reported an association between migraine and autoimmune pathologies.[11] Something mysterious is happening between these ailments. The general prognosis for autoimmune disorders was similar to what I was told about my migraines: They are chronic and lifelong, symptoms can come and go, and there's not much that can be done. The symptom set varies widely between autoimmune diseases, but the common denominator is that the immune system targets and harms itself.

I imagined my cells, little rocket ships whirring in the black void of my inner body. What had tricked them into attacking me? I felt their utter confusion. The task they were created to do, repeatedly, until the day I die, is keep me alive. And yet here they were, recklessly attacking themselves. Could the presence of the Earth help rewire their distortion back into healthy function? Could the sensuous living world show them how to love me instead of harm me?

Being so aware of my illness felt, at times, like too much. But in the West, it's not that we feel too much; it's that we feel too little. Of what matters. With technology and around-the-clock information, our bodies are both overstimulated and desensitized at once. We have become psychically numb in an oblivion of noise. It's a particular form of cruelty to be bombarded with images of genocide alongside American capitalism in the same breath. We are not wired to accommodate such dissonance. When I am overstimulated, I try to numb or dissociate to bring my body back into regulation and protect me from further overwhelm. The downfall of this strategy, though, is that it cuts me off from my vital heart, even in my attempt to shield it.

Left unaddressed, these coping behaviors can rob us of our sensual sensibilities, including pleasure. Pleasure is experienced in the body. If I am out of mine for whatever reason, and there are many justifiable reasons to escape one, I cannot feel what's here.

A study published in the *International Journal of Mental Health and Addiction* indicates that elevated phone use reliably increases emotional dysregulation, nonacceptance of emotions, and inability to achieve goal-directed behavior.[12] How can we engage meaningfully in the living world from such a place? The phone is not erotic. Our animal bodies need more quiet to feel and sense their inner and outer worlds. Psychic space, stillness, and quietude are antidotes to the noise. In that reprieve, our bodies can gingerly discover safety, creating an inner courage to sense, feel, and experience the sensuous world. In this calm, we come home. So when you can, turn off your devices. Take a fast from information. Go outside with no agenda. Immerse your sensing body in nature and see what arises in this sacred space. Allow your system to settle into its own silence. In that receptivity to the subtle, pleasure can find you once again. The French mystic and political activist Simone Weil says that "Absolute undivided attention is prayer." Do we want to pray to screens or to the Earth?

The invitation in this chapter is to practice light explorations of what feels good with the Earth. We're not necessarily aiming to resolve trauma here, but to welcome back more innate aliveness. Because some traumas do not resolve, and we do not have to be "healed" in order to feel good. Pleasure is our birthright.

To do so, we can begin by resensitizing our bodies to the language of trees. Everything around us is an embodied form of life. Let life touch us. As we do so, these latent sensorial capacities will awaken, offering cosmic and Earthly tenderness. Our bodies heal when we are *in touch* with the Earth. Let's allow the Earth's gentle seduction to melt away the armor that blocks our embodied awareness and tune in to softness. In so doing, we will develop an inner vocabulary for what feels good. From this base language of noticing sensations through the topography of our body, we will naturally begin to be more aware of our emotions, too. That is how body awareness works. Each step builds on the next. In my research, I found that the dimension of interoception called emotional awareness is the most statistically important in creating a kinship with the Earth. But we cannot be aware of what we are feeling if our bodies cannot sense sensation. It starts there.

When we listen to what feels good, we are gathering attention back into the body. We are reorienting to sensation as a bridge to connection, consent, and our erotic nature. We are returning to the garden of our body. We can practice simple questions as we move through our days: *Does this feel good? How do I know?* Even the mindful sensation of washing our hands, for example, can bring us into contact with our yes. I have found that being attentive to the quality of how I interact with my soma throughout the day is a good starting point of feeling pleasure, of awakening to my eros. I call this mindful, self-compassionate touch. Expressing loving-kindness to myself through intentional, physical contact has been a profound practice.

"I touch my own skin, and it tells me that before there was any harm, there was miracle," writes activist adrienne maree brown in *Pleasure Activism*.[13] The erotic implicates the relationship between ourselves and our bodies. Yet there I was, poking and prodding mine to find a cure. In so doing, I approached my body more like an "other" to be controlled instead of with curiosity, consent, and care. What was my animal body trying to say?

I wondered if I really had the ability to come close to my own desires as Lorde describes. Could I honor the pulsing yearnings of my animal being? Did I even have any idea what those were? Could I feel with the whole of me?

In the doctor's offices and blood labs, life felt quite literally leached out of me. Endless medical examinations are incredibly disembodying, even as they apparently center the soma. It's distortion and fragmentation, not sensorial wholeness. And in these spaces, I was certainly not connected to the Earth. I'd also seen and experienced trauma that made it very scary to feel. If I opened to that grief, would there ever be a bottom?

I wanted to hold basketfuls of berries, all juicy in my fingers, but instead I felt like the living dead.

I feared that my learned and forced disembodiment had contributed to my autoimmunity. I was only just beginning to reckon with the patriarchy's impact on my life. Which is to say, in my midthirties, I was only just starting to recognize all the ways society had taught me to silence my yes to survive. While I will not now, and will not ever, blame sickness on the sick, systemic intersectional injustice replicates like disease through our bodies. Internalized patriarchy corroded my capacity to be freely and erotically embodied. That is, until I gestured to say *No, I will not be a carrier for this gene* and started the lifelong process of unclipping the wings of this maniacal, historic ill.

Every encounter with the living Earth invited me to detangle the destructive systems that had taken root in me. Where the medical industrial complex was sterile, the Earth was sensual. Where traditional Western medicine told me I was broken, the Earth said even my aberrations were perfect. Where doctors told me I could not do much to improve my quality of life, the Earth beckoned with endless possibilities for joy.

I do not want my body to be a host for the systemic diseases that make us and the planet ill. Even still, could I really hope to live in sync with my pleasure with all my embodied complexity? Of course, I wanted to. But the erotic? Is there a place for the erotic in sickness?

Eros always finds a way. Is it not the impulse of desire that motivates the stigma to receive pollen in a microscopic embrace that has sustained life for millions of years? Is it not eros that brought the very first cells together, dancing in their embrace? Is it not eros that helped plants evolve flowers to attract pollinators, animals to develop songs and displays for courtship, and humans to create art, music, and ceremony to touch the divine? Is it not the sheer torque of creation energy that miraculously joins a sperm and an egg into a zygote that will create the mystery that is a human being?

The Aspen's white trunks glow like moonlit skin. Underground, their roots intertwine in an intimate embrace in an endless exchange of giving and receiving. Eros is the pulse of life. Desire is at the heart of existence.

Banishing our thirst only drives us to fulfill our needs in distorted ways. No, it is not desire that is to be feared, but the lack of it.

I was on a night walk in the Maroon Creek valley, which I relished. The onyx shadows of trees, contours in shapes I'd never seen, wound into mesmeric patterns. Suddenly, I noticed that an unusual motion sensor light had been tripped by the animal stable. I approached.

I saw the body perched as if on the precipice of a pyramid. Perfectly still like a cloud, the llama rested in snow, white on white. Except the red midnight oil of itself, which spilled everywhere. A fox upturned their head when they heard me, stealing a glance away from their quiet feast, so as not to disturb this little life. I was witness to a Rocky Mountain *Pietà*, the grandness of the llama's dying body descending with the same ease as the Carrara blue-gray marble sculpture of Mary holding the slain Jesus.

I could almost hear the heart of the fox, racing as they finished their stolen meal. I looked back once over my shoulder as I walked away. These creatures seemed captured in amber, the stillness punctured only by the trees' figurines falling over them in long striping shadows.

The next day, they told me it was a mountain lion that did it. *Hungry*, I thought, *so very hungry in this long winter.*

Later that night, I heard a single shot.

"They got him," they told me later.

I felt neither relief nor disgust. But rather the deeper pulse of the force of life vibrating in my hands. There and then extinguished. I couldn't stop thinking about that mountain lion, wild, as it should be. And the quarried marble stone body with feathery gray veining, so decorative and tragic all at once. Isn't it like that? The irony that it is our desire that might get us killed, but it is also the neglect of that desire that surely will?

The lion brought me face-to-face with my own nature. The animal's primal yearnings gave me permission to touch my primordial aches. We are animals. We are hungry. We have to satisfy that hunger, or we will not survive. Even in sickness, if I reach deep enough, I can contact the pulse of my own appetite.

Our animal nature doesn't have to make us vicious; instead, it is where all of our sensitivity and reverence exist. We forget our animal because we can't remember what it is to be feral. We forget our primal because we can't recall what it is to be a primate.

Getting in touch with our yes threatens the status quo because it wakes us up. The systems that perpetuate inequalities and injustice of all kinds thrive on people staying asleep. Separating us from our hungers perpetuates numbing amnesia. I think of the billions of people watching screens instead of trees. Scrolling instead of rolling in the dirt with the unruly burst of dandelions. Buying things instead of staring dumbstruck at the moon.

I want to paint myself in yellow pollen. Drench myself in a river. Decorate my hair with Pine needles, bluebells, and tears. The overculture conspires to keep our desires small. Maybe it's not that we want too much; it's that we want too little.

This is not to say all desire is weighted with moral equivalence. Of course not. I am not suggesting we indulge deviant yearnings that could cause harm to self or another. Rather, I am speaking to that part of us erotically woven into the Earth that might need the invitation, the *permission*, to wake up. In this, I am assuming a baseline of human goodness. However, having documented crimes of war, I am too familiar with how desire can be warped into horrific cruelty. I would say to that, though, that even in what a perpetrator might think is desire is actually a disconnect from the fruit of nature, which is measured by kindness, sharing, reciprocity, conviviality, and mutual flourishing. If desire does not lead us to those values, it is not eros but greed and exploitation.

If the erotic is akin to "life force," according to Lorde, and is a principal bridge to creative power and feeling, then the climax, so to speak, is a life lived in sync with one's yearnings. And why is this dangerous? Because people who are awake will see the truth of how our society and culture are destroying human bodies and the planet. Sober, bright-eyed, conscious communities might challenge patriarchy, capitalism, racism, imperialism, colonialism, and more. I venture to imagine what kinds of protests, changes, and shifts we would uprise together in the name of love.

Thus, the erotic is not an individualized self-fulfillment quest. The erotic is fierce—it is power—it is creation energy. To be in touch with one's aliveness is revolutionary. Ultimately, erotic ecology is an orientation to welcome and protect life, wherever it is found. For in communion with the erotic, we will not accept the degradation of our bodies or the Earth body. In communion with the erotic, we will protect the lifespring of shared life because our life depends on it. Lorde culminates her argument: "Recognizing the power of the erotic within our lives can give us the energy to pursue genuine change within our world, rather than merely settling for a shift of characters in the same weary drama."[14]

Eros, then, is a radical principle of ecology that, when cultivated, will provide the fuel to generate right action in the world. In this way, erotic ecology is both a worldview and a contemplative practice.[15] It basically says this:

My body is the Earth body.
I welcome my YES as an act of defiance to separation.
I welcome my YES as a gesture of loving-kindness for all beings.

May it be so.

The Redwood tree elders created a spider's web of darkness, fog, and air. On the forest floor, there was night that day did not touch. The silence was not silent but packed full of a thousand sounds. And yet, I was quiet.

I noticed a felled and rotting Redwood. Struck by lightning in some year, this being was now a beast. Char snaked up the dead bark toward their heart of hunger, which had exploded in one dazzling blast. The dead mother tree was surrounded in a perfect circle by about five other Redwoods. Were they shielding?

Watching? Waiting? *Your mother is dead*, I wanted to tell them. But they already knew.

I needed to be inside them. I squeezed myself like a pressed flower in between the trees to get into the center of their assembly. I stood right on top of the dead mother. What I wanted to happen didn't: The Redwoods did not welcome me with open arms; the leaves did not shake in my presence; the sun did not shine on my face. I was an intruder, and I knew it.

I waited and listened like sand on the shore, numberless and infinitely regular amid such fathomless grandeur. The Redwoods were so tightly woven around this dead tree that I nearly missed her. This was not a passive gathering, but a summit. Was this a séance to draw the dead mother tree back to life or bless her into eternal sleep?

The Redwood encircled this creature in an orbit of electricity. Pulse. Heat. Flame. I succumbed to the winged god's weapon. I began to move in rhythmic patterns in response to what I felt, swaying with the energy that was there. I found myself dancing with the dead mother, her lovers, and the liminal Earthly radiance I could feel in their presence. There was no other way to say it: I was penetrated by the Earth's eros.

Even while sick, my erotic and embodied ecology with trees pulsed and grew, creating an ecosphere of enlivenment. Together, we became a revolving constellate burst of desire. As the trees pursued me, and as I responded to the primal yes in my body, love (eros) and soul (psyche) became one.

We are entangled with the Earth. Our pleasure, our desire, and our futures are connected. We inhale oxygen that is exhaled from the trees. We are alive only because the Earth is alive. Audre Lorde insisted that feminism and racial justice cannot be separated. Neither can erotic ecology nor racial and environmental justice.

In an interview for my PhD research, Detroit-based environmental activist and artist Liz Kennedy says that eco-eroticism and intersectional justice are intertwined. Scholars like Donna Haraway, Andreas Weber, Alexis Pauline Gumbs, and many more say the same. A sacred relationship with the Earth is not just for private pleasure but, rather, is meant to catalyze collective emancipation. Eros is reciprocal. It's not just about us waking up to our own pleasure, but becoming receptive to the eros of the Earth. What pleasure does the Earth desire? What life are they fighting for? What makes them feel good?

Love is for liberation. Eros, therefore, dissolves individual love into an interspecies quest for freedom. Such sensual encounters serve to trouble binary frameworks, echoing scholar T. J. Demos's invitation for the human and more-than-human to stretch together toward an "emancipatory horizon."[16] Erotic ecology enchants and heals our individualism.

Eros is our fuel to love, tend, and care for all the living beings we are connected to, from the underland to the overstory. Absolutely no one and nothing is left out. We have yet to imagine what the Earth would do if we opened ourselves to the creatures and critters, plant life and ocean life wanting to dream through us along the waterways of our collective desire. I see a radical reorientation of bodies and ecologies that fully express our entangled love. I see new ways of living springing to life through co-emergence. I see more life for all life.

The Earth is reaching their arms out to bind us to one another, so we all may exist free of exploitation. Difference and multiplicity are the praise of the Earth. Just as the lark is not the same as a bluebird, nor an Aspen the same as a Cottonwood, love honors and respects difference. Love does not seek to reduce us into sameness.

May we witness the love inherent in the Redwoods who encircle their dead mother, in the courage of the mountain lion haunting the wintery night for sustenance, in the bumblebee falling into the flower. These are signals, lights on the emancipatory horizon calling us to acknowledge and honor our erotic intelligence. What are you attracted to in nature? Can you trust that?

The Romantic lyrical poet John Keats famously wrote, "Beauty is truth, truth beauty,—that is all / Ye know on earth, and all ye need to know."[17] Indeed, the eros of the Earth is all we need to remember.

Come, taste the wine of the Earth's erotic body. Come, allow beauty to pursue you. Come, let the Earth become your lover.

Body Practice: Welcoming Back Embodiment

So often parts of ourselves or our entire bodies might be in exile from the conditioning we've received from the overculture. In this practice, we will work to undo this exile and allow our own being to be the beacon welcoming us home.

Opening attention to the sensation of water is a helpful stimulant, so I invite you to complete this practice in a body of water. If that is not accessible, choose a place of ease, even if that's just lying down in bed. You can adapt this practice by bringing your attention to whatever is touching your skin, be that water, clothing, or bedsheets.

If you do decide to practice in the shower or bath, begin by turning on the water to a pleasurable temperature.

As the water washes over you, tune in to the sensation of it on your skin. What do you notice? What is the temperature and pressure of the water? What is the feeling state of the sensational experience?

Wiggle your toes and feel the water drip through them and squish in the bottom of the shower or bath. Notice the water sliding down your back and onto your legs, running through your hair and down your face.

Take a few moments to map the sensations in your body and name them out loud, observing what it feels like to be in your body in this moment. Perhaps your feet feel warm, or there's a tightness in your belly, or your face tingles in response to the water's touch.

Now begin tapping (or gently slapping) your feet with your hands. Find the pace and pressure that feels best to you. Bring your full awareness into your feet, noticing what the contact feels like in that area. Then, out loud, say, "These are my feet. Welcome back."

Then move up to your ankles: "These are my ankles. Welcome back."

Move up slowly through each part of your body—your lower legs; your hamstrings and quads; your hips and pelvis; your belly; your torso and chest; your back, arms, and shoulders; your neck, face, and head—and give each part a gentle welcome: "Welcome back, welcome back, welcome back."

Move through every part to bring presence back in while reclaiming your connection to your body.

When you're ready, transition out of the practice slowly and gently by bringing loving awareness to whatever action you'd like to engage in next. Now that you've welcomed your awareness into your body, send it some gratitude and love for the ways it supports you. If anger or sadness arise because your body is in pain, see if you can meet that with gentle awareness as well. Perhaps your body is trying their absolute best to support you. Perhaps extending just slightly more loving-kindness can deepen a sense of belonging.[18]

Tree Practice: Touching the Tree

In this practice, you are invited to explore the world of sensuous pleasure with a tree and open your awareness and sensory landscape to the feeling of the tree's physical form. Go ahead and approach your tree and ask for permission to touch them. If you do not receive a yes, consider simply spending time with the tree without touch.

If you feel that you have been given permission, approach the tree and touch them. Explore the textures of their skin. Get closer and smell the tree. Run your fingers down their spine. Explore their leaves. Are they flat, needle-like? What color? Texture? Go low to the ground and touch the soil. As you notice what feels pleasurable about the tree, also bring your attention to your own body and feel the sensations that are occurring within. Track the flow from the tree to your body and back to the tree. Allow yourself to explore. Perhaps press your cheek onto the tree's trunk and stay awhile.

Once you have spent some time touching them, take a moment to thank them. Notice what arises in you from this contact and the opportunity to get to know them more closely. Offer a gesture of gratitude.

Growing Deeper

1. "Welcoming back" my body feels _____.
2. One thing that felt pleasurable was _____.
3. Describe an erotic experience you've had with the Earth. If you have not, what did this chapter bring up for you?

4. What did you notice about attraction, desire, and pleasure during the practice of touching a tree?
5. What did you feel when you touched the tree, and how did you notice that in your body?
6. Think back to a moment you have had in nature that felt pleasurable. What was that like? How did you know it felt good?

5

Kinship: Secure Attachment to the Earth

Remember, you are this universe and this universe is you.
Remember all is in motion, is growing, is you.

—Joy Harjo

My original heartwood is my grandmother, Betty Joyce. She had baby blue eyes like the Mediterranean Sea on a May morning, shining and clear. Her giggle shook her whole body like ribbon, and her hands were gnarled like tree branches winding around the sun, turned into curious shapes from rheumatoid arthritis. Before I went to bed, she would press her finger pads made of clouds affectionately on my face. "I love you," she'd say, her hands moving across my skin as if kneading bread, as if to say *We make each other.*

Taco Bell hot sauce packets jammed the drawers in her kitchen, and Folgers coffee canisters lined the counters. Atop the ledge over the sink sat an indoor thermostat made of colored bubbles and glass hummingbirds that floated surreptitiously up and down to indicate if it was 71.6 or 73.2 degrees. She tended to the lavender plant on the windowsill with utter devotion, a beacon of wildness amid suburban development. Her ecological tenderness seemed to rewild the concrete and strip malls out her window. She would excitedly convey the interesting phone calls she got during the day.

"So many nice people," she'd say.

"What do they want?" I'd ask.

"To sell me something. Or maybe, I think they just want someone to talk to."

She made jewelry with those impossible fingers for the local Christmas church bazaar. She never missed a year. Beads were everywhere in that apartment: in between the seat cushions, in the bed, under my feet.

She resides in the densest, innermost part of me. And this is a biological fact. The ovaries of my mother, which contained the egg that would contain me, were carried in her body. This means that my grandmother's world, her likes and dislikes, formed my DNA.

She survived the deaths of three husbands and moved her young family across the Texas and New Mexican plains. I see now that I was not just loved by this woman, but by all the ecologies she loved, too. The Colorado Rockies, the New Mexican desert, the Texan bluebonnet. These lands reached right through her body into mine. The language I learned from the ecology of her heartwood, with rings of human and beyond-human care, was one of unconditional love.

Our relationship was what child development scientists call a *secure attachment*. That's why I see her as my heartwood. She was the sturdy center in a world of chaos. This bond eventually gave me the blueprint to create loving relationships with the living world. She had *shown* me how, without *telling* me how.

Relational attachment theory originated with Mary Ainsworth and John Bowlby's now famous Strange Situation experiment in the 1960s.[1] They witnessed what they called "patterns of attachment" between children and their primary caregivers that created a new understanding of the role of safe and enduring relational bonds and the differences they observed between them. They found that relational attachment patterns are important predictors of well-being and health and follow us throughout our lifespan. Even just one secure attachment for a child, like with my grandmother, can weather the storms of other, more difficult bonds.

In the decades since, myriad scientific studies indicate that attachment security makes people healthier and even leads them to be more compassionate and helpful to others. Secure attachment creates a fascia of loving ties, knitting together a world of goodness. Such relationships satisfy one of our most core psychological needs: the need to belong. Secure attachments are also foundational for developing body awareness and emotional regulation. Psychologists, neuroscientists, and sociologists alike believe that secure attachment is so important that it "may be the psychological equivalent of a broadband antibiotic."[2]

Relationships are the most important part of our lives. The Harvard Study of Adult Development, one of the longest-running studies on human happiness and health, found that relationships influence our well-being more than money and career, and that the *quality* of them, not the quantity, is what matters.[3] Close relationships protect our physical and mental health throughout our lives and are the single most important factor in our joy. Yet, human relationships are extraordinarily difficult, romantic and family bonds particularly so.

Bowlby and Ainsworth's original research discovered the behavior profiles for what are called secure, avoidant, and anxious patterns of attachment. In the decades since, therapists and psychologists have used this model to improve their efficacy to help people overcome challenges in relationships and develop lasting, close connections. What follows is a brief overview of the patterns, although it's best to understand them as a spectrum, not fixed categories.

Securely attached people form happy and healthy relationships that function as a "secure base," from which they can venture out and explore the world. Their nervous systems feel safe when close and safe when apart. Anxiously attached people have overly active nervous systems in connection and often misinterpret distance as abandonment. Avoidantly attached people prefer distance and can feel threatened when coming too close. In both anxious and avoidant patterns, the nervous system is stressed.

There is a fourth category that emerged a decade or so after this initial research: disorganized attachment. This style includes signs of both anxious and avoidant behaviors in chaotic and unpredictable sequence. The body of a disorganized child undergoes physiological distress from human relationships, and their nervous system struggles to find regulation with either distancing or proximity-seeking behaviors.

None of these styles are "bad," and they are not meant to be understood as a hierarchy. But in recent years, attachment styles have become popularized as a diagnostic and co-opted by pop psychology. Avoidant attachment, in particular, has been misunderstood. Child development psychology research indicates that these styles are not fixed, and one study published in *Attachment and Human Development* followed participants over a six-year period and found that the styles are characterized more by fluidity than stability.[4] All human beings desire and need connective relationships, and everyone is capable of building them. One's attachment style is malleable and fluid and can change, meaning everyone can learn how to create "secure attachments" and find the joy, love, and happiness that they bring. In every case, the relational style is connected to one's embodied nervous system capacity. Relationship, just like the language of sensation, is built from our bodies.

I grew up in an alcoholic home, and even though there was sobriety, which is a remarkable feat in and of itself, some of the behavioral dysfunctions of addiction were still present. This led to an unpredictable relationship with my father. Chaos was common. I adapted by becoming hypervigilant and hypersensitive to his shifting moods. I could read a room with laser accuracy, but I could not identify my own feelings, wants, or desires. As I got older, this led to challenging intimate relationships. In some sense, I suffered from disembodiment. The closer I'd get to someone, the more I would be filled with an impulse to run away. The more distant we became, the more anxious I would become. Another language resided below the surface of my skin, the language of sensation, but I did not know it yet.

One afternoon about ten years ago, I was sitting on a rickety metal chair outside the laundromat with a giant blue awning on Fulton Street in Brooklyn. The chair and table were pink. The table had an umbrella. I forget the color. My partner of three years at the time sat opposite me. He was restraining my arms because I'd just tried to hit him. I can't remember what the initial argument was about, but I was so angry. Childish words spilled out of my mouth: "No!" and "I hate you!" among them. I threatened to leave. I threatened to stay. But he was steady and did not react. It was obvious to him, if not to me, that this had nothing to do with either of us. Not really.

What was happening inside my body was a disorganized attachment pattern. I felt overwhelmed with impulses I could not reconcile. How do I maintain connection *and* keep myself safe at the same time? In that tension, my body interpreted bids for closeness as threats, and slammed the fear center in my amygdala like a panic button: FIGHT. FREEZE. FAWN.

I wanted to stay close to people I loved, but my body had trouble with it. Our brain's emotion and behavior regulation center does not know linear time, and processes threats at a young developmental age. As a consequence, cognitive and somatic development do not always sync up. When a young child endures developmental trauma, the resulting core wound, usually having something to do with the fear of abandonment, has trouble surfacing as an adult, because the body is too busy scaring itself. And so, the pattern stays stuck and buried.

These kinds of impacts and responses are not at all uncommon. There is also a link between childhood experiences and adult health. The Adverse Childhood Experiences (ACEs) study, for example, surveyed over seventeen thousand adults about their exposure to various forms of childhood adversity and found a connection between these experiences and chronic health challenges like heart disease, diabetes, and cancer.[5] Adverse childhood experiences, like having an incarcerated relative and enduring emotional abuse and mental illness in the household, can create chronic stress in the body of the child, leading to long-term immune system dysregulation. Children with higher ACE scores are also significantly more likely to have autoimmune diseases compared to those with low or no ACEs.[6] I recognize that it can be reductionistic to say everything comes from your childhood, and it can satisfy the impulse to try to fix a constellation of symptoms that may not go away, but in my case, perhaps there was a connection.[7]

I parked in the strip mall in Santa Monica and walked up the spiral garage driveway. I squinted my eyes against the beating drum of the sun. I paused in front of a full-length mirror on the landing. I looked like a woman who was tired of suffering.

Next thing I knew I was on the table. Emblazoned in red-and-black silk, a bewitching dragon stared at me overhead. Apparently, they would witness my first colon therapy session. I shifted a bit on the table and rumpled the paper below me. Crick, crackle, pop. A friend with multiple sclerosis (MS) swore by this practitioner. She said colonics are good for the gut, which is part of autoimmune dysregulation. And out of all the treatments she had tried, she said this had helped her the most. This friend was a graceful creature who you would never guess lived with something as hard as MS, so I thought I would try it for my autoimmune condition.

After explaining the mechanics of how the colonic works, Violet, the self-described "metaphysical colon therapist," asked for my permission to clear and then read my energy.

"Sure?" I shrugged my shoulders on the table.

"I see a parental figure," she began. "You need to forgive this person."

Of course it was my parent. I was more annoyed than anything. Who *doesn't* need to forgive their parents?

"Think of what forgiveness means during the session," Violet added.

I felt resistant, but I couldn't escape now.

"I will begin, so just relax, and tell me if there is any cramping." Violet started to massage my lower belly.

As my insides inflated with water and then emptied out, so too did my emotions. I felt the physical talons of this complicated relationship in my body. The rage. The love. The gripping. The disorganized attachment. I didn't do anything except let the experience happen to me, which is to say, to let what I was sensing be felt and allow what was leaving my body to *leave*.

It felt cathartic, though usually I am suspicious of that. The process of release can inadvertently put people over their nervous system's threshold and carries the risk of conflating purging with healing. Release does not necessarily mean emotions have been processed or integrated. But it can feel good to get things out.

Trauma-informed somatic care does not urge people toward big tears and screams as requisite for healing. Rather, slow shifts, in pace with one's own nervous system, are found to lead to more sustained change over time. Psychologist Jean Piaget taught that growth happens when we move from state experiences to stages of development. I didn't want a fleeting state of healing; I wanted a stage of change.

What is undeniable is that emotions have an impact on our physical health. For example, numerous studies have linked negative emotions with higher inflammation.[8] There is also epidemiological evidence linking emotions to diverse health outcomes.[9] So whether our emotions are from yesterday or thirty years ago, the body experiences them in the now. Emotional and physical health are intertwined.

Forty-five minutes later, it was over. Something had definitely happened. For the first time in months, my head felt crystal clear, and my energy was vital. The lights had been turned back on. Could this be a gut dysbiosis reset? A recalibration of serotonin, of which more than 90 percent is produced in the gut? A reduction in inflammation? Or had I actually forgiven my parent as Violet and the dragon stood guard? Did my emotions really affect my physical body this closely? As I drove away that day, I thought to myself, *Maybe forgiveness is not something you do, but something you allow. Over and over again.*

This experience helped me tend to what are called attachment injuries. Every human being has them. They are emotional wounds from close relationships, particularly where there has been a violation of trust, safety, or security, like betrayal, abandonment, rejection, or neglect. Most parents truly do their absolute best, and it is impossible to avoid some of these wounds. This is not an indictment on parents, but rather an invitation to tend and repair the impact of how our lives invariably touch and affect each other.

Attachment wounds have lasting effects on the nervous system, our body awareness, and, subsequently, the ability to develop secure relationships. Studies show that these wounds predict both how close we can feel with self, place, and others and how satisfied we are with life.[10] We are wounded in relationship, and we heal in relationship.

Somatic therapy, eye movement desensitization and reprocessing treatment, psychedelic-assisted therapy, and spiritual direction are some of the other modalities that have supported me to address these wounds. But what was remarkable to me about the colon therapy experience was that it occurred primarily at the level of sensation, combined with emotional awareness. Through listening to the wisdom of my body, I was brought into contact with difficult emotions that I was then able to allow. These sensations do not need narratives. I found that freeing. It could've been about my father. Maybe it wasn't. Does it matter? What I realized is that if I can't feel, I can't connect deeply to myself, others, or the Earth. And it's in that kinship ecology that healing unfurls. By allowing and experiencing what I am feeling, greater connection is possible.

Yet the West continues to live deeper into disconnection. For example, loneliness levels in adults have steadily increased with each calendar year over the last forty years in the United States, according to a meta-analysis of over three hundred studies.[11] And people's relationships are getting worse, too. About a decade ago, another meta-analysis analyzed nearly one hundred studies and found an unfortunate trend over a thirteen-year period: a 15 percent decrease in secure attachment, along with a 56 percent spike in avoidant attachment and an 18 percent increase in anxious attachment.[12] Relationships are hard. And they are getting even harder. Perhaps part of the problem is that we are forgetting about our relationships to the living world, too. In fact, recent research published in the journal *Earth* finds that human connection to nature has declined by 60 percent in the last 200 years.[13]

In *We've Had a Hundred Years of Psychotherapy—and the World's Getting Worse*, Jungian psychologist James Hillman and cultural critic Michael Ventura write, "You can't change yourself without changing your relationship to the world."[14] The myth of individualism destroys our relationships to our bodies, each other, and the Earth. And attempting to heal just ourselves without addressing our kincentric ties to the entangled world is a fool's errand.

Just as the mycelium network, whale song, and Aspen root system each function as one living organism, the chain of the sun's photons and the moon pulling both the oceans and wombed bodies into elegantly paralleled cycles shows us, we are not islands. As much as Western culture would sell us otherwise, *we belong to one another.*

But when confronted with human-driven climate change, it's clear our individualism has caused such a mess. We are more like a poison or a virus to the Earth than a participant in the fabric of being.

I'm thinking about how our fossil fuels caused such enormous forest fires in the heart of the Amazon basin that particulate matter floated all the way to the United States and choked the lungs of people in Los Angeles. I'm thinking about how, at the time of this writing, forest fires in Oregon, Washington, and Canada are pushing smoky air so far south that the Roaring Fork Valley in Western Colorado is blanketed in haze. Outside, the air is putrid pink, a harbinger of the death of trees in faraway places. With every breath, I inhale dying trees. And soon, *those* places might be this very canyon.

We live in a window, a sliver of time when we can still revive the relationships necessary to preserve love's ancient architecture, to protect all living beings. Through a kincentric lens, humans and the Earth need one another. We are in this together. But since humans are responsible for the damage, it is up to us to garner the courage, vision, and heart to change course. We can yet restore our relationships with the living world. We can still find our way back to connection. If we are still breathing, it's not entirely too late.

As I walked up the path toward them, my mind was fixated on the future. I would be leaving to go back to Los Angeles soon. Just the thought of being so far away from my Aspen family generated a familiar sensation: pain. Nausea rose up from my guts and slithered around my throat like a boa constrictor, pulling tight. My breathing slowed to the pattern of a sputtering engine. Separation anxiety, but worse.

I arrived at the hearth of my family. The snake slithered off my body, and my breath returned to long, clean inhales and full, smooth exhales. I was haunted by a question: *Could I trust these trees? And if I left, would our love remain?*

I stood in front of the smallest Aspen. I could hear the river—sprinting—right through my veins. I could feel the sun—sultry—syncing with my own pulse. Their bone-colored trunks were like a set of vertebrae. I could imagine that, together, we formed some kind of whale skeleton, big enough to contain the human and the more-than-human. Big enough to hold my questions.

I had read about the *Perucetus colossus* once, otherwise known as "the colossal whale from Peru." Each backbone weighed more than 100 kilograms, and each rib measured 1.4 meters long. Since a whale has nine pairs of ribs, that's 12.6 meters of rib bone, or 41.3 feet, a bit more than the length of a London bus. All that bone, just to be able to breathe.

These trees were a part of me. Together, we breathed in unison. I reached out to the baby Aspen, my fingers enormous around such delicate, spidery limbs. We began an interspecies waltz while standing completely still. The tree and I—palm to palm—listened in a language we both could speak.

I sensed my small place in the order of life. I beheld myself, the trees, and the entire forest in each exhale. While they did not respond to my question directly, my body knew the answer. I did not need to be certain that the trees would never hurt me, leave me, or abandon me in order to feel safe enough to trust them. They were with me. That was enough.

Kinship brings relational repair. The Earth can teach us the deep and lasting refrain of relief of belonging to an ecosystem. My desire for certainty was displaced by something greater: a relaxation into a type of love that is not precipitated on promise, but premised on presence.

The trees taught me how to be in relationship. By sensing my place in the universe's tender geometry, I embodied a feeling of safety and felt free to move toward connection. Fear keeps us separate. Presence brings us close. This is how I learned secure attachment.

Over time, I started to come to the trees with my emotional and physical needs. They became my sanctuary. My nervous system felt easeful, relaxed, spacious, and calm. As I deepened my awareness of my body, I could listen to the language of sensation and gently unwind the calcification that had numbed my sensitivity to connection. That is to say, trees rewired my ability to feel secure. And as my attachment with them deepened, my body fed off this goodness, which spilled over to my human relationships, too.

Imagine if the challenges of our most intimate human relationships could be attended to not just by another human, but by the *more-than-human*? Philosopher David Abram first coined the term *more-than-human* to point us toward the broader ecology as a community of intelligent presences. Everything is alive. And everything speaks. If we had a deeper connection with the Earth, there might be less pressure on our human bonds. We could spread out our need for love into the vast forest and find what our animal bodies crave. We could meet the wider world's gesture toward connection, too. The ache at the heart of the severed relationship with the Earth is a loss of the vitality and conviviality of the more-than-human world. At the same time, every rock, tree, flutter of wind, and spinning hummingbird invites us to reawaken to the erotic relation that moves through us. The sensuous world awaits.

I started to believe that yes, trees could be a secure family system. With them, I felt steady, calm, and peaceful. Scientists call this a "safe haven" or a "secure base." That's not to say secure attachments do not face challenge or conflict. It is just that the relational containers can withstand the storms because the nervous system feels mostly relaxed instead of threatened or hypervigilant. A secure attachment offers the freedom of mutual autonomy and sovereignty within connection. The Earth extends such a safe haven to us.

My experience with the trees invited me to reimagine relationships altogether: Can humans create secure relationships with the living world? Can these relationships shift human security patterns with other humans? But this view is still anthropocentric, so taking it a step further: If so, can such relationships be healing not just for humans, but for the Earth?

In a study I conducted on attachment and nature connection, I found that yes, relationships with the Earth can parallel secure human bonds.[15] I further found that such kinship is connected to our body awareness, motivates environmental care, and improves all our other relationships. The Earth can shift human attachment toward secure relationships, even in the absence of a human bond. This is enormously helpful for those who do not have a heartwood like I found in my grandmother. But we all have the Earth. *All of us.*

The Earth can indeed teach our bodies how to be in right relationship with everything and everyone else. Further, by flipping the focus from what we can get from them to what they can receive from us, we can complicate attachment theory and widen the proposition of desire, love, and relational kinship. For example, what possibilities for desire and intimacy emerge when the boundaries of what counts as "legitimate" human attachments are dissolved? How might challenging rigid human-centric notions of bonding transform an understanding of who and what can participate in relationships of love and care? Of our responsibility to the Earth in relational kincentricity?

The bio-erotic diversity map of desire escapes classical biology, for the Earth is myriad and polymorphous with modes that are not human modes, underscores eco-forester Alan Wittbecker: "Our direct intuitions tell us that the Earth is strange."[16]

This strange Earth is our safe haven. Through this refuge, the Earth can love us as our more-than-human family system, where the pain and history of human relationship is not the dominant relational model. Trees don't supplant our human families, but rather add to them, because they are our kin, too. Through their atmosphere of safety, trust, and reliability, despite change, our attachment wounds can gently move toward stability. The gift is attachment security, which leads to deeper and more satisfying relationships with all kinds of life. Previous studies have documented the benefits of nature contact and exposure[17] and identified important pathways to connect to nature,[18] but experimental work had not investigated our relational attachment to nature.[19] Not until now.

How do we create such secure relationships with the Earth? And how do we ensure these are mutually beneficial? We begin by practicing our body awareness, speaking the language of trees, and cherishing the land of our bodies so that we can create the foundation of a coherent bodily self and become more capable of developing an enduring kinship with the natural world.

Living with a chronic health disease challenged my ability to be a secure base for others. My symptoms made it impossible for me to be reliable and consistent. I felt grief that I could not always offer the refuge to another that I wanted to. I felt grief that I could not necessarily show up for the Earth in the ways I longed to, either. When you are stuck in bed instead of free to meet the trees, what then?

The Earth is somehow consistent, even while constantly changing. The Earth embodies flux while maintaining center. Uncertainty and unpredictability are in the epigenetic memory of the trees. They are not shocked when the seasons shift. They are not startled when the strong wind blows. They know that steadiness and change are intertwined. The false binary dissolves in the

Earth. There is a mutual understanding of change and growth. The Earth is so very aware, so very available, in every moment, that even the erratic is not sabotage.

The Earth is present. The lakes to the trees, the trees to the ground squirrels, the ground squirrels to the foxgloves. Presence is the pathway. Even in sickness, the bridge to connection isn't to force consistency—because not even nature is static—but rather to become so attuned and available, when we can be, that we can ride the waves of change together.

This time of year, sheaths of old snow hold rainbows of last year's Pine needles in their frozen breasts. One day it snows, and the next, the sun blasts right through the white ocean of ice. Not winter, not spring, but something else perfectly ripe and round. I wanted to eat this season between seasons like a purple-hearted plum. I wanted to spread myself like a chasm to fit into the middle of it. I wanted the juice to drip down my chin.

Spring is lauded for its baubles and flair, but this is the stolen time in between. In Colorado, it's called mud season—a gentle transition—when the Earth prepares itself for the intensity of spring. I wonder if it's the Earth's way of finding safety.

In mud season, the Aspens go through their own delicate transition. Between bud and leaf, there is a middle step: the Aspen's catkins. Catkins are fuzzy caterpillar-looking things, two inches long, that dangle from the branches. They are clusters of tiny flowers that contain seeds. And although new Aspen trees can grow without them, and mostly do, sprouting from the common root underground, the catkins offer another way to adapt to change. For a few weeks only, the Aspens wave these little pom-poms in the air as if to say *We believe in life.*

Seeing the catkins makes my heart burst because it's the first proof that spring is indeed coming. I wouldn't want to miss their billowy hands gesturing in the April air. It's their way of finding their footing in flux. And if they feel safe enough, they will bloom. The Aspens embody steadiness and emergence. I want to do the same.

Nothing is certain in this world. And with climate breakdown, our rhythms of life will face unprecedented changes. Places previously considered safe from extreme weather will not be. Already, fishermen can't keep their catch cold enough on the streets of Cairo. Already, people are dying from the heat in Delhi. Already, fires have ravaged Altadena and the Palisades in Los Angeles. Already, floods have swept away children in the middle of the night at Camp Mystic in central Texas. We will lose and already are losing homes, lives, and each other to these disasters. How do we build a relationship with the Earth if we are angry at the Earth? How do we grieve alongside the Earth, who is also experiencing the loss of their beloved kin? We need each other. We must find a way together.

Secure relationships with the Earth can help us do this and come in many forms: companion, a close and comforting friend; lover, a passionate and erotic partner; healer, a tender and compassionate caregiver; elder, a wise and spiritual teacher; family, a welcoming and unconditional safe haven; and refuge, a protective and trustworthy sanctuary. And so many more than I can name here.

Place is always ready for relationship if we are. Whatever the relational model, they all offer a host of psychological, emotional, spiritual, and physiological benefits. The Earth arrives at the doorway of our bodies, able to meet our exact design. Safety is co-created. We can't do it alone. We knit the generous threads of connection together. Like the mycelial universe, we conspire in this effort to renew and rejuvenate ourselves in an ongoing interweavement. This is no small wonder.

How could a tree be safe unless the rains came to nourish them? How could a bee survive unless a flower opened their petals to share their sweet nectar? Every creature cares for the biological world by expressing their fullness through their particular forms.

I look to the trees, the lichen, and the whale to teach me about becoming safe in an unsafe world. They are under constant threat from our fossil fuels and the warming planet. But they persist. And they offer an irreplaceable piece of the structure of life that is essential for its function. The architecture of a seed creates the passageway for a flower to eventually move through the soil. A catkin preps the leaf for bloom. There is a relationship between form and life, process and emergence.

Therefore, it is the relational structure itself that creates safety, where life can flourish and flower. If a tree stopped being a tree, humans could not breathe. If a lichen ceased being a lichen, trees would be exposed to damage, and animals would lose their food source. Every being matters. Every relationship adds up.

The profound freedom of each being humming in vitality within the field of awareness renders the organized universe touchable, even though ever unfathomable. "Nature Alive," says philosopher Alfred North Whitehead in his lecture and essay, arguing that reality consists of processes defined by their relations to other processes, thus rejecting the notion that reality is constructed by independent bits of matter.[20] This holistic framework shows us nature's true face: not passive but purposeful, not mechanical but creative, not fixed but flowing with conscious agency. We *are* nature. We are nature, alive.

Indigenous worldviews like kincentricity and collectivity have long lived by these principles. According to Indigenous knowledge systems, relationship to self, others, and all beings in the living world is the foundation for both understanding and being in the world.[21]

N. Scott Momaday, a Kiowa novelist, poet, and Pulitzer Prize winner, writes, "the Earth is not only our mother but a living, breathing entity with whom we have a deep and sacred relationship."[22]

Instead of the Descartian maxim of "I think, therefore I am," Indigenous knowledge systems say, "We are, therefore I am."[23] *We are, therefore we are.* We are family. Secure attachment, through a kincentric lens, is therefore bigger than an individual; it points to a system of entanglement, a relationship that is not just one to one, but one to many and many to many.

Kinship is a cacophony of microbiomes, fungi, and friendship—a field of loving presence that we can participate in unconditionally. We are a heap of relationships. My grandmother, my Aspen family, the heartwood, me, you. These bonds spin into a communicative power: an erotic and ecological creativity. A numinous and evocative strength that can speak. We move toward them because, yes, in connection we find safety, pleasure, and joy, but what can kinship set in motion?

Refuge with the trees might incline us toward gratitude.
Refuge with the trees might incline us toward reverence.
Refuge with the trees might incline us toward *love*.

Already, the Aspen trees are growing their buds for next year. Already, they are storing them until spring. Even now you can see them on the twigs. The Aspen trees live out their promise to us.

Life.

Growth.

Beauty immeasurable.

What is our promise to them?

Body Practice: Heartbeat Awareness

In this exercise, you will gently practice becoming more attuned and connected to your own heartbeat. You can do this practice anywhere you feel comfortable. Take about five minutes to complete it either first thing in the morning or right before bed. These are the times of day when the body is most still and we can hear most clearly.

Begin by taking a few deep breaths. Quiet your body, and

when you feel calm, lightly bring your awareness to your heartbeat. Tune in to it.

Wait for a while until you can actually sense the subtlety of this sensation. The speed, frequency, and strength of your heartbeat.

If you cannot sense it, place a hand over your heart or your fingers on the inside of your wrist and notice the sensations. Simply stay with sensing your heartbeat for a few minutes.

Now let the focus go. If you do not sense your heartbeat, that is all right. Try again another time. Sometimes it can take practice to be able to sense our inner heart.

Did paying attention to your heartbeat increase it? Decrease it? What did you sense?

Becoming aware of the accuracy of our own heart's rhythm is a core foundation of interoceptive awareness. Doing this practice for a few minutes every day, with the goal of listening deeply, will increase your interoceptive awareness overall. It is a wonderful—and simple!—practice.

Tree Practice: Family System of the Earth

For this practice, spend about twenty minutes with the tree you have been building a relationship with, with the intention of exploring your familial tie to one another. You may have already felt a different relational role with the tree you are getting to know, but for this practice, lean in specifically to the notion of *family*.

Sitting or standing near your tree (whichever is most comfortable), take a few deep breaths and settle into mindful awareness.

Now, consider the qualities of a family system that you notice in the tree and the forest or area around them. For example, is there a parent? Elder? Child? Are they close in proximity? Can you sense how these trees take good care of each other? What is the role of a family system in a forest?

Now, bring the word *safety* into your awareness. What does it feel like to experiment with finding that with the tree? Do you notice when safety arises? What is it like?

If safety is a core aspect of a healthy relational system, see if you can locate that sense somewhere with the tree or within the forest.

Now, flip the exercise. Does the tree feel safe in your presence? What do you need to shift about your body posture, energy, or intention so the tree can also feel safe with you? What sensations arise in your body that let you know this?

If you have a few extra minutes, tune back in to your heartbeat in the presence of the tree.

After about twenty minutes, close the practice by thanking the tree. Take a few moments to write down what you noticed about the idea of *family*.

Growing Deeper

1. When listening to my heartbeat, I noticed _____.

2. Practicing tuning in to my heartbeat was _____.

3. How I sense trees as a family system is _____.

4. What relationship in your life has been secure and safe? What are its qualities?

5. Describe a time you experienced those qualities with the Earth. What was that like?

6. When you listen to the Earth, what does the Earth need from you in order to feel safe?

6

Heart to Heartwood: Listening to the Soul of the Earth

> *Listening with the heart means hearing not just the words of the land but its silence, its pauses, and its deep, unspoken feelings. It's about creating a relationship of trust and mutual respect.*
> —Leanne Betasamosake Simpson

A lone mountain bluebird sang their dirge, piercing the morning with a rapturous keening. Their feet were coiled tightly around the trees like a second skin. Each serpentine, meandering branch was dressed in one inch of perfectly diaphanous ice.

As they hopped back and forth on the high branches, a wedding veil of snow fell sideways across the air, all smeary and blurry in flight. The pale pink morning light bloomed like a Georgia O'Keeffe painting into botanical visions of a lost paradise, always in motion of becoming. My heavy heart had no chance. That seed of awe buried in my breast started to glow.

On my walk, I saw the bird's cousin, the snowy bluebell wildflower, one of the very first blooms in early spring. Their bell-shaped heads swung right above the fresh, unfrozen soil. The flowers seemed to sing straight into the ground: *Wake up, sleepyheads.*

I passed the ferns, their wide green leaves unfurling like scrolls, just about to let me read them. Farther on, an Aspen tree had been pulled up by the roots, probably by a mini avalanche last winter. A part of the heartwood was fifteen feet away from the rest of the trunk, displaced during their open-heart surgery. I knelt to the ground to inspect. The center of the big chunk of tree was fibrous and almost soft, and there were no tree rings. Because of the faint, white-colored bark, it was hard to tell how old they were from the inside.

I felt the impulse to reunite the heart with the body—but I didn't—knowing that already they had become a host to insects, fungi, and other creatures, who, in the tree's death, would find their own lives. I was transfixed by a thin white webbing, now home to a grand palace of other creatures eating, dying, surviving. This was a white-rot fungus, and it would eventually eat every last bit of the tree. White rot is the only fungus that can eat it all, breaking down a tree's tough outer layer of lignin as well as their cellulose and hemicellulose layers. Who knew something so plasmodial could be such a very hungry animal.

I sensed a fault line of heartbreak in me. Who was the forest losing? What would they become? As I beheld this decaying tree, they took on a regality and grace. Like an elder, they offered one final teaching through the generosity of their dying breath. I heard: *If you give your heart away, no matter where it lands, the whole forest will benefit.*

How do we listen with our hearts? How do we comprehend the unspoken of the Earth? To listen, we must pay attention, with the whole body. Attention regulation is one of the eight dimensions of interoceptive awareness and points to the capacity to be intentional with where we place our consciousness. Attention starts within and extends without. A relationship of trust with the Earth might be no more complicated than this: *I am here; I am with you; you have my attention.*

The best antidote I've found to the theft of my attention is to be a student of the subtle. The finest grain detail, the infinitesimal change. The microscopic makes way for the universal, and the other way around. Reliably, I am pumped full of awe. Without fail some new color, texture, or movement erases every memory or seeps out of the old one's edges, and we start again. I go out into nature to begin anew. I am never not welcome.

A dynamic interplay of emotion, sensory awareness, attunement, and receptivity creates the right conditions for us to hear the Earth. And to pay undivided attention to them. Attunement is central to the language of trees and can be thought of as a skill of mindful awareness. In his book *The Mindful Brain*, clinical professor of psychiatry Dan Siegel proposes that interpersonal attunement in relationships leads to more neural integration, which refers to the process by which different parts of the brain communicate harmoniously and explains how mindfulness promotes both relational and internal well-being.[1]

There are two predominant types of mindfulness: focused awareness (such as on the breath) and open, or choiceless, awareness (such as emphasizing a state of allowing). Both are regulating and potent. Yet the allowing/open awareness type of mindfulness is more relevant for attunement, because if we want to speak to the trees, we must widen outward toward the dynamic processual liveliness of the whole forest. Instead of being mindful only of our internal state, we stretch that attention to encompass a wider field. Offering our awareness to nature is a good gift. Other beings can sense when attention is being bestowed upon them. Not *to* an object, but embedded in a phenomenological, embodied experience *with* the living, simmering, breathing world. In this perceptual immersion, we can begin to live from inside a dynamic ecosystem as co-participants. To attune, in essence, is to listen very deeply, with the whole body.

If attunement improves neural integration between people, could attuning to the Earth improve our brain's harmony too? In a phenomenological study of the relationship between humans and the Earth, heightened sensory attunement to the natural world reduced anxiety.[2] Participants cited that their mode of being in the world was primarily sensory, that being with nature was integral to their sense of self, and, further, that this relationship led to a profound impact on their well-being. Therefore, moment-to-moment awareness with the Earthly surroundings was shown to lead to a profound sense of connection and care. We can access more joy by attuning to and with nature.

Trees also attune to each other. Recently, a team of dendrologists used a technique called isotope tracing, where they covered Fir trees with a shaded cloth to block their ability to acquire nutrients through photosynthesis. But instead of dying, scientists tracked as nearby Birch trees gingerly and deliberately sent them sugars. How did these trees know that their neighbors were hurting? How did they intuit exactly what to give? The trees were listening.

Just like human beings, trees are sensitive to certain frequencies. In fact, studies indicate that radiofrequency electromagnetic fields damage trees, including yellowing or browning their leaves.[3] The type of energy they receive from their environment affects how they will grow, just like us. What energy do I emit when I am with the trees? What energy do they give to me in return?

Like all living beings, trees also have electrical activity in their cells, and they even emit electromagnetic radiation at low levels. When I am heart-to-heartwood, the variable rate of my human heart and the rhythmic frequency of a tree begin to synchronize. Scientists call this process entrainment, and as we sync up, our connection grows. We can perceive the rhythms of trees through a variety of vibrations, such as sound, light, temperature, atoms, molecules, and cells and begin to integrate these rhythms with our own using sensory feedback into a spatiotemporal coordination and calibration mechanism.[4] We then become entrained, entwined, interwoven with the natural rhythms in nature like birdsong, the sound of tree leaves, wind patterns, and water movement at multiple levels—circadian, physiological, and even cellular. We are drenched in expressive resonance.

The sonorous moan of the tree's trunks adjusting to changing temperatures. The groan of the leaves as they whir, spin, and quake. The rhythmic flow of a forest canopy, the pulse of the primeval mycorrhizal universe. Trees contain rhythms, and our human systems can sense them.

Entrainment can even improve heart rate variability (HRV), the variation in time between heartbeats. The higher one's HRV, the faster one's body can recover from stress. Where chronic illness creates incoherence in heart rate variability, the Earth can literally do the opposite. Studies show that even just walking in the forest can decrease the heart rate and increase variability.[5] The heart-to-heartwood connection is not just sentimentality; it is physiological healing. And if these benefits happen with just passive engagement with trees, what is possible with mindful, attuned, embodied awareness? What might unfold when we speak the same language?

The 1925 book *The Music of the Spheres* invited readers to imagine what musical notes might ring out from celestial bodies. Before space science had mapped planetary sound, this poetic invitation incanted what harmonies and holy songs might be carved by stars' arcs through galaxies and beyond. What is the song of the moon? What is the chord of Jupiter? What is the chorus of a shooting star?

Today, we know there is a music of the spheres, whether we can hear it or not, and these vibrations interact with our own—creating either dissonance or resonance. When two sonic or energetic wave forms collide, they interfere with each other, either amplifying or reducing amplitude, with complete cancellation occurring only when waves have equal amplitudes and are exactly out of phase. This is a fundamental law of physics.

Nature's waves create resonance with our body's biological ones. Such physiological coherence can amplify our body's innate healing rhythms, leading to harmony. The climbing sun, the dappled light on the Aspen's leaves, the unimaginably tender press of rain. Energetic waves are dancing all over us. Not just among the stars. But in—and through—our Earthly connections, too. Everything shines.

Entrainment with a tree is essentially this same process: Energetic signatures emit from our bodies, wrap around each other, and compose a unique, ephemeral song, a music that has never been heard before and will not be sung again. It's as if the geographies of our bodies can recognize each other and duet at will. We are instruments in the Earth's music, participants in an arching spherical orchestra. Beauty ad infinitum.

My health symptoms started with a very loud sound. I was at a month-long yoga teacher training in Portugal, and it was a day of silence. I was reading the seminal text *Light on Yoga* by B. K. S. Iyengar on a warm, *silent* April afternoon. Right in the middle of a passage about dharana, or single-pointed concentration, a ringing sound suddenly erupted in my left ear. I could not have made that sequence of events up, but it happened exactly like that. And I've had the ringing ever since.

Doctors call this tinnitus, the perception of sound without an external source. Diverse root cause theories proliferate, such as that the little crystals in the inner ear are off-balance, or the neck is misaligned, or that maybe it's the voices of ancestors trying to say something. I'd steamed my ear, gotten it examined, received a chiropractic adjustment, and listened to my inner child, my dad's inner child, and even *his* dad's inner child. No luck.

I feared the sound would erode my sanity. But instead, it taught me about letting go.

Mindfulness techniques served me the most, by helping me become aware of my mind's habit of fixating on the sound and to laugh at myself as I did it for the one millionth time. Would the sound hurt me? No. Was it annoying? Yes. Over time, my reactivity decreased, and it stopped bothering me as much. I felt like a good little Buddhist.

In 2020, living in Los Angeles, the tinnitus suddenly got worse, coinciding with the start of my migraines. The noise woke me up at night, so I started to fear going to bed. This created a cascade of nervous system dysregulation. Two or three weeks in, I was at a feral fracture. Apparently, after thirty-six hours without sleep, you can start to experience hallucinations, and after forty-eight hours, depression. Sleep deprivation can kill you because the body's systems will just break down.

I followed my instincts and went to Griffith Park. I barely made it through the gates. Right past the entrance, next to the public restrooms, I collapsed on the Earth, wet from a recent rain. I felt the soil, raw yet firm. Recognition happened instantly. The matter in me recognized the matter in the Earth. This was elemental—oxygen, carbon, potassium, calcium, magnesium.

I sensed the tree roots, curling lithely underneath the Earth's surface, creating webs of stability, anchoring the trees securely in the organic matter, mineral particles, and living organisms. A mantra came to mind, and I repeated it silently: *I am the Earth, and the Earth is me.* I resisted the urge to narrate or psychologize my pain. I tried to listen from both within and beyond my body. Was I experiencing the resonance of the Earth's energetic wave forms? Was this entrainment? All I knew was that I felt held. Impossibly near in a manner I could not replicate otherwise.

Sound animates the world. And ironically, it was through an unwanted sound in my body that I developed the listening capacity to hear beyond it. I was, in effect, practicing open awareness without knowing it, emphasizing the allowing quality inherent in mindfulness. When you are in pain, noticing the discomfort has limited value on its own. But by falling into an allowing awareness state, the phenomena have room to dissolve.

When in pain, though, all I want is for sensation to go away. I don't want to move closer to it. But there are skillful ways to approach sensation, even pain. Through patience, deep internal listening, and the intentional act of creating more space between a sensation and a reaction to one, our stress response can be down-regulated. Since the brain is where pain originates, not necessarily in our tissues or nerves, by calming the amygdala through open awareness and messages of safety, the pain mechanism can be reduced.[6] Of course, more often than not, pain is chaotic white noise, not distinct notes, and there is no time to choose a reaction. And yet, even in that wall-to-wall chaos, by mindfully slowing down, space miraculously emerges, puncturing the totality of the pain experience.

What is the sound of pain? Can the Earth attend to our cry, wail, moan? Scientists have now captured the songs of fungi, the communication highways of trees, and the sonic pulse systems of whales. When we listen, truly listen, we can hear the harmony of the dawn chorus, the crash of the ocean waves, the buzz of the hummingbird's wings, the creaking of the ground melting from winter to spring, or the faintest sigh of the jasmine flower bowing in the Santa Ana winds. Their voice can soothe our lament. Or perhaps, our heart's howls can crescendo together, an arrangement of resonance. A quartet of gravitational power.

When energy moves through substances in waves, we experience sound. When energy moves through vibrating electric charges, we experience light (although technically light is a particle and a wave). The Earth speaks through sound, and these songs can be medicine.

The acoustic universe of the Earth heals us. For example, in one study, scientists played birdsong for hikers on one trail and ambient noise for hikers on another. They found that those who heard the birdsong experienced increased well-being compared to those who did not.[7] Since 2.9 billion *fewer* birds exist in North America than fifty years ago,[8] it's hard to fathom all that we are missing. For we don't even know the songs of the birds we've never heard. What was the acoustic ecology of our ancestors' ancestors' ancestors? Well, for one, it had at least 2.9 billion more songs.

The field of soundscape ecology chronicles this music and warns us that many of our ecosystem's sounds, or "biophonies," are becoming distorted. Biophonies are the collective sounds made by organisms in a given habitat. When we listen to these soundscapes, we can hear the health and dynamic shifts of whole ecosystems. With practice, we can learn to listen for ecological balance and biodiversity.

For example, humpback whale songs can travel up to ten thousand miles. But commercial ships, seismic testing, and oceanic oil drilling cause such a cacophony of noise that the whales go silent. Their complex, distinct, thirty-four-sound breeding songs just disappear. Not only do the creatures of our breathing world need to hear one another, but so do we.

I couldn't stop thinking about the orca whales deliberately capsizing, and even sinking, fishing and sailing boats in the southwestern European and North African waters. The attacks started in 2020 and more than tripled in the last two years. Perhaps the rising sea temperatures in the area were to blame?

The Iberian Peninsula is a big zone of atmospheric high pressure and has been gaining strength with increased levels of CO_2. The stronger and bigger this pressure system, the less rain and the warmer the waters. Scientists have found that these large high-pressure events are occurring more frequently now than in any other century in the last 1,200 years.

In this hot, hot, unstable sea, orcas are literally ramming their heads into boats during the summer months. Maybe they are mad at humans for what we've done. Maybe they understand that what's going on in their home is madness. Maybe this is their way of saying *Stop*.

Orcas, the apex predators of the sea, target the boat rudders, in some cases even breaking them. One Facebook group with sixty-five thousand members details accounts of the orca interactions, while in another, users share tactics to stop the attacks. Deterrents like throwing sand in the sea don't work, and there are plans to test an acoustic device to get them to swim away.

Although a recent open letter cosigned by close to eighty marine biologists suggests the orcas are just "bored teenagers"[9] and that these attacks are their way to play, I don't buy it. They further say that "science cannot yet explain why the Iberian orcas are doing this." For now, researchers and authorities say the only solution is to leave the area.

The way I see it, orcas are making themselves heard as a critically endangered species. Could this be their way of speaking to us?

We exist.
We are still here.
Help.

I wonder if this is whale body intelligence, turning fear into expression and transforming their untenable circumstances into resistance. To send up a last signal flare to the world, even when that sign is a broken rudder. I don't want the only apparent solution to be abandoning them. They are a siren from the sea reminding us that we are made of plankton, too; we are mammal and animal. The whales want us to know; we are connected. When we learn to hear the world, we can respond to their needs in kind. We can be good kin.

May we feel with our whale hearts, may we sing notes we never knew were inside us. May we come closer to them, wrapping our spirits around their slippery bodies, and tell them *We see you. We're listening.*

After all, only 0.001 percent of the deep sea has even been explored. What do we really know about being a human or whale? To breathe water or air?

The heart of a blue whale is the largest of any animal on Earth. At over four hundred pounds, and over five feet high from the top of the aorta to the bottom of the lowest chamber, this heart is a world. *Teach us*, creatures of the deep, how to feel with a heart as giant as yours. How to welcome life inside our chambers. How to ensure the Body of the World has all of the blood they need.

Tinnitus, when it was at its worst, caused me so much grief because it made silence impossible. As a meditator, I relished the quiet. Without it, I experienced the acutely negative impact of focused awareness. Noticing pain is easy; widening outward beyond what is loudest is difficult. However, by working closely with the tinnitus as a sort of mindfulness teacher, it taught me that there was a much wider sensory landscape to listen from than simply an obnoxious sound. Over time, I have practiced letting go of the impulse to fixate on the noise or fear what it may foretell. In turn, the volume has decreased. And today, I barely notice it, and I can hear silence once again.

Acoustic ecologist and sound recordist Gordon Hempton documents and advocates for areas of natural silence, or "quiet places," which he argues are becoming increasingly rare due to human activity and noise pollution.[10] These areas are characterized by their natural soundscapes and biophonies, where the impact of industrial and urban noise is minimal or absent. Hempton has committed his life to protecting these rare environments due to their ecological and psychological benefits. But while he advocates for the preservation of ecologically diverse sound, Hempton himself has experienced significant hearing loss. Despite his profound commitment to capturing and preserving organic ecological biophonies, he is losing his own ability to hear what he fights to preserve.

Yet, even without the faculty of hearing, listening is still possible. The other senses intensify, helping us "hear" through vibration, touch, and sight. I experienced this with my tinnitus, too. As if the rest of my body learned to hear in ways I'd never dreamed. We could learn from people who are Deaf, and listen with our mouths, our bellies, our hands, and our hearts. The Earth speaks to everyone.

Perhaps we need to become enchanted with the world as a path into deeper listening. If enchantment in Latin means to sing upon or cast a spell and disenchantment means to be without singing, quite possibly, our disconnection from the Earth is the loss of our shared song.

The swallows fly in playful, aerobatic loops high in the sky. Their swooping forms soar way above the uppermost reaches of the tree crowns and drop in dashing, raffish falls. Sunshine surges through the wings of the birds; plummets between curling branches, leaves, and Pine needles; and falls straight into the waiting hands of the silvery lupine and Colorado blue columbine. The light pools there, dripping through the petals, pistils, stamen, stem, taproot, and woody rhizome. Below that teems a world of fungi, bacteria, protozoa, earthworms, beetle larvae, and ants. The O horizon (humus) gives way to the A horizon (topsoil) and eventually descends straight into the R horizon (bedrock). Each profile of soil tells a story about the life of the place. Each swoop of the swallow, effervescent in impish flight, tells a story about the life of the place.

If we listen, what song would we hear?

In my PhD research, I had the pleasure of interviewing philosopher Bayo Akomolafe. He talked a lot about "cracks": the trauma of ecology, the trauma of the body, and how the myth of sanity got us the atomic bomb and slavery, which is not exactly a testament to health. In contrast, he spoke in a melodic and calming way about "blueing boundaries" and "finding cracks." He said that it is inside these fissures that alternatives to toxic systems become possible. Cracks are not problems, but portals to new realities.[11]

I look back at myself prostrate in Griffith Park, at the numberless doctor's offices and wonder, *What if my migraines, what if my tinnitus, what if my pain, was a "crack"? What if my sickness was somehow a portal to a different world?*

In a way, this reframe helped me ensoul my suffering or widen my participation in animate life. Psychologist James Hillman critiques psychology's limited views of healing, highlighting the field's lack of imagination and soulfulness, and its perpetuation of a reductionist, materialistic view of the psyche.[12] In contrast, the trees, and that heartwood elder, cast aside by human eyes, but still teaching their ecological kingdom, helped me move away from seeing the body as a physical structure that needed to be fixed. Ensouled participation, ensoiled in the roots of the Earth, is the healing I'm interested in.

The life we live, I am certain, happens beyond just our physical form. Instead of asking *How can this pain stop?* I am more captivated by questions like *What songs are the trees singing? Can I join them?*

Songs of participation, sharing, community. These melodies heal my individualism and upend my materialist reductionism. In their loving company, I unlearn human exceptionalism and taste the ordinariness of being yet another speck of biological life. I feel great relief in that.

When I was twenty-five years old, my grandmother gave me her beloved wildflower guidebook. Mint green and delicately bound, it holds her decades of discoveries. Meticulous notes are scribbled into the margins: *Not ready this year. Yes! Found it! Must see next June.* This book is the closest thing to an heirloom I ever want.

Now, as I find my own face in the Earth studying the latest wildflowers to grow in the Colorado Rocky Mountains, I feel her mindful listening through my bones. Wildflower season is an endless undulation of discovery and surprise. Over three thousand species grow in just about three months. Watching them stagger and then burst becomes an oceanic experience. I am a diver watching their remarkable hues, contours, and textures rise and fall back into the boundless expanse. Even slight changes in elevation delay or expedite their arrival. On one walk I can traverse through time. Their ethereal and sublime becoming is a perfect teacher in open awareness. My grandmother was a genius to choose them as her elders.

Her attunement, her love, her eros for these mountains spills out of me. She makes me want to listen so completely, from my heart to the Earth's heartwood, that I let myself be reconfigured by what I hear.

And when I get very close to the ground with those baby bluebells, I hear their gentle whirring and sonorous bloom, I hear a music of the spheres: a song of whale-hearted love, a song not of other worlds, but of this one.

Body Practice: Mindful Awareness to Sound

Find a comfortable seat and relax your body. Take a few deep, centering breaths, then allow yourself to tune in to your inner bodily state. What sensations are there? Buzzing? Tingling? Heat? Coolness? A heaviness? A lightness?

Now, turn your attention to the exterior world. What sounds do you hear? Out of all the sounds that you might be aware of, choose one that feels the most pleasant and tune in to it.

Now shift your awareness to sense how the sound travels into your body. How does it shift or change as you allow it to resonate inside? What does hearing that sound feel like within your body? What is the texture, color, tone of that sound?

Now see if you can tune in a layer deeper.

What emotions are present? Can you name or identify any of them? There's no need to overidentify with them or try to change them. Just continue to focus on the sound itself with a soft inner gaze and explore if there is an emotion or feeling that it's connected to.

If listening to a sound feels agitating in any way, you can adapt this practice to instead listen internally for a sensation first and stay with your own inner soundscape until you feel ready to widen that listening to include an external sound.

Once you have linked a sound (or sensation) to an emotion, let your focused awareness go and return to a more open, allowing form of awareness. You have just practiced a core interoceptive awareness skill: being mindful of sensation as it connects to emotions and then recognizing how these change and shift as your attention does.

Complete this exercise again in the presence of your nature place and observe if it is easier or more difficult to link a sensation to an emotion.

Tree Practice: Listening to a Tree's Biophonies

For this practice, you are invited to develop more awareness about the biophonies, or acoustic ecologies, that live within and among the tree you are building a relationship with.

To begin, greet the tree and let them know you want to get to know their biophonic landscape. Listen, attune, and become receptive to your tree. Get to know the biophonies that your tree lives within. Listen for various sounds. Are there animals? Wind? Weather? Is the tree in an urban setting surrounded by the sounds of cars and people or in a forest surrounded by the sounds of their kin?

Perhaps there are specific species of birds that live nearby, or maybe the trickling of a creek lulls your tree kin to sleep each night. Spend twenty minutes with your tree with the singular intention of listening to their sounds and the sounds of the world they live within. If hearing is not available, listen through your other senses.

In reflection, how does tuning in to their soundscape help you know them better? What do you notice from this practice?

Growing Deeper

1. When I practice mindful awareness to sound, I notice _____.
2. What sensation were you able to link to an emotion? What did this sensation or emotion tell you about yourself?
3. What did you notice about the biophonies of your tree?
4. What did you notice in your body when you listened so deeply?
5. What stood out to you by listening heart to heartwood?
6. What is one way you can practice more open awareness in your daily life?

7

Composting Grief

The heart that breaks open can contain the entire universe.

—Joanna Macy

I dared myself to go down to the river deep in the woods under the new moon. For three nights every month the forest is darkness absolute. I had to face the cosmogonic oblivion. I didn't know what else to do. The hurt was huge inside me. Like a pressure, a sea filling me from within. I thought I might burst, spilling sadness over the side of my shores. It was terribly hard to live in a body that was so unpredictable. It was terribly sad to navigate so much of that on my own.

When I got to the bridge, I said a prayer quickly over the side, tossing it into the inky waters, and then ran back up to the road into the twisted arms of the velvet tree shadows, where I could finally exhale. I didn't know what might meet me in that opacity, but it made my heart race. I went into the moonless night to practice facing fears that had nothing to do with my body's pain.

I went into the hollows to grow my snakeskin, so I could slither through it. But grief is more layered than skin.

Grief is difficult to write about. It slips through my fingers. Concepts do not hold it well, and sentiments are broken by it like sediment. The more I look directly at it, the more prismatic it becomes. Grief seems to take on infinite expressions. One moment the despair of my corporealgia loudly goose-steps all over me. Another it's the faintest hum. We learn to live with these augmentations to our realities. We adapt to grief, even if it means growing around the pain instead of welcoming it inside us. Grief changes us.

To live, and to love, means we will inescapably feel and face losses of all kinds. This is a fact of life. The tree grows because they've learned to hold their ongoing dying at the center of themself at the very same time that they keep on living. That is what the heartwood is. Grief is food for growth.

We can't avoid the losses of our lives. Yet coming close to our aches is not just important for our own souls; it matters for the wider ecological world, too. Western culture teaches us to hide, bury, and sublimate grief. We have been conditioned to numb or dissociate from what is hurting. Yet avoiding pain and turning away from heartbreak does not make it disappear.

Psychotherapist and "soul activist" Francis Weller explores grief through the lens of alchemy in his book *The Wild Edge of Sorrow*.[1] He presents what he calls "the five gates" of grief as inevitable sources of pain in our human lives. Each of these liminal crossings are difficult to digest, but they hold the same invitation: *Come closer*. If we refuse, pain will bury itself in our bodies and our hearts, coming out sideways as painful symptoms, lifelessness, and soul anguish. If we feel what's here, even when it hurts, there is no promise that it will lift. But likely, it will *shift*.

Grief is a phase between worlds. Transpsychic and transcendent, it presses us impossibly toward facing loss. This process becomes its own doorway. But how do we approach such a threshold? We must walk toward it, and then we must traverse through it. There is nowhere to hide when radical sorrow unravels the fabric of our lives. I know. I, too, tremble at the sight of it. I, too, have slid on my bathroom tile, clutching my belly in so much pain from grief, I did not think I would survive. The body doubles over from loss. We can be flattened by a force that seems to erupt from a gap in the cosmos, designed specifically to take us down.

Grief can feel deadly. But since grief and love are two sides of the same face, as the poet Pádraig Ó Tuama writes in his poem "The Facts of Life," "...you might as well live, and you might as well love."[2] Becoming intimate with our sorrows is an essential part of being human, and of being more than human.

I can't even remember the exact moment the Earth became my partner in grief, but the practice is now so familiar, it's as if we've always done this. Just yesterday, my heart felt sunk with sorrow. Grief had tunneled inward, carving paths into corners I did not know were there, eating my guts as it went. Grief can be a hungry ghost.

I was on my walk when I came across a fallen tree. The bottom part of the trunk was on its side, the roots flailing into the air. The tree had been cut to make way for the trail. Gray bark, smooth and soft like the tender underbelly of some creature. I did not recognize the type of tree. Perhaps during all the rains, their particularities had been wiped clean. Perhaps they were slowly becoming geological. Perhaps they were already some unwavering stone.

Even on their side, the size of the trunk rose to hip height. Perfect for draping. I laid myself over them and surrendered to the Earth's quiet pulse. As soon as my body landed, tears came. The tree beneath me had motion, even in their stillness. As I cried, I thought about how I did not want to burden the tree with my grief. But they could hold what I carried.

Shhh, I felt from within. *This is not a burden to me. Come, lay your heart down. Rest a while. When you are ready, the whole forest will walk you through the doorway of grief. You are not alone.*

A sheath of fluffy white cotton from a fireweed flower descended through the air over me. Fireweed is a nearly six-foot-tall flower with purple and pink blooms and is known to grow primarily in disturbed areas, or places that have survived disasters like avalanches or fires. In August, it turns into a parachute, distributing up to eighty thousand seeds from a single stem. The luminous organza floated aimlessly by me. How beautiful that this flower tended exactly to the places that hurt the most.

The tree was soft, so very soft. And it offered me the simplicity of steady presence. A strong enough container to hold me as I fell apart.

On my way back in the other direction, I placed an Aspen branch I'd found on the tree's belly. A gesture of gratitude. The little green leaves put their own hands on the tree then. As I walked away, I knew they would hold each other, come what would and what may.

Where grief can feel so complicated, here the tree made it very simple. They held me. They witnessed me. I wanted to trust that bond. I knew it was our healing ground. Where unwitnessed grief causes much more pain than the original wound, their kinship was the elixir. "Those who love us never leave us alone with our grief. At the moment they show us our wound, they reveal they have the medicine," writes Alice Walker.[3]

During my chronic illness and my years of witnessing immense injustice through documentary filmmaking, I felt that I had walked through all of Weller's five gates of grief, over and over again.[4] You may have walked through many of them, too. I thought I could "process" them on my own. But grief must be attended to ecologically. The tenor of grief can be heavy and dense, raw and piercing, vast and oceanic, ancient and primal, fluid and unpredictable. How do we attend to something so wild?

Our living world is the community of witnesses we need—they hold the power to share what hurts. The Earth's wisdom holds out an invitation to us: *Bring me your deepest pains*, for they are powerful food for transformation. Arm in arm with the Earth, we can enter the inarticulate pain together.

Grief is like a seed. Inside its hard casing and brittle exterior is the potential for new life, the living pulse of love. When we take the risk and open to it, the water can nourish, the sun can revive, and life can surely grow. But if we avoid the opening, the seed stays buried. What if every single sorrow we ever had was simply a seed?

Some enter the gates of grief by choice—through childbirth, meditation, or psychedelics—but many times we are thrust through them by illness, loss, and unforeseen life circumstances that no one would ever choose. Whichever way we get there, softening around our seeds of grief will invariably bring us face-to-face with all there is to mourn. The fourth gate of grief, according to Weller, is the sorrows of the world. This includes ecological collapse, species extinction, and all that befalls our planet. Opening to this grief can feel especially hard. The West does not have cultural practices that honor and hold such pain. How do we open our hearts to a planet in ecological peril? How do we soften around that tight, tough seed? We start small, with what is right here.

A concerto of voices from my Buddhist eco-chaplaincy cohort filled my apartment in the early-morning light. Outside, a faint buzzing sound kept distracting me from our discussion on decolonization. Something was going on. I peered out the front door, all quiet. I looked out the kitchen window, and there it was. A man was eye level with me on the second floor, tangled in the trees that lined the back of my building. He was sitting in the bucket of a chip truck. And he was lobbing the tops off the trees.

My heart started to race, and my body filled with an itchy, sandpapery sensation. I *loved* these trees. They created a sanctuary by hemming me in from the concrete sprawl of Los Angeles. The California scrub-jay and the mourning dove nested in them, and violet purple and iris blue morning glory flowers bloomed all over them.

Instinct took over, and I abandoned the Zoom call. I ran outside and up to a pile of treetops scattered on the asphalt, surrounded by a group of men. A chipper-shredder truck was decimating the carcasses. I had to scream over the din:

"*Excuse me*, hello, I live here!" I shouted, pointing at my building. "What are you doing?"

"WHAT?!" one of them yelled back.

"I *said*, what are you doing?"

"WHAT?!" he said again.

Another one flipped off the chipper-shredder. It ground to a halt.

"I said, I live here!" I continued to wag my finger like a flag of surrender. They looked at me blankly. "Why are you cutting down the trees?"

"Ma'am, the owner called us in," one man said as he lazily gestured to the house next door over his shoulder. "Technically, these trees are on his property, and he wants them cut back. They are getting too wild."

Too wild? Dumbstruck, I inspected how they were shoved in between two buildings like thin dividers in forced lines. There was no space for them to turn feral.

"But these won't grow back correctly." I stuffed my hands into my pockets. "Please?"

I looked up at the remnant. The man in the bucket was about two-thirds of the way done. If he left the trees as they were, the remains would be about eight feet taller than the others. It looked ridiculous.

"I'm sorry, ma'am, but we have to finish the job," he said while shuffling his weight in annoyance.

I saw another man with a chainsaw going for the lower branches.

"That is on *our side* of the property," I said defiantly, using terms of ownership.

He backed away.

We were in a stalemate. Bucket man hoisted high in the heavens. Me in the pile of branches. Them waiting for me to leave them to it. I had no power. I did not "own" the property next door.

But who owns the trees? Who gets to decide their fate?

"Can we finish our job now?"

I turned around, deflated, and went back up to my apartment. The grinding continued. I put a pillow over my head. I had failed.

When it was completely silent, I went out to survey the damage. The birds had gone, the flower petals hugged the dirt, and the remaining trees were wasted thin. Where there had been bursting life, color, and entanglement, now there was precise control, boundaries, and bodies. This was not tree trimming. This was murder.

"Tree topping" is an improper trimming technique, whereby the trees' most dominant trunk—or branch leader—is cut at random. The attempt to reduce the tree's height results in unhealthy and unsafe conditions for the tree. When the crown is topped off, the tree can no longer support itself. Basically, their spines had been cut in half. I knew the trees would have a stress response to the whole thing, one day resulting in spindly, weak branches sprouting in a mass at the end of the cut.

If you know what to look for, decapitated and deformed trees are all over urban areas. They have those signature blobby knobs of branches growing out of stumps. This is evidence of tree topping. It's the same as permanently deforming the tree, reducing their life and ruining their future. And yet this is how humans and trees live together in many urban areas.

The Earth's ecosystems are dying all around us. Forests are being clear-cut, reefs are bleaching, species are going extinct, ice caps are melting, and freshwaters are drying up. And all because of human activity. As massive amounts of carbon that had been safely buried under the Earth's surface for millennia are released into the fragile atmosphere through deforestation, and as carbon emissions increase from fossil fuels and livestock, the oceans acidify, and the balance needed to sustain a livable atmosphere becomes increasingly impossible to maintain.

Ninety percent of the climate's heat goes into the oceans, disrupting its cooling system and regulatory power over the climate. Some scientists have stopped using the term "global warming" and instead call this the era of "global boiling" to elucidate the escalating intensification of thermal conditions. For example, as of this writing, July 2024 was observed as the hottest month on record, according to the National Oceanic and Atmospheric Administration (NOAA), surpassing all previously recorded global climate data.[5] The world is getting dangerously close to a long-term breach of the 1.5°C mark, a goal put in place to avoid the worst impacts of climate change. In fact, the first twelve-month period to exceed this average was February 2023 to January 2024, according to Copernicus Climate Change Service.[6] We are already here. It is not long until that is the permanent norm.

Though this number may seem abstract, every fraction of warming matters. Exceeding 1.5°C could trigger multiple climate tipping points, such as the breakdown of the ocean circulation system, abrupt permafrost thawing, and the total collapse of the tropical coral reef system.[7] What this means for human life on planet Earth is a rise in global public health emergencies and an increase in extreme weather events like floods, wildfires, heat waves, droughts, and heavy precipitation, according to the Intergovernmental Panel on Climate Change (IPCC).[8] We are already seeing that occur. From 1980 to 2024, an average of nine extreme weather events occurred annually in the United States, each costing over $1 billion in damages, according to the NOAA.[9] However, that average has jumped up to twenty-three events per year over the last five years (2020–2024). This represents a significant acceleration in extreme weather frequency. Additionally troubling is the announcement from the current administration that they will no longer be updating this data set.[10] Yet the blatant and dangerous choice of blind ignorance in the face of climate collapse will not save us from the weather events that are certainly on their way.

As the ecological crisis deepens, resource wars and climate migrations will increase due to a hotter and less abundant world for certain populations. People in the Global South are the most at risk, with climate change disproportionately affecting those who are the least significant emitters of fossil fuels.

A recent study by *Lancet Planetary Health* found that the countries in the Global North who are the largest exploiters of the Earth's resources are also responsible for 92 percent of global emissions.[11] Yet every corner of the planet suffers this uneven extraction. And what is this all for? Economic growth? Lifestyles of convenience? What will it take to curb imperial capitalism?

Living with climate change in such harrowing times is akin to witnessing a prolonged death. In the last half century, global biodiversity has declined alarmingly. More than forty-two thousand species are now at risk of extinction. And since we are the Earth, when we lose another species, we lose a part of ourselves. What happens to the Earth happens to us. How do we possibly turn toward grief at this scale?

I do not have the answers. I honestly am struggling alongside you with how to navigate such unfathomable loss. I find refuge in Buddhist approaches to being with suffering because avoidance will only amplify the pain. Being with ecological loss, mindfully, with a loving open heart, however small, is not meaningless, and is something all of us can do.

Living with these realities is very anxiety-inducing. It hurts to be so open to the living world such that witnessing a drought, for example, is felt. I cannot unsee the impacts of climate change all around me. Sometimes I wish I could. It's hard. *Eco-anxiety* and *eco-grief* are two newer psychological terms that attempt to grapple with these psycho-emotional-spiritual impacts of climate change. *Eco-anxiety* is the behavioral and emotional experience related to environmental crises, and *eco-grief* is the human response to ecological loss. In a global survey of ten thousand children and young people in ten countries, more than 45 percent said worries about climate change affect their daily lives.[12] Eco-anxiety is a normal response to ecological crisis, and thus treating people for anxiety disorder is a categorical error, a moral mistake. Pathologizing individuals for their appropriate emotional distress instead of holding systems accountable is another way capitalism and imperialism oppress us.

Climate anxiety also surfaces in response to ecological disaster. Will there be another fire? When? We are living in a rapidly changing world where there are no climate safe havens any longer. We need more human communities that can acknowledge, honor, and hold such precarity as well as the anticipatory grief of what might come, so people are not alone in their heartbreak. We need to turn to the Earth to help us hold it, too.

Part of bearing witness to grief is developing the body awareness capacity to digest what feels like anguish. To digest emotions, we can: move our bodies, spend time in nature, seek support from sources of resilience, and engage in ritual. Digestion also implicates our physical guts. This is metaphorical, mythopoetic, and very biological.

The human microbiome is a collection of microbes, bacteria, viruses, and single-celled eukaryotes that contains about 3 million genes working to metabolize food, protect the body from invaders, and modulate the immune system. If the gut doesn't work, food cannot be converted into energy. Many autoimmune diseases have root causes in the gut. Mine certainly did. I had a parasite that would *not* go away. I tried natural treatment, antibiotic treatments, and more, until finally it cleared. Once that happened, many of my overall chronic health symptoms started to improve. A meta-analysis in *Nature Communications* created a MicrobiomeHD database spanning ten diseases and found evidence for the hundreds of clinical studies that have demonstrated associations between the human microbiome and disease.[13]

A tree also has a digestive tract. "Tree food" is formed on contact with sunlight and CO_2, converting it into chemical compounds such as sugars that sustain the tree. Their digestive system is made up of elements within the soil that flow through microscopic ducts in the sapwood and stretch from the tiniest root hairs to the most distant leaves. Without proper nitrogen metabolization, phosphorous utilization, and micronutrient processing, trees won't live. They are dependent on their alchemical powers.

The entire living world has their own intelligence to respond to loss. They grieve, too. There is evidence of this. For example, Tahlequah (J35), a Southern Resident orca, carried her dead calf on top of her body for seventeen days and over a thousand miles through the ocean in the summer of 2018. This extraordinary display of grief captured global attention and became a powerful symbol of animal mourning. When forests are clear-cut, nearby trees experience enormous stress through mycorrhizal and root damage, nutrient deficiency, and even hormone changes that alter growth patterns. Tree mortality rates spike in the first few years after adjacent clear cutting. The Earth also mourns. I wonder, can we grow the eyes to see their pain? Can we witness their animate and articulate utterances?

If we thought of grief like a potential food, then how we process it together in ecological community is what will determine if the pain transforms into nourishment or fossilizes into a deeper wound. Together, with the Earth, we can learn how to make medicine from mourning.

One way to do this is through ritual and ceremony. Weller says that any wound suffered without a container is life threatening. In contrast, life-giving rituals can create the structures through which grief can be liberated. A breathing vessel where we can face what must be faced. Like the psychosis of an overculture bent on annihilation and the horror of many dying trees. A living membrane where kincentricity can be awakened within us by the dreaming body of the Earth. What might emerge in such a living womb?

I studied their form, about six feet in length. They lay haphazardly where they fell from several stories up. Somehow, this one was spared decimation by the woodchipper machine. Here was the top of the tree, erratically cut. Their green leaves were still bright, and they had not yet started to die. I was seized by an overwhelming desire to not leave them alone.

I did what any sensible person would do. I dragged that six-foot treetop down the street, up the red staircase that wraps around my 1920s Spanish building, past the archways that peek onto the Jacaranda trees, through my front door, and into the middle of my living room. I dropped it right there on the white wool rug. The tree made a crucifix shape with the rug's edge. As the leaves shook into stillness, the room closed in on us or grew bigger, I couldn't tell.

I followed my instincts and laid my body down on the tree lengthwise. We held each other, their branches a broken nest for our embrace. I cried into their breast, bearing witness to the death underneath me and the dying outside my kitchen window. Whole families would be no more. I could not tell if the tears were mine, theirs, or ours. I felt foolish, but maybe only because the overculture would call a woman crying over a dead tree a fool. Who cares?

I needed to sweeten my heart because it felt broken. I had the impulse to dip my fingers into a pot of honey, and I smeared it on my chest, right over my heart space. I sprinkled dried lavender from New Mexico over the honey and lay back down next to the tree.

I had never done something like this before or since. My body performed a bereavement ritual like a dance I didn't know was inside me, dragging the tree to a sacred, quiet space to be witnessed, taking my limbs and wrapping them around the dead body. That's not to say I didn't have agency, but something else was going on. Theater, death, and the imaginal are not that far apart. The ritual said to us both, *You are not alone.* The ritual showed me how a tree and a human know in our heartwoods how to work with the prima materia of pain, how to ferment grief's dark matter together, and how to allow it to break us open to a profound sense of love.

The sheer enormity of all that we are losing is impossible to transform on our own. "The sorrow, grief, and rage you feel is a measure of your humanity and your evolutionary maturity. As your heart breaks open, there will be room for the world to heal," writes Buddhist environmental scholar and activist Joanna Macy in her *World as Lover, World as Self.*[14] I hold on to this notion.

We need each other. Together, we can move with the surprising grace of rivers, carrying us through our collective mourning. There is life inside every living being, even if oil companies and governments say otherwise. Like grief itself, what seems to be the most dismissed landscapes are perhaps the exact places that are teeming and bursting with life. We know the truth about these things.

The Earth can be our refuge to hold the pain of the destruction we've wrought against them. In old French, circa 1775, the word *refuge* meant "a place of shelter or protection." In fifth-century Latin, refuge meant "sanctuary" or even "the right to sanctuary." The living world is not an object of extraction, but *a living sanctuary.*

And we all have the responsibility to nurture the garden of this refuge so it can offer a haven for generations to come.

This makes me think of the three refuges, also known as the Triple Gem or the Three Jewels of Buddhism: the dharma (teaching), the Buddha (or Buddha-like nature), and the sangha (community of all beings). The three refuges are often chanted at the start of practice to remind people of what to rely on for support in a challenging world. When I was training as a Buddhist eco-chaplain, we explored as a sangha (community) how to support others to find refuge in the greater sangha, the community of *all* beings.

We can find sanctuary by letting ourselves be held by the more-than-human collective. Both the forest and the houseplant, the community garden and the night sky. Urban or rural, mountain or ocean, there is no place where we are not touched by nature. If you are breathing, you are as close to the Earth as you can possibly get. Nature is inside you, because the Earth *is you*.

May we venture out and find the fellowship of animate life daily, in regular, nondescript fashion, and trust that this co-presence will weave the safe harbor we both need. The consistency of everyday, mundane moments is what makes a relationship a sheltering grove. With a childlike curiosity, we can approach the Earth that is around us and listen with every sense we have.

A soft bed of moss is waiting to hold you. A river is waiting to kiss you. A bird is ready to serenade you. If the community of living beings is our sangha, and if we can indeed take refuge in them, then we must provide the same to the Earth. How can we be a warm embrace of friendship for our animal, botanical, dendrological kin? How can we give the ocean space to breathe, the trees soil to flourish in, the mountains silence to stand in? They need us, too, to weave a hollow of intimacy with the listening world—in which they can thrive, unfold, and become.

We've done so much damage to the Earth, but I believe we can become a source of refuge for them once again.

But what do we do when the world itself is the source of our hurt? When that hurt is hurting, too? When the Earth—through natural disaster, extreme weather, flooding, or fire—causes loss to our homes and lives, multiple wounds are created at once. The grief of bearing witness to myriad intersecting corners of devastation. The grief of wondering what world our children will inherit. The grief of homes floating away in floods. The grief of livelihoods burned to ash in moments. The gift of witnessing humanity show up for each other in these disasters with such exquisite care.

"Can we love what will swallow us when we are gone?" asks Chickasaw poet and environmentalist Linda Hogan.[15] "I do," she says. It's up to us. We can face the latest ruin caused by human-driven climate change, hold the immensity of that pain close, and, despite it all, choose love anyway. Or we can amplify the division, greed, and damage of climate collapse by perpetuating it. Doing nothing is not nothing. That inaction has consequence.

The Earth is not our enemy. The Earth is our home. We are the Earth. If we are to move through this disaster, we must do so in alliance with them.

Joanna Macy spent her life advocating for ecologically conscious grief practices because she believed they are the core missing capacity in Western society that prevents us from meaningfully addressing climate collapse. In her program, Work That Reconnects, she teaches that a spiral of grief can help us develop this ability. And surprisingly, the spiral starts with gratitude. Filling our hearts with reverence creates a base of support for the next steps of opening to pain, digesting it, feeling it, and composting it. If we move around the spiral, we will begin to see with fresh eyes and invariably become a wider container of love for the world. But that new vision and committed action does not spurn from veneers of care, but rather spills from broken hearts.

May we be so very brave that we choose to dilate our hearts beyond our individual griefs. May we gently approach the gate of ecological collapse. May we move through this gate together, which is so essential for collective renewal.

Joanna Macy also translated many of the works of beloved German poet Rainer Maria Rilke. This poem has long been an anthem for me.

> *I live my life in widening circles*
> *that reach out across the world.*
> *I may not complete this last one*
> *but I give myself to it.*[16]

Can we give ourself to the widening circle of grief? The beautiful promise is that as we move into and become intimate with it, it will not stay in the original form we found it. Grief will transform under such loving attention. It's physics. Grief will transfigure as it spirals through those widening circles. We can keep the material of ecological loss "warm" with our attention. And when we become the exact vessel to hold it, alchemy happens, as Weller points out in his *Wild Edge of Sorrow*. The grief will morph, dislodging age-old pain, expanding the heart, and stretching us to contain more love. Of course, this must happen in our own timing, and no, there is no rush. *But*. Grief is a portal, grief is a doorway, and love is on the other side.

Compost is another way to think about grief alchemy. It brings us into the soil, straight inside the rot and guts of the Earth. Could our pain contain the exact nutrients the Earth needs? Could our pain be composted into flowers, trees, and life? What if, as we offer our grief back to the soil, the Earth could change it into mutual nourishment? Maybe we are food for our Earth kin.

When I found that Aspen graveyard made by the avalanche, I was reminded that the Earth knows how to respond to loss. The side of the ravine packed with new trees so suddenly after disaster seemed to say *We will surround this place with as much life as we can muster*. And the other side of the ravine, which had barely grown an inch, seemed to say *We will go slowly to honor what's been lost.* There is no right way to mourn. But what matters is that in both instances, no tree was left alone.

If we are to continue widening, spiraling our hearts outward, we do so not because, as Rilke writes, we will complete anything. But rather, because that's where love is found.

The Earth is longing for us to listen to their grief, to participate in their healing. We can also become a container solid and boundless enough for their softening. We can give *them* the space to fall apart. If the trees' topsoil can compost refuse into nutrients and new life, then may our hearts become fertile ground that can transform human greed into kinship. My prayer for those of us who are courageous enough to feel ecological collapse is this: *May we become good compost for all the love that longs to grow.*

The LA fires destroyed over ten thousand homes. These fires were so massive that they earned the designation "conflagration." Instead of spreading from structure to structure, intense winds propelled them into utter chaos. They also burned up almost a hundred thousand acres of land, home to myriad creatures: the Coastal Live Oak, Palm, and Sycamore; the raccoon and coyote; the milkweed and manzanita. Many living beings found themselves suddenly displaced.

In the aftermath, if you look at photos of the neighborhoods, you will see that many trees, somehow, survived. The human homes are ashen heaps, but the trees stand. How? Oaks have such thick bark and remarkable water retention capacities that they were fire-resistant guardians. The Oak's genus name, *Quercus*, comes from Celtic roots meaning "beautiful tree." I can't help but think of the staggering beauty of their endurance. Not all trees survived. Certainly not. But some still rise, standing sentinel with their beautiful bodies, transforming destruction into life.

I don't know what is coming next. And as an environmental psychologist and eco-doula well aware of the urgency of our uneven times, it is easy to feed fear. What other trees will be topped at random? Will anyone honor their deaths? Is another fire coming? Will the trees survive that one? I don't know. But I take enormous heart from the Oak trees, loving, collaborating, and giving themselves away—in life, in death, and beyond it. Their courage and tenacity even defied fire. May I never cease to be surprised by the intelligence of the living world. May I never indulge, too long, in ruminations of despair.

If there is life here, there is still life worth living for. *What a beautiful tree.*

Body Practice: Rhythmic Tapping

There are many things to be worried or anxious about every day, from our personal lives to global problems. In this practice, take some time to tune in and become familiar with an experience of anxiety that is present within you right now. If you can, choose a worry that has medium intensity—not the most stressful thing but not the most benign, either.

Find a comfortable position to be in, whether that's sitting or standing.

Extend your arms in front of you, palms down, then cross them, resting your hands on opposite knees.

Here, begin to rhythmically tap one knee and then the other at a consistent pace and pressure that works for you. Tap your knees like this for one or two minutes. If you notice any tension or discomfort, please stop.

When you're done, take notice of any shifts in sensation. If you feel more relaxed or grounded, how do you know that? What signals does your body give you?

If you do not feel any different, that's fine. You can try it again at another time, or simply practice a few deep breaths, during which you extend the exhale at least three counts longer than the inhale. Do this deep breathing for several minutes. Now, see if you notice any shift in your sensation of anxiety. Perhaps the anxiety is still present, but has the tone of it changed? The sensation? The intensity level?

Once you have completed the practice, let go of the breath or tapping and rest in the development of your body awareness capacities.

Tree Practice: A Letter to Grief

Everyone grieves differently, and science collapses in the face of the mysteries of the heart. There is no map for the landscape of loss, no established itinerary, no cosmic checklist, where each item ticked off gets you closer to success. You cannot succeed in mourning your loved ones. You cannot fail.

—MIRABAI STARR[17]

In this practice, you are invited to write a letter to your grief. This may be physical, relational, ability-centered, identity-focused, or something else in origin. Write as little or as much as you sense is needed. Take time in a quiet place to write your letter. You can allow this entire process to become its own form of a ceremony, being mindful and intentional with each step.

Once your letter is written, I encourage you to bring it to your tree. Ask them for permission to share it. If you receive a yes, share your grief with your tree, reading it out loud and pausing long enough between each line to listen for their response. If you heard a no, perhaps the letter is meant to be buried in the soil instead of read, or respected in a different way. Tune in to your body to listen for any subtle invitations on how to honor this letter you've written.

Afterward, you may wish to ceremoniously burn the letter and offer the ashes to the Earth or a body of water. Ultimately, this exercise is an exploration of how you can decompose your pain so it can become good compost for all we want to grow.

Growing Deeper

1. When you look closely at your life, do you see any strategies or behaviors for keeping pain at bay? What are they?
2. Rhythmic tapping felt like _____ in my body.
3. Writing a letter to grief and sharing it with a tree was _____.
4. What did you notice energetically in your body before and after you shared your letter with the tree?
5. In what ways does holding grief with the more-than-human world feel different from holding it all by yourself?
6. Has the Earth ever held you in your grief? Have you held them?

III
Embodied Cosmology

8

Spirals of Belonging

*Continents and countries come one after the other
and the earth feels—not small, but almost endlessly
connected, an epic poem of flowing verses.*
—SAMANTHA HARVEY

It's never too late for love. My grandmother met Bob at seventy-eight, swooned over their shared affection for deer watching, and quickly married, despite his children's protests. He was legally blind, but he always said she was the most beautiful woman in the world. I called him my grandfather even though he was technically my step-grandfather. But he is the only one I ever knew on my mother's side.

When I asked him how he was doing, no matter his latest physical challenges, he would brighten up like a shooting star. "I am faaaantastic!" His effusive, buoyant spirit won him all kinds of awards at their senior living center. Most positive. Best attitude. And once, they were crowned king and queen.

My grandfather's father was Native, but he didn't know that until he was an adult. As a kid, he had never understood why he didn't look like his siblings. Finally, it made sense.

Since all he knew about his father was this one, very important fact, he began researching the various Native communities that might have inhabited rural Wyoming in the early 1900s. He listened to Native music and read Native literature. I could see he was trying to locate himself in these cartographies and shed a lifelong lie. But how would he find himself without a map?

He spent his final years trailing a thread that was not traceable to a singularity. The belonging he sought was Earthly kinship with all his relations. A story we are all waiting for, long after we find it. Though he didn't exactly arrive, there was some solidarity and solace even in the seeking. He was left with a pan-Native approach to understanding himself. But even still, watching him struggle through unknown landscapes with his blinded eyes, it was clear to me he was guided by a piercing vision—the heart.

According to Four Arrows, a deep sense of reciprocal relationship and responsibility comprise Native belonging, not a percentage of blood ancestry or even a specific tribe. Belonging is much more expansive. I think my grandfather could sense that.

Bob and my grandmother had twelve beautiful years together. When he was ninety-two, he suddenly started to decline and entered hospice. My grandmother sat at his bedside, stroking his face. I saw both the young maiden and the crone in her tender touch. She had buried every single one of her lovers, and there she was about to do it again.

The night Bob passed, I will never forget tucking her into bed. "Thank you for being here," she said, as her little frame folded under the weight of her loss. I could hear her tears as I closed the door gently over the plush carpeted floor.

When he died, my grandmother wilted. His absence drained the water out of their shared ocean. There was no buoyancy anymore. When she moved to hospice, I went to visit her.

As I entered her hospital room, a pristine brightness illuminated her face. She was resplendent. Her skin glowed; her heart beamed; everything sang. My body felt the luminosity of her presence, as if her form was now a radiant circuit, a bridge to the beyond.

I could feel her entering an ephemeral liminality, where the known and the unknown lose their meaning. It was essence and movement, little thought. I felt an energy open and then swallow us both. She was swimming in the seas of planets with many moons. As her spirit started to move beyond matter, wisdom spilled from her cells.

"I have things to tell you." The sunlight splashed over the hospital bed in dappled light. "We are all going the right way." These simple words filled me with a profound peace. I believed her.

She moved her arms through the air like poetry. Is this where we were going? Into the sky? Woven into each other through invisible motion?

Reaching, beckoning, dreamlike—her limbs were tree branches, and she turned into a pillar of authority.

It was as if one simple swipe of her arm had the power to reconcile a lifetime of learnings, loves, wounds, joys, and regrets. Her tiny body was a live wire—stripped down to the essential voltage of being, the raw current that runs through all things.

"I love *everybody*," she continued.

A tear rested in the crook of the folds of her face. I leaned in close to brush it away or hold on to it forever.

"Are you scared?" She didn't answer. We both knew.

I felt the largeness of her love fill the room. There was simply no space for anything other than the ineffable.

A few days later, as I was preparing for a film trip to Ghana, my phone rang.

"She's gone," my mom said.

The words hung in the air. They couldn't land. If they did, they'd be real. So I kept them suspended until gravity brought them down with a crash.

I went outside and stood in the rain. I needed it to consume me, to absolutely pummel its fists on my body and wrap itself around me. To feel the clap of thunder vibrate off the walls of the canyon and into my spine. To know I wasn't alone in my weeping.

My grandmother and grandfather belonged to the clouds now, to the rain, to the wildflowers that were coming into season. They were reunited in a place that is no place, where time is not time, where there is no start or end to all things. I could sense that my grandfather had found his belonging there, that maybe he even met his real father. I hoped there'd been some sort of healing in that big chasm that runs through so many whose belonging has been robbed from them. I felt my grandmother was there, too, setting up the little green dishes for tea, waiting for me to join them.

Stories can help us remember to whom, and to what, we belong. And since stories are the oldest form of human learning, and the norms of these tales shape our behavior socially and culturally, they are very powerful tools. In my PhD research, participants said that an important "ancestral technology" for Earth kinship is what are called *origin stories*.

Origin stories, or cosmogonic myths, are symbolic narratives of how the world began, how humans, animals, plants, trees, and everything that is here came to exist, and how we relate to one another. These stories are vital tools for understanding our place in the order of things. And our responsibility to that order.

My grandfather's lost origin story pained him. And yet, I watched as a sense of the kinship cosmogony did somehow come to him, carried by the instruments of music and narrative. This story was not written down but rather lived like impressions, a watercolor painting, an opaque sense rather than cold, hard fact. But he could move from inside that art. The story started to become inextricable from his breath. A stone falling into a pond sending ripples in every direction. The entirety—the wholeness— was felt rather than understood.

Origin stories are essential not just for our inner sense of homecoming to ourselves but also for our connection to the Earth. Because our very first home, our original belonging, is *here*. Narratives can act as a propellant to forge a sense of deep entanglement with land and place. Such power becomes a salve to dissolve the tentacular reaches of the myth of individualism. Our collective human and more-than-human origination and continuation is our true kinship.

When asked where one comes from, the answer is often equivalent to the geography of one's residency. Such a narrow and linear story contracts belonging and disregards the rhizomatic, nonlinear, nonhierarchical, and entangled nature of human and Earth relations. We forget—we belong to the Earth. As the heartwood belongs to the trees, we belong to the family of life.

The next time someone asks me that, I want to startle them: *I come from the understory. I come from the Aspen forest. I come from the Weeping Willow. What about you?*

In the West, those in the dominant culture can be haunted by a feeling of rootlessness. Those who survived genocide can live with the yearning to be rightfully reunited with their lands and waters. In the United States, where most people are living on stolen Native land, and most Native people are not living on their original land, that ache is amplified. How can we come home? How do we find belonging?

We begin through an honest examination of what happened here—in, on, to, and through this very land. Settler colonialism's reach into our bodies, spirits, and relations is immeasurable.[1] The first great and ongoing loss is that of Native history and ways of life. Through the combination of genocidal violence, land theft, displacement, and epidemics, languages were destroyed and oral histories were lost. In addition, because of violent assimilation policies, even more was expunged. Native children were taken from their families by force and placed in residential boarding schools run by the Catholic church, where they had poor living conditions and inadequate food and medical care, and often endured sexual and physical abuse. There were over 350 such schools in the Western United States alone from the late nineteenth century to the early twentieth century.² Such horrific policies suppressed and nearly eliminated Indigenous spiritual practices and ways of life.

Everyone is affected because we are all connected. From settlers to the displaced, from the land to the sea, each expression of life feels this incalculable loss. And for the dominant culture, to prevent the perpetuation of such violence moving forward, the wounds must be tended. Both within the human and the more than human.

Did the Redwoods not weep when they lost their loving caretakers? Did the buffalo not mourn when they were banished from the prairies? All of life carries the impacts of separation, holds the embodied wounds of colonial empire. Lovingly addressing the absence of kinship belonging with each other is an inoculation against acting unconsciously from that terrain.

What if we look further back than colonization, industrialization, and imperial empire? What if we lived out of an origin story that rightfully restores us into a nonhierarchical relationship with our Earth kin?

To tune our hearing toward deep time isn't bypassing. Rather, it's a practice to reimagine our entanglement. To let this ancient tapestry vibrate in our fingers. To let the tree, stone, and bear teach us the stories we are still a part of. To allow humans to become unexceptional for once.

This story will not be found in books. Before there was written language, there was oral storytelling. The pitch, fall, and pace of rhythmic tales and mind-bending epics shared in community, face-to-face. Colossal, crooked, branching tales wound their way through bodies, relations, and lives. Instead of being pinned to a page, stories were constantly unfurling. They had shape, weight, and blood.

If we came from the trees, what would that story sound like? Feel like? What is its breath? Tenor? Pitch? The tree and I are not the same, but we are also not other. We are in motion. The tree in their infinitely slow decay. Me in my encircling little life. An experiment of belonging, return, and embrace; of what and how is body; of to where and whence body flows. Geographical knowing emerges from the cuts and cartographies of time through a slow polymorphous listening. I think of a river: Where does it begin? The rain falls from space. Does water start on some distant planet's sea? Can we ever know? Does it matter? All that remains is that it's alive.[3]

We can find belonging through our senses. Forget identity and nation-state for a moment. What do you hear? How can the exact sound of the wind tell us something about to whom and to where we belong? The sensory topography of the river is speaking a story of belonging. Can we hear it?

The more we surrender to the story of kinship, the closer we will move toward multispecies eco-justice. The more we inhabit that living community of animacy, the more human individualism and exceptionalism will become unthinkable.

We are part of an ecosystem, blended into and belonging to other life forms. A sense of home transcends every human civilization and is a story longer than our spun and known universe. We are intrinsically woven into the Earth and to the cosmos, deep in the land of our bodies. Such a mysterious origination is our birthright. Our ancestry structures grow and expand through interactions and connections across time and species. Belonging is not contingent on owning land, having a family, or even *feeling* like we do. We just belong. If we have a body, we are made of the Earth. And so, we can be at home here. Like the stars are our children and the trees are our elders, so too are we wrapped into the matrix of life. We cannot be rejected from the code of aliveness.

In contrast, the most influential Western origin story is simply that humans are the center of everything. How dull, vapid, and thin. When we are but one creature of 8.7 million species, how could we possibly be the epicenter?[4] The marrow of the world is multiple.

Within this narrative stem myriad strands, like Medusa's head. One is the myth of "progress." The more, the better. The faster, the better. Do people today generally have access to more convenience than at any other time in human history? Yes, but at what cost?

Until 2019, Amazon refused to release data on their carbon footprint, but rulings have made it imperative for them to share. As of 2023, Amazon is responsible for emitting 71.54 million metric tons of carbon dioxide yearly.[5] For comparison, that is nearly the same emission load as the entire country of Ecuador, and more than the countries of Bolivia, Mongolia, the Democratic Republic of Congo, Switzerland, and Norway combined. The supremacy and centrality of the human is a dangerous tale. The myth of progress is killing the planet.

Further, the wealthy of the world consume more resources than everyone else, which drives climate collapse at uneven rates. We are living in a time of kleptocracy and oligarchy. But not everyone in wealthy countries consumes the same amount of resources. For example, a recent study published in *Nature* quantified the link between wealth disparities and climate impacts to shed light on climate justice. They found that the wealthiest 10 percent within the United States and China contributed 6.5 times more to global warming than the average person.[6] Instead of *more*, what if the wealthiest 10 percent valued shared equity and well-being? Imagine that a flourishing planet is actually good for everyone?

If the following excerpt from an 1848 speech attributed to Chief Seattle of the Suquamish tribe was a warning bell then, it is a clarion call now:

> How can you buy or sell the sky, the warmth of the land?
> The idea is strange to us.
> This we know; the Earth does not belong to man; man belongs to the Earth.
> This we know.
> All things are connected like the blood which unites our family.
> All things are connected.[7]

The Judeo-Christian origin story of Adam and Eve has also shaped thousands of years of social norms and behavior that underwrite disconnection between humans and nature. These stories are epistemological failures that seed separation. But what if this tale is not fate? What if the Garden of Eden is right here? And what if we could nurture that garden every day in our polymorphous interactions, exchanges, and care? The garden is not some utopia to reclaim, but a reality to reembody. We *are* the garden. This is Eden.

In utter contrast, in Norse mythology, humans originated from trees. The story goes that Ask and Embla were the first human beings, created by gods from trees on the seashore. How would we live if trees were our gods today? If our allegiance was to tree intelligence, wisdom, love? If we were their star seed?

This makes me think of the beautiful line from Richard Powers's tour-de-force, *The Overstory*: "This is not our world with trees in it. It's a world of trees, where humans have just arrived."[8]

Returning to such a forest of kinship echoes the work of biologist Rupert Sheldrake and his controversial but intriguing hypothesis of morphic resonance. He argues that certain habits or patterns of behavior within natural systems can persist across time and space through a collective memory. If that is the case, then the biological world, including humans, inherits a collective memory from all previous similar systems. Could origin stories be a way nature's invisible memory drives how living systems develop and behave? Could these narratives redefine the terms of livable intimacy between humans and nature? Perhaps, but we'd have to remember them.

What if we could hear the origin stories that live in the collective memories of the trees, mountains, and oceans? What if we could listen so deeply to the stones, for example, that we could hear the song of their remembrance? What if we could shed our human-centric slumber in favor of beautiful stories fit for beautiful worlds?

The logic of climate change is a ferocious tale, and contending with its origin is part of how we subvert it. The global rate of nature's decline is unprecedented in human history and is directly linked to human actions, with 1 million species threatened with extinction and 69 percent of animals already having been lost since 1970.[9] This peril has been perpetuated by now ubiquitous—and largely unchecked—origin stories. Like that humans are the most important creatures in the universe, that we are here to dominate nature, that growth, progress, and wealth are the preeminent jewels. If we want different worlds, we need different stories. Feminist Donna Haraway urges that we must "struggle within the belly of the monster"[10] to unravel destructive ideologies and binaries and instead foster imagination, theory, and action that weave through genealogies, kin, and species.[11] In short, to be better storytellers.

In order to refigure beyond the Western binary epistemes that serve colonial and capitalist projects and justify various forms of exploitation, we must escape hegemonic discourse, practice, and storytelling. We must remember how to dream. Take ecotones, for example, a transition area between biological communities, a place where they meet and integrate. Ecotones are a place for possibility and friendship. They are edgy and blurry, soup-like and teeming with surprise and improvisation. Perhaps we need to listen far outside of the multifarious normalized frameworks and instead press in toward the stories within the processes always unfolding between humans and nature in such in-between spaces. For example, Indigenous scholar Vanessa Watts presents the concept of "Place-Thought," which echoes the idea of an ecotone to me. She writes, the "land is alive and thinking and that humans and non-humans derive agency through the extensions of these thoughts."[12] Again, who we are and what we are is precipitated on our relations with each other. Could we "think" anew if we inhabited such fluid and shared sentience? Could we subvert dominance over nature by remembering that we are the Earth's way of sensing? That our flesh is a continuous flesh of the world?

This makes me want to listen differently. What is happening in the marginal zones, fringe regions, periphery places, and borderline areas? What creatures and critters are passing along their memories through their particular forms at these edges? What teems within our shared Place-Thought? What if the language of trees gives us access to the stories in these liminal thresholds? What wisdom is waiting there?

Indigenous communities have long lived by cosmogonic myths that center kinship with all of the Earth's relations, and these stories invoke ongoing kincentric care today. These narratives deconstruct the nuclear human family unit to include more-than-human life, like rivers and other lands. A creation narrative this replete with multispecies relations might forge a capacity for celebrating instead of sublimating difference. In my PhD research, one of the participants, Niria Alicia, a Xicana water activist, shared one such narrative.

The Winnemem Wintu people, stewards of what is now known as Northern California, nurture an origin story centered around salmon. They believe that at the very beginning of humanity, it was salmon who gave humans a voice so they would protect them. In their community, humans are not the beginning of creation; salmon are.

Today, facing the disappearance of salmon runs, Chief Caleen Sisk of the Winnemem Wintu started the Run4Salmon, a prayerful three-hundred-mile journey and advocacy ceremony to restore the salmon, protect the waters, and honor their Indigenous lifeways.[13] Their prayer journey is a ceremonial way to "bring the salmon home." They are currently protesting two tunnels that would divert water from the Sacramento River and expand the Shasta Dam. These projects would kill the largest estuary on the Pacific coast, flood future spawning grounds for the salmon, and destroy Winnemem Wintu sacred sites. The Shasta Dam, which was built seventy-five years ago, has already destroyed the salmon's homecoming journey to their ancestral watersheds. The only remaining genetic descendants of these salmon are now in New Zealand. Bringing the salmon home is an essential, kincentric duty and joy.

In a remarkable victory, for the first time in 112 years, the Chinook salmon are now swimming freely nearby in the Klamath Basin in Oregon. Indigenous advocacy achieved the largest dam removal and river restoration project in US history. Their unwavering persistence, advocacy, and alliance-building led to the removal of four dams on the Klamath River in late 2024. The sheer torque toward liberation was propelled forward by their kincentric narrative. Such a victory serves as a living hope for Indigenous leaders, activists, and biologists. Stories have power.

May the Chinook be a harbinger for the salmon to also return to the Winnemem Wintu ancestral watershed. May their relatives come home soon.

Salmon are not just a character in an origin story. This tale teaches ecological wisdom. Salmon matter for ecosystems, bringing essential nutrients to the waterways, forests, and lands. And so, this origin story explains not only how humans came to be here but also what their responsibility is to other creatures. There is a cultural, spiritual, personal, and social basis for their activism. Stories like this motivate eco-centric versus anthropocentric worldviews and eco- versus ego-centric living. Since worldviews then shape human values, behaviors, and societies, what they're made of really matters.

What would happen if everyone could remember an origin story that didn't start with the human? What if those who already live by such a cosmogony were celebrated and honored for their eco-centricity? What if our lives could be in service to such ecological legends instead of human-centric stories that justify the domination, extraction, and obliteration of the planet? What if we had the courage to let the trees, the oldest organisms in the world, tell us who we are?

Humans do not just belong to the Earth—the Earth also belongs to themself. Ecosystems have found a way to find home with each other across and because of difference. There are over seventy-three thousand different tree species in the world, with nine thousand species yet to even be discovered.[14] The Baobab, Giant Sequoia, Joshua, Bristlecone, Dragon's Blood, Rainbow Eucalyptus, Banyan, Pacific Yew, Beech, Cypress, Weeping Willow, Ginkgo, and so many more. The complexity, diversity, and creativity of these beings are remarkable. We will never know them all. Forests are also home to 80 percent of the world's amphibians, 75 percent of the world's birds, and 68 percent of the world's mammals.[15] There are billions—maybe a billion billion—of these glorious companions in every corner of every land. Our planet hinges on the health of our trees. Our forests are home to us all.

In the Roaring Fork Valley, Aspen trees and Cottonwoods coexist symbiotically. They tell me a story of belonging. Cottonwoods have heart-shaped leaves that, due to their flattened petioles, shimmer in the wind. So, in this valley to which I belonged, I was surrounded by my heartwood trees and their neighbors with heart-shaped leaves. They do not just tolerate each other. I often see them wrapped up and through one another. A dendrological hug. A full-body embrace of each other's wholeness.

Belonging celebrates—instead of suppresses—diversity. This is no small difference from the dominant culture, which is set on homogeny. The infinity of biological life terrifies empire. Because what is sovereign is not easily controlled. The diversity of biological life is exactly what creates the enduring relational networks that support it. The pursuit of sameness, in comparison, often justifies violence against those deemed as "other." Throughout human history, difference has been weaponized again and again. Contorted versions of sameness destroy people and planet. Monoculture crops, the Aryan race in Nazi Germany, the supremacy of Hutu over Tutsi in Rwanda, and so many other examples. Difference is not to be feared; sameness is.

Take the Cottonwood and Aspen trees. They are both members of the *Populus* genus but look and function differently. Aspens are more crucial in upland forest environments, enhancing soil growth through leaf decomposition. Cottonwoods are essential for water sources, preventing erosion and regulating water temperature for aquatic life.

However, they can be found growing together, in the same place. How do they navigate their divergent purposes? They both form extensive underground root systems through grafting, allowing them to share resources such as water, nutrients, and even chemical signals. They both create habitats for myriad animal species and are food sources for insects and other invertebrates.

And like all trees, Aspens and Cottonwoods both reduce the impacts of climate change by downregulating the amount of greenhouse gas concentrations in the atmosphere through sequestering carbon in their biomass. They are part of a symbiotic ecosystem and have evolved to not just cooperate but collaborate. Diversity is essential for resilient ecosystems. This is how they belong. Here are these two trees, completely other in appearance, lifespans, and in some regards, ecological roles, yet *they belong together.*

Following their lead, how can we collaborate, just like the trees do, in service of our collective well-being? Is this the key to finding our belonging? Mutual aid brings us in touch with how we can feed, nourish, and support one another. And yet, how do we belong when we have such thin attachments to place?

Even though I found belonging in the Roaring Fork Valley, I had not spent all of my life there. The quality of rootedness for those who have tended to the same land for decades, multiple generations, or even thousands of years, is deeper. I have lived all over the world, and one gift of this experience is a sense of kinship with many places: the ancient Beech forests in northern Europe, the Teak and Mahogany trees of the Congo, the Silver Birch in England. However, as I age, I yearn for slower living in a smaller radius. And since kinship is not one-directional, how can I be responsible and accountable to that many places? To that many trees? I think it is quite impossible to be deeply connected to land if I am moving too quickly to hear, listen to, and know that land.

Sometimes at night these trees from around the world visit me. I feel their pyramidal, columnar, crooked forms. The effulgent green of the Brazilian Pepper tree, the slick high-gloss coppery bark of the Tibetan Cherry tree, the elysian shapes of the African Baobab. I dream of us all living together in a giant terrarium. Oh yes, I remember, we already do.

I woke up to an orange sky, thick as toffee. At midday, the Jaffa orange blended into rust, and the entire horizon became a caramelized onion. The sun was a blurry orb, pumping what should have been light through the miasma. The outlines of human beings floated through the campground. Intermittent coughing, gasping, and chattering about what was happening leaked through the smog. Our phones all got alerts at once. The Bell, Caldor, Monument, Glen, and McFarland wildfires were growing. Evacuation was possible, and we were told to stand by.

I decided to go on a walk through the nearest Redwood forest, to hear what they had to say. As I careened through the trees like a salmon, pressing my attention close to the soil, I studied these giants—astonishing and unmediated—their arms and hands were as large as caves. I paused in the crook of a ravine. Here we were, Redwood and human. The smoke from the nearby fires was all over us; inside the canopy, it could've been afternoon, night, or tomorrow.

The Redwood in front of me was an absolute giant, a grandfather of a tree. With his arching arms, he reached out and over me as if he were about to bow or fall on his knees. His leaves trembled, but there was hardly any wind. In my body, I felt it as panic. *Of course*, I thought to myself, *they smell the smoke that is choking the oxygen out of our lungs. Of course, they know their brothers, sisters, mothers, and fathers are dying in the forest nearby.*

Time collapsed then, and I became very, very small inside myself. I could sense their kin in pain, disappearing in flames and ash. I could sense the grief this grandfather was feeling, his body a cathedral to hold their disappearance. He was speaking, but there weren't any words. I could feel the remnants of the dying trees being entombed in this silence. I could touch the Redwood's requiem.

"I'm sorry," I said into the amber air.

"I'm sorry we have forgotten we belong to each other."

"I'm sorry you are suffering our forgetting."

Carbon dioxide emissions from boreal fires that year shattered previous records. The causes varied, but with appropriate rainfall, they would not have happened. Climate change is killing our forests, which ruins our air, which harms humans and every other living thing, and around and around we go.[16]

When the Earth hurts, we hurt. The human body is made up of the same elements that comprise stones and rocks, the same material that makes up asteroids and the cores and rings of other planets. We are 90 percent water; most of us is freshwater river, high alpine lake, mountain runoff, and glacier. Our bones are made of calcium, just like the Earth's crust. Our body is filled with carbon, just like how carbon makes up more than 50 percent of a tree. We belong here.

I am entwined with water, both as a physical collection of chemicals that perpetuates life and as a surrender to flow. I am braided with trees, both as the source of the air I breathe and as the companionship to endure the impossible uncertainty of a world we are destroying. By being in contact, our corporeal belonging reweaves itself. We can only know ourselves in relation to the living world. I want to embody an origin story where the trees and I stand side by side; where I, too, am woven into the Earth; where I, also, am connected at the roots.

I wondered, what if the Aspen tree is the start of my cosmogony and my life is in service to them? I let myself try on that story, letting it seep up through the topsoil and into my skin.

What narrative is buried in the lichen under this rock? What whisper of connection can this monarch butterfly infuse in me as they fly up to three thousand miles every year? What quality of the heart does the old crone nightingale telegraph every evening as they keen into the setting sun?

Let us forgo the centrality of the human. Let us touch, taste, and smell the fruit of what Earth kinship belonging could do to us, and to our futures. Let us use the full force of our collective imagination to dream differently. But to dream from a different landscape, with different content.

What if we let ourselves be composted? Otherwise, we might continue to recycle the same imperialist colonial fantasies that have gotten us here in the first place. May we conjure and reverie from our shared roots. May we be ceremonial and fluid and feel into the corners and places that need air, to let the Earth grow a loving cosmovision out of the compost heap of our lives.

In my chronic illness, I struggled to relate to the word *belonging*. How could I, when I could not belong to my own body? My body was a house of pain, and I wanted to escape through the ceiling. But when I imagine belonging as something that happens sideways, and is rhizomatic and mycorrhizal, the burden disappears. A sense of homecoming reaches from the bacteria in my gut to the bacteria in the soil, from the blood vessels of my lungs to the trees' root system that looks just like those branching veins. Illness teaches me that as I let my body commune with the Earth, I become kin with the trees, the clouds, and those I've loved and lost. *We're all going the right way.* I can feel them reaching into my body to hold me when I'm hurting, and I can do the same for them.

My human grandfather and the grandfather Redwood tree had something in common. Their land was stolen from them both. They tended to that rupture the best they could. My grandfather used his imagination and felt senses to cast a kinship story that had room for him inside it. The grandfather Redwood held space for a funeral for his kin, teaching humans how to stand together until the end, and beyond it. Belonging requires so much courage.

I am thinking about that fire again. I am imagining myself kneeling in the dirt next to the Redwoods to ask them, *How do we create a world where your lives, and ours, are not under constant threat? How do we foster belonging that goes beyond blood?*

They might say something about not forgetting the smell of that smoke. They might remind me how, in their dying, through their communal loving, they taught us how to live.

Body Practice: Inner Belonging Through Toning

This exercise introduces the practice of toning, bringing intentional vibration to the vagus nerve. The vagus nerve is the longest nerve in the body and is responsible for creating nervous system regulation. Through toning, you can explore the sensation of inner belonging. Before we can belong to the Earth, we need to touch the feeling of belonging to our bodies.

Find a comfortable position, whether sitting or standing. Begin by breathing in deeply, then exhaling completely. Do this a few more times to ground and center yourself.

Bring your attention to the center of your belly, and on the next exhale, make a sighing sound out loud like the word *om* (or *aum*), which is thought to be the first sound of the universe.

Again, inhale and speak the tone out loud on your exhale, varying the pitch or speed if desired. Allow your tone to reach the very last extent of each breath as it vibrates your vocal cords, which are connected to your vagus nerve.

Repeat this for a few minutes, hearing your own voice. Once you have completed the practice, let go of the toning and return to mindful awareness. Notice how you feel as the vibrations settle in the body and you return to stillness.

Take at least five minutes to complete this practice. If it feels good, you can do it more frequently. To really experience the benefits, try toning every day for a week and take note of how it shifts your sense of inner belonging.

Tree Practice: Kinship Origin Stories

For this practice, you are invited to spend time with your tree and allow space for imagining origin stories that would explain both of your existences. This is meant to be playful and imaginative.

Begin by approaching your tree. Share that you would like to playfully dream up a story about how trees and humans came to be. As you spend time with your tree and mindfully notice them, see what story emerges in your togetherness. This can be in the genre of fairy tale, fantasy, science fiction, or anything else. Let yourself move out of the rational mind and into a felt sense of embodied co-creation.

If this is not coming easily, spend some time simply observing how the tree belongs to itself and the forest. Notice any parts of them that indicate hardship, loss, or change, like burn marks on the bark or felled trees nearby. Study the traces of resilience, strength, growth, community, and kinship that already exist in your tree kin's environment.

How did you and tree come to be? Perhaps write down the origin story that came to you. Once you feel your story is complete, thank the tree and let the practice go.

Growing Deeper

1. In what ways do you feel that you belong to yourself? In what ways do you sense your belonging to the Earth?
2. How could you belong more deeply, more intimately to the Earth?
3. When you reflect on your own origin story, what are the dominant myths that influence how you understand your place in the universe? Are those helpful or unhelpful to belonging to the Earth?
4. When you consider how certain origin stories have shaped your experience in the world, what does this bring up for you? If there is grief, consider spending time with your tree to seek refuge and support in processing this pain.
5. What did you learn about the nature of belonging as you studied your tree's resilience?
6. What origin story came to you when you were with the tree? What does this story feel like in your body?

9

Sacred Reciprocity

The time has come for acts of reverence and restraint on behalf of the Earth. We have arrived at the Hour of Land.

—Terry Tempest Williams

The fluttering flap of wings says it's summer. This is a welcomed return of the world of sound. In the morning, the broad-tailed hummingbird makes such a herald with their high-pitched vibrations, I nearly leap out of bed. All day, the rhythmic trill of these red-breasted, teeny-tiny birds keeps me company.

The monarch butterfly also arrives in the early summer to breed in the Rocky Mountains. They have one of the longest migrations of any insect species. And it's multigenerational to go roundtrip. They use environmental cues like the position of the sun and the Earth's magnetic field to find their way to the same wintering sites each year, despite never having been there before. In Mexico, the monarch's return marks the start of the Day of the

Dead celebrations. In Colorado, their homecoming announces summer's arrival.

I was on a walk when one fell from the sky and landed on my arm. As they settled, I quickly studied their black-rimmed wings with yellow geometric shapes, the mosaic ceiling of their private cathedral, but better. I could hardly believe this delicate creature had flown all the way from Mexico, an astonishing three-thousand-mile journey.

The gentlest rain could have pierced their paper-thin wings. How do they fly so far? I felt anointed by their visitation, and as they folded up their patterned sails and fell backward into the sky, I was left speechless, having touched the divine.

Monarchs are marvels. Like bees, they are pollinators—their dance is essential for ecosystems, agriculture, and human health, and they contribute to the reproductive success of over 75 percent of flowering plants. I like to envision the flowers nodding their stems in gratitude to the pollinators, and the monarch batting their stained-glass wings to say thank you in return. Without pollinators, we would not have vegetables and fruit. Their existence allows the ecosystems around them to flourish. Such generosity is reciprocity in action.

The Earth is built on a sacred reciprocity principle, which is at the heart of sacred relationship. To make kin with one another, we must tend to and care for each other with the utmost love. We must nourish each other from a rooted acknowledgment of our shared sacredness. Reciprocity is not a utilitarian exchange. Rather, it is the most natural response to the kincentricity of all life.

The concept of reciprocity has its origins in Indigenous worldviews. In their book *Restoring the Kinship Worldview*, Wahinkpe Topa (Four Arrows) and Darcia Narvaez offer twenty-eight Indigenous precepts for rebalancing life on Earth. They define reciprocity as an embodied ethic, a mutual give-and-take with the Earth, rising from intentional relationship. Indigenous cultures—while outrageously diverse in their beliefs and lifeways—often value giving and receiving as a deep biological and spiritual instinct, which supports the delicate, subtle balance of life.[1] Their attention is not on what they can get from the Earth, but on how their braided existence can help each other thrive.

Indigenous worldviews center reciprocal generosity as a way of life and believe that we are mutually dependent on one another, viewing the Earth as benevolent and loving.[2] Generosity is the lifeblood of the Earth. Basil Johnston of the Wasauksing First Nation says, "We owe the Earth our all, more than we can take in, more than we can say. We can never return anything but our respect and thanksgiving."

When we view our bond with the Earth as a bidirectional or even multidirectional relationship, reciprocity helps us tend to that bond. To maintain harmony and restore power where it should be.

Reciprocity is therefore not a sentiment—it is a foundational, ecological, biological, and evolutionary principle. And it requires practice. Four Arrows and Darcia Narvaez say that reciprocity is modeled after the laws of nature, including listening to plants and animals, understanding the cycles of life, living from a landscape-grounded morality, and maintaining the continuum of being embedded in the natural world.[3] To say thank you, *all day long.*

Where Western culture and dominant worldviews have perpetuated extractive and one-sided ways of relating to the Earth, sacred reciprocity upends human superiority. For if *all beings are equal*, then none are privileged to exploit, extort, and extract the rest. Without giving back to the Earth, we legitimize a utilitarian and anthropocentric view of nature, which contributes to the commodification of the Earth and backfires on ecological conservation. Environmental movements and activism are not immune to dominant worldviews. They creep in everywhere.

Let us ask ourselves: *What can we give back to the Earth?*

Take the Aspen, for example. Their bark has similar properties to aspirin and can treat inflammation and pain.[4] The white powder that covers the Aspen is a substance of shedding bark cells called bloom, which contains a natural sunscreen.[5] Indigenous peoples discovered these therapeutic properties and lived in reciprocity with the trees in a loop of medicine and blessing. The trees take care of the people as the people take care of them.

The Earth is full of good gifts. Last summer, I noticed these scarlet puffs growing low to the ground in the Rockies. They were red clover, and I learned they can be brewed into a tea to help with hormone balance. I started drinking red clover tea daily and experienced a wonderful ease of some of my symptoms. I was reminded: The Earth has what we need. But if the delicate resources are overharvested, there will not be enough for everyone. We must share. Nature's calibration is a living symphony.

Like the pollinators, whose existence hinges on how skillfully they can give everything away, we can also practice such generous, loving living. We can learn to say thank you to the Earth. We can take seriously that right relationship with them is precipitated on mutuality. We can slow down, connect to our Earth kin, and find gratitude there. And when we do, we will want to respond in kind.

I came across a tattered sign taped to the back gate of the Topanga State Park. It read: ADOPT A BABY OAK TREE. There was a QR code printed underneath. I scanned it, which pulled up a spreadsheet listing all the baby Oak trees available for adoption in the area. Each tree had a number, and each number had a spot on the map. California State Parks had initiated a replanting effort after the most recent fire, but there was not enough rainfall. Volunteers were needed to make sure these trees got sufficient water to survive.

I could feel the thirst of the land. All around me, the Earth had bowed its head. The Manzanita, Chemise, Sagebrush, and scrubland plants were brown and dehydrated. California had hit a 126-year low for rainfall.

"Bring one gallon of water every other week," the sign said. I scrolled through the spreadsheet.

"Put your name next to the tree you are adopting."

Some rows in the spreadsheet had names, many did not. How strange to see these trees digitized into a grid, waiting for a human to care.

I was already in the park, I thought, so I might as well find a tree. Down a little hill and into an absolute gaggle of dry brush stood a tiny baby Oak, surrounded by a metal mesh fence to protect its growth. A round tag swung from the grate: #100.

The tree was maybe four inches tall, its spiny leaves barely breaching the soil. How vulnerable. *Yes, this is the one.* I put my name down on the spreadsheet to make it official.

I walked down the dusty, arid trail a week later, finding my way back to #100 with a gallon of water in my hands. Consistent water is essential during the first few years of an Oak's life. The water coaxes the roots to grow ever downward, helping to establish their footing. It will take twenty to thirty years for this baby Oak tree to reach adolescence, and already in their infancy, they had known so much struggle.

My belly felt sunk with stones. Rain should be nourishing this child, not a human. The longer I stared at the metal fence around the tree, the more enraged I felt. Anger is a taboo feeling because society lacks an imagination for it. The overculture does not understand what power really is. I felt anger at big oil, industrial agriculture, and factory farming, anger at politicians, anger at the "bottom line," anger with the human condition, anger with myself. I felt angry that this tree might not make it. I felt angry that the ones before them did not. Electrical charges coursed through my nerves. But the heat did not make me feel bad—it made me feel alive.

Trees, even that little one, have their own sense of strength. They do not exert power over other living beings like humans do, but rather, they source it for their own presence and find a sense of resilience there. They know how much they can endure—not through dominance, but through harmonious relationships. They know they can survive as long as they're with their kin.

I poured the water on the dull leaves—splash—and in a flash they turned shiny, sparkling in the slanting sun. It was as if the tree responded to their thirst and my care in a continuum. I felt immense appreciation for this little life and the ones connected to them. I realized that though this act was small, for this tree, it mattered. A whole lot.

The more I work with the emotions associated with ecological loss, the more I am convinced they are not to be quickly discharged, regulated, or breathed away as soon as discomfort sets in. Maybe we are meant to hold our spine straight and feel them. That day with the baby Oak, I realized that the movement toward anger and love are not that far apart.

We are living in a polycrisis, in a period of time where environmental, social, economic, health, and political crises intersect and mutually reinforce one another. I, too, have contributed to greenhouse gas emissions through my lifestyle. I, too, have lived most of my life in a human-centric worldview. James Baldwin, in his *Notes of a Native Son*, writes, "People who shut their eyes to reality simply invite their own destruction."[6] Having the courage to see our personal complicity in these intersecting tragedies helps us to have the vision to fathom solutions at scale. To commit to sacred reciprocity as a fundamental principle of our existence. While no single individual is responsible for climate change, our collective love for the Earth is an essential mechanism to motivate the type of large, systems-wide changes needed to protect the planet.

At the time of this writing, there are more than fourteen wildfires burning across the state of California, and more than sixty-six thousand acres have already disappeared. Such a frequency is four times higher than the five-year average—and fire season has only just begun.[7] Global warming has led to higher-than-average temperatures, which dry out vegetation and soil faster, creating increasingly combustible conditions. Our planet's lungs have become a tinderbox.

As Zen master Thich Nhat Hanh says, "We are here to awaken from the illusion of separation." We are the Earth. When the planet suffers, so do we. Living from reciprocity with nature is a dynamic force to repair what has been broken. Because so much is out of balance now.

The matrix of ecological breakdown is a reflection of deep and systemic imbalance. As ice shelves melt into the ocean and climate disasters increase in scale and frequency, dysbiosis is all around us. One culprit is capitalism, and below capitalism is greed. And capitalism has made greed into a virtue.

Today, every ecosystem on the planet is out of balance because globalized extractive capitalism takes more than the Earth can possibly sustain. In essence, the exact opposite of reciprocity.

Such disequilibrium is also reflected in a pervasive chronic health crisis. For example, even though the United States spends the most on health care, it has the lowest life expectancy, the highest infant and maternal mortality rates, and the highest rates of avoidable and preventable deaths compared to other developed nations, according to a report by the Commonwealth Fund.[8] Overall, the US ranks last in health-care outcomes compared to eleven other developed nations. The richest country is the sickest.

Where the Western medical model places the burden on individuals to heal themselves, despite poor outcomes and unbearable financial hardship, it is an unreasonable expectation for anyone to be well in a sick society. My illness, in all its impossibility, pain, and confusion, is ironically the exact pathway that helped me understand that it was not just me who was ill. An Australian Aboriginal approach to mental health says, "If the land is sick, you are sick."[9] I would gesture indeed, we are all suffering. For the land is not well.

The Earth is asking us to develop something that is unfathomable to the Western psyche: restraint. Where humans look for power in our supposed human superiority, we will conversely only find it through equality. Reciprocity offers us an astonishing sight: Come and rebalance the Earth through relationship; come and allow the Earth to be in equilibrium with us.

Trees are already reciprocal, using their power skillfully. Forest scientist Suzanne Simard published a groundbreaking study, proving the mutuality of trees for the first time. The cover of *Nature* that August 1997 featured "The Wood-Wide Web," to indicate the vast interconnective system within forests.[10] Since then, further studies have found that there are mycorrhizal networks that facilitate trees' ability to share resources, communicate, learn from, and remember one another.[11] These networks form a "scale-free" pattern so that older trees become the hubs of the network, while the younger trees act as satellite nodes, much like the pattern of a modern-day telecommunications network.

In Simard's book *The Mother Tree*, she further explores the entanglement of forests. The Mother Tree is the largest and oldest tree in a woodland, who share resources with all the younger, smaller trees around them to ensure the health of everyone. Simard investigates the implications of this belonging: "We found that trees could recognize their own kin and were more willing to support their relatives."[12] Trees know each other. Trees embody reciprocal kinship.

Simard's work was pioneering for many reasons, but most notable was that she turned the idea of trees as competitors upside down. They don't compete. They don't fight. In fact, they collaborate. In a forest ecosystem, survival is based on how communal, co-creative, and emergent trees are, not which one is the strongest and tallest of them all. There is a moment-to-moment mutual awareness occurring below the soil. Each sugar exchanged is a step toward balance; every milligram per kilogram of phosphorus transferred is another degree closer to harmony. Forests are reciprocity in action.

To speak of collectivity in forests, we have to talk about fungi. Fungi are fundamental to the reciprocal life of forests. In Merlin Sheldrake's *Entangled Life*, he emphasizes how they serve as the reciprocal bridge between different species and ecosystems, creating opportunities for symbiosis. Fungi decompose organic matter, recycle nutrients, and form co-beneficial relationships. They attach to tree roots and make sure that nutrients are taken up by the soil. Phosphorus and nitrogen are exchanged for carbon. The fungi and the tree are in a mutual exchange to make sure they both have everything they need.

Mycelium, the vegetative part of a fungus, are composed of tiny filaments called hyphae, microscopic structures that create vast and extensive underground networks. According to one study, as Sheldrake points out, if a hypha were as wide as a human hand, it would be able to lift an eight-ton school bus.[13] They are multifunctional and vast, serving as the highways to transport sugars between trees that Simard measured. Mycelium form a world under the surface of the soil, and we are only beginning to understand their sweeping significance.

Fungi, argues Sheldrake, are intelligent, too, just like trees.[14] "Mycelium is ecological connective tissue, the living seam by which much of the world is stitched into relation," Sheldrake writes. Further, they teach us that there is no such thing as an individual. We are in a constant intertwined existence, whether we see it or not. A seminal study on the symbiotic view of life finds that there is no such thing as a biological individual by any anatomical or physiological criteria, challenging how living entities have been characterized.[15] We are not the raindrop. We are the field of rain falling in haphazard unison from the sky to the sea. We are the surface of the pond thrust into spasmodic delirium. We are heaps and heaps of intimate microbial relationships.

Trees, mycelium, lichen—the entire biological world lives out the sacred reciprocity principle. They are healthy examples of power, agency, and balance. They ensure that every being has what they need to survive. They make sure that resources are distributed equitably. But when the human-built systems in which we live are based on extraction and exploitation, how can we move toward a life of reciprocity, ensuring that those who come after us have a world to inherit? How can we be good ancestors?

Reciprocity is less about what we give and more about where the gift comes from. "How you do anything is how you do everything," says Father Richard Rohr. When the giving is born out of a kinship worldview—honoring the Earth's sacredness with respect for the cycles of life—both the gift and the process of giving can become nourishment to the Earth.

I came out to Topanga Canyon to sleep alone under the stars, to mark the end of a year I frankly did not know if I could endure. I had finally received a diagnosis, yes, but I was very far from well.

I went outside the tent and was greeted with a chorus of crickets and katydids in full operatic reverie. It was as if they recognized all I'd carried. I could hear their voices telling the stars what I'd lived through. When I looked into the night sky, knowing that the light was evidence of the past barreling toward me, I let myself drink up the feeling of being hopelessly and deliciously small.

Their music moved me. As the sky pressed its thumb of darkness over my body, I cast otherworldly shadows on the side of the tent. Gigantic figurines swayed, twisted, and pitched in circles. Together, we blocked the light of the full moon. I became a winding, feral serpent, my blood quickened with the clarity that I could not wait until I felt better to live.

The next day, I walked myself to the edge of a cliff overlooking the Pacific Ocean. The sea rolled out like a taut canvas. Memories from the last year rushed up from the valley floor. When I nearly crashed my car because my vision was obliterated by raven-black sheets with no warning. When during one migraine so severe I tried to call an ambulance, but I couldn't reach my phone. When I'd wake to the sound of whimpering and realize the tears were my own. When I grasped my own hand in the darkness and whispered, *I'm here*. How badly I'd wanted certainty. How, certainly, it had eluded me.

All of it was a strange curse. All of it was a strange blessing. But here we were, the Earth and me. I was proud of us both. Where I'd felt so alone, I wasn't. The Earth had carried me.

The Earth was my compass, refuge, beloved companion, family, and lover. I wanted to say thank you. For guiding me through the underworld. For being the lamp in my bardo. My myriad-toned twisted puzzle of a body somehow didn't feel so pressing to solve. The Earth was my blue hour.

I pulled out a velvet-soft peach, still cold from the darkness of my backpack. I felt the juice drip down my chin and into the soil. My body was less like a barrier now and more like a membrane.

I knelt on the edge of the cliff to build an altar. Dead eucalyptus for my lifelessness. Bright peonies for the life that still lived. I stood up to read a poem I'd written out loud. The dry air swollen, now expectant in heat. Perhaps the Earth was reading it back to me.

> *when the pain returns,*
> *(because it will), don't worry.*
> *Instead, become a dahlia,*
> *all mad with photosynthesis.*
>
> *Colors like pinecones, so generous with*
> *their seeds opened from fire. And like the nightly*

> *ritual of the sleeping sun, the pain will be gone,*
> *sliding down the backside of the blue whale,*
> *all rough and soft at once. An anthem that*
> *you too can breathe underwater.*

I inhaled deeply. One day, the pinecones, the flowers, and my own body will compost back into one shared biomass. I exhaled and imagined trees growing from the center of my chest.

Reciprocity brings us closer and closer to balance, dropping us straight into the heart of symbiosis. Symbiosis is the foundation of life. From the pH balance in our cells to the specific range of the ocean's temperature, every ecosystem is designed to thrive within a very precise range. Symbiosis is not perfection, but it is just the right amount of mutualism to promote biodiversity, health, and flourishing.

That ritual on the cliff brought me closer to kinship symbiosis through reciprocity. The result was a state of muditā, a Sanskrit and Pali word that translates to "empathic joy." Muditā is one of the four divine abodes. This is a joy that multiplies in the presence of another's wellness. I felt happy because the Earth was happy, and the Earth felt happy because I was. To the degree we embody sacred reciprocity is the degree to which our joy can grow, compounding on each other ad infinitum. No matter the circumstance.

Studies indicate that generosity increases our well-being by helping us to be happier and more generous to others.[16] It's a continuous loop. Relationships that are based on sharing versus transactional exchange improve the quality of our connections and even the quality of our lives.[17] If we seek to share because we love instead of because of what we might get in return, our relating will be transformed. Likewise, across four studies and two experiments, gratitude-motivated altruism was found to be the foundation of care for nature.[18] Gratitude is the fuel for sacred reciprocity, and we can nourish it daily.

How do we develop such gratitude? Studies have found that it depends on how frequently we have meaningful contact with the Earth, and to what extent we perceive the Earth as animate and sentient.[19] Ultimately, we learn to tend to relational qualities with the Earth by making it a daily spiritual and ecological practice. We start by nourishing what we appreciate. We begin by allowing that appreciation to grow.

I was transfixed by the newest flower to arrive, this one blushing pink, thin, and veiny. I tracked the growth of the lacy miracle day by day. Their effervescence enlarged every time I paused in praise. I am grateful that I can dissolve into nature and forget myself. Even for a moment.

If generosity can improve human well-being, then it can improve the Earth's flourishing, too. Indigenous philosopher and climate and environmental justice scholar Kyle Powys Whyte argues for this perspective. Whyte says that deep attentiveness to the relational qualities of our relationships is absolutely paramount for protecting the Earth from climate collapse. In a seminal paper, Whyte flipped the focus from preventing the ecological tipping point of a 1.5°C rise in global temperature to arguing that the planet is dangerously close to what he calls a "relational tipping point."[20]

According to Whyte, attending to the relational qualities of reciprocity, consent, trust, and accountability is the way we build the foundation for climate justice. This is a radically different view from mainstream environmental movements that may still be rooted in dominant worldviews. The colonial project of "hope" can perpetuate white saviorism and extractive relationships, even when it attempts to "save the Earth."[21] For if efforts like activism, protest, conservation, and policy are done under the guise of the relational qualities inherent in colonialism and imperialism, they simply perpetuate the same harms they are trying to remedy in an ongoing coloniality.

Whyte, by contrast, along with many other Indigenous scholars and activists, says that if we want to help the Earth, we must first tend to the quality of our *relationship* with the Earth. Our reciprocal bond is where climate action begins. Robin Wall Kimmerer agrees, suggesting that this cardinal anchor is the place from which all our activism, advocacy, or conservation should stem. Where modern environmental movements prioritize acting on behalf of the Earth, Indigenous wisdom asks us to pause and ensure that we are acting from love *alongside the Earth*. Sacred reciprocity acknowledges the importance of our *relationships* in climate justice, not just the actions to stop climate change. And since the West has historically enacted abuse and violence against the Earth, this requires deep care and practice.

Sacred reciprocity invites us to give gifts to the Earth out of a spirit of mutual kinship. Through body awareness and speaking the language of sensation, we can attune to what this might look like. Deep, slow attention to reciprocal relationship is the pathway to protecting the relational tipping point, to ensuring we do not repeat the harms we want to protect against. But how do we know what gifts to give the Earth? How can we be sure they are coming from these relational qualities?

We evaluate the gift based on its reciprocity. Reciprocity is the pinecone scattering its seeds, promising new life despite the fire it survived. Reciprocity is the altar on the cliffside, giving me gratitude as I offer them mine. Reciprocity is bringing back native plants and not forcing nature into human designs. Reciprocity is freeing the Earth from the suffocation of concrete. Reciprocity is mindful consumption, cultivating hearts of compassion, advocating for justice, and living more lightly on the Earth. Reciprocity has infinite expressions flowing from the ecological creativity of our love for the living world. Reciprocity centers the relationship with the Earth, rather than the hubris of thinking we can save them.

When you are in right relationship with the Earth, how to give and what to give will become evident. These gifts could be as subtle as a song, a prayer, and your love, or as practical as advocacy, restraint on consumption, organizing, and climate justice. Just like in our human relationships, it becomes obvious how to show one another care as we get to know each other more deeply. Kindness, reverence, and respect. If you don't have any idea how to show the Earth reciprocity, that probably means you need to get to know the Earth better first. It all starts in that sensuous, kinship relation.

I was thinking of Oak #100, two years after we first met. Two years of water visits and water prayers. The act of bringing nourishment to this tree was about the tree, of course, but it was also about me. It did something good for my heart to participate in giving back to the Earth. To put my body in motion toward our interconnection. Water enlivened us both.

I felt #100's spiny branches inside me. I knew I loved this baby tree because I wanted them to live. And if I listened closely enough, I could hear them say *Yes, I love you, too*.

Engaging in sacred reciprocity as a way of life will change us from the inside out. I can see that one day this tree will support others through their mycelium. I can see that one day another generation might have a tree to rest under, too. Their heartwood was getting sturdier by the day. I felt a leaf sprung with gratitude unfurl inside me. A slick thread of kincentric webbing handfasting me to the Earth in love. A spiny palm that I can hold with my own.

Body Practice: Gratitude for Our Embodied Life

In this practice, you are invited to intentionally thank your body for holding your life, carrying you, and caring for you. This practice is intended to foster a sense of gratitude, knowing that reciprocity is rooted in it.

Find a comfortable position to be in, whether sitting in a chair or on the floor, or standing up.

Take a moment to tune in to your whole body, from your toes to the top of your head. This body, imperfect as it may be, struggling with any number of symptoms or ailments as it may be, still carries you through every day of your life on Earth. Your body is the vehicle for you to experience aliveness. This body is your home. As you bring your awareness to this fact, do you feel a sense of gratitude, care, and love for your body? It's all right if you don't, but try to slowly open to welcoming in a sense of gratitude. To help with this, maybe choose a part of the body that is not experiencing pain. Sometimes I focus just on my feet. I can feel grateful for how they carry me, allowing me to experience the beauty of the Earth.

Now gather attention into your body. Bring your awareness to a sense of the whole body breathing. Spend a few moments thanking your body, even if you currently are experiencing discomfort or pain. See if you can find three things to be grateful for right here right now.

As you bring those three things into your awareness, notice what other sensations come up in response to this gratitude. There might be pleasure, or perhaps a level of discomfort or unease.

Take a few deep breaths right into those pleasurable or uncomfortable sensations. This is your body. This is your home. After about five minutes, let the practice go. Notice what is present for you afterward.

Next time, try doing this practice in your nature place and see if you can tune in to the wider sense of the Earth body. What kind of sensations does this bring up?

Tree Practice: Offering the Gift

In order to mindfully be in reciprocity with the Earth, you are invited to begin tuning in to what gifts might be yours to offer them. When you are with your tree, let them know that your intention is to offer a gift. Communicate that you desire to embody reciprocity.

When you are ready, take some time to listen deeply for what your gift might be. I recommend carving out twenty minutes to spend time with your tree with the sole intention of listening for the gift that is yours to give. Out of the spaciousness and open heart of being present, perhaps something will become clear to you and arise. If you are finding it challenging to identify a gift, ask your tree for help. Your gift could be a song, a prayer, water, or whatever creatively emerges.

Once you have a sense of what your gift might be, practice offering it. Listen for the tree's response to this gift and notice how it deepens the relationship. When you have offered, thank the tree. Notice what has shifted in your body and between you and the tree from this practice of reciprocity. When we learn to practice reciprocity with just one tree, perhaps we will become creative to be in reciprocity with the wider Earth.

Growing Deeper

1. What are three things you are grateful to your body for?
2. How has your sense of reciprocity shifted through this chapter? What are the relational qualities you want to grow with the Earth?

3. What is an offering or a gift you gave your tree?
4. What does reciprocity feel like in your body?
5. How did giving an offering to the tree shift your relationship with them?
6. What other gifts would you like to give the Earth? What is yours to give?

10

Cosmic Entanglement

Empirically speaking, we are made of star stuff. Why aren't we talking more about that?
—Maggie Nelson

LiYan and I became fast friends in the Buddhist eco-chaplaincy training. Tree people see each other. She preferred the dry Oaks to the giant Redwoods—she said they were too gloomy. Her voice hummed with wild herbs and sugar—so very, very kind. During one of our endless Zoom sessions, she privately DMed me:

"Hey, love, just want to make sure I heard it right. Did you say be a toucan to trees?" I laughed.

"Haha no, I said be a *true kin* to trees!"

"Ah, haha, glad I asked!"

"Maybe a toucan IN a tree!"

"I thought that was lovely."

As the months went on, her presence changed in our Zooms. A little less bright. Like the luster had been rubbed off a pearl. She had cancer, and it was advanced. LiYan shared her pain with us—a raw, unflinching ache—and the late nights filled with worry over her six-year-old son's future. She was a landscape architect, and while she'd spent her career designing places for humans and nature to coexist, now she needed the landscape to architect on her behalf. To wrap her in a forest of care.

After seven months of digital pixels, we were finally in person at what one friend affectionately called Buddha camp. We applied dharma teachings from the Buddhist tradition to the emerging field of eco-chaplaincy. We approached loving the Earth as a palliative act. We wrestled with inquiries like *What is suffering? What is liberation? What role do we have in both?*

We'd just spent time cultivating fearlessness in contemplative practice through listening to the refuge of the Earth. It was LiYan's turn to share.

"The Redwoods found me in my cancer." She turned her eyes toward the crowns of the trees, which created sky islands far above the forest floor. There were worlds within worlds up there.

"Different trees find us at different times of our lives." Her elegant frame was silhouetted by the light moving through the forest in sloping, deciduous lines. For a flash, she became them.

"There's a song about this." As she started to sing, even the insects were listening. A Tibetan mantra about the five elements became a drum beat pounding deep within the Santa Cruz Mountains: Air is connected to the heart, wind to the lungs, water to the kidneys, fire to the liver, and Earth to the skin. As she poured out her tender heart, everything else fell silent. A ballad of entanglement, of belonging, spun from tree to tree. It was not language but an essence that flowed through her, making the words materialize the intention of them the second they left her mouth.

The Redwoods were no longer gloomy, or ornamental, but kind. They became part of the song as she sang. Her voice was a spell that in an instant made something out of nothing. Or rather, revealed the everything that is always here.

A few months after our program ended, her condition deteriorated. Hospital, then hospice, then home. Her husband wrote our eco-chaplaincy cohort and asked if one of us knew the name of the song from the retreat. Someone shared a video. Someone else suggested we record a meditation for her. I volunteered.

Trees are utterly divorced from the scale of human time. "From one lover of trees to another, this meditation is for you," I began. "As you breathe, inhaling through your nose, exhaling through your mouth, imagine dropping below your body, below the top of the Earth, down and down, until you find roots. Roots belonging to beings that we humans call trees."

LiYan knew she might be dying when she signed up for the eco-chaplaincy program. But she wanted to devote herself to the Earth, even as her body moved closer to joining it.

She passed peacefully at home. Zen priest Gil Fronsdal, the director of our program, had spoken to her a few days prior and said that she'd found deep support in the Earth as she prepared to let go. I imagined that the trees held her through her final moments.

We are interwoven. Tree, human, love, loss. All of it. We are born, live, and die side by side. There is no end to the communion we are a part of.

Witnessing LiYan face death with unwavering care was radical dharma incarnate. She allowed her grief to guide her into the refuge of the Earth. She welcomed the dissolution of her individuality into the profound care of the whole. She let herself be stitched into the sinew of the living world. Being by being. Bit by bit. She reminds me we are more than that; we are entangled—porous, breathing, and alive—all of us, without exception.

Entanglement is our ecological reality, which is a movement of *actions*, not static interrelations between systems or beings. This is no small philosophical turn and has biological and metaphysical implications. Nature is an event that never stops. As William Bateson, who coined the word *genetics*, observed in a 1917 lecture at Cambridge, "A living creature is a vortex of chemical and molecular change... We commonly think of plants and animals as matter, but they are really systems through which matter is continuously passing."[1]

Life forms are not inert entities that touch at discrete intervals—no, we are all ever-moving, ever-flowing, ever-changing rhythms. We are more river than water. We are more storm than rain. If we had eyes to see what was really happening at the microscopic, subatomic levels, we would understand this.

I am drawn to entanglement because it dissolves the boundaries between human and more-than-human. It awakens the vision that we are life processes in process. It makes relationship a very powerful cauldron. Entanglement, therefore, connotes something beyond interconnection, something even deeper. The prefix *en-* means "to make," while the prefix *inter-* means "between." *Entanglement* is the ongoing act of co-creation—a fluid, messy togetherness—whereas *interconnection* highlights separateness and inadvertently underscores dualism. There is no way to isolate where time starts or ends, or where a human body originates and dies. What is a forest? The visible trees? The roots? The water that sustains them? The entirety of the cosmos? We are an undefinable heap of endless relationships, and we make life together in a million immeasurable ways.

Knowing we belong to the Earth upends the human-centric worldview. Reciprocity roots that belonging in a mutual give-and-take of love. Entanglement is the next ring on the tree. Out of the joy of giving our love back to the Earth, because we belong to the Earth, we then stitch ourselves into the fabric of *becoming with* the Earth, stem by branch by leaf. And then just like that—*poof*—we are on the move again.

Billions of years ago, a celestial body exploded somewhere and became a star. During that explosion, almost all the heavier elements, like the oxygen in our lungs, the carbon in our muscles, the calcium in our bones, and the iron in our blood, were made inside these stars before they died. Our bodies are made of stardust. In fact, we are built of the same matter as butterflies, trees, rocks, and soil, too. Death happens as a necessity in order for life to exist, not the other way around. Every element is in everyone and everything all at once. This is our entangled body. We are the body of the Earth. Even more, we are the body of the cosmos.

As I lay flat on a frozen glacial lake of snow, the galaxy spun in operatics overhead. I had the piercing clarity that the constellations could fall straight out of the darkness and pin me in place. There was a circle at play. The astral fires fall, make pinpricks of light in my body, go straight down into the Earth, and thread the needle back up through the roots of an Aspen forest, bursting through the leaves, turning into oxygen, and blowing fresh air back up toward the cosmos. The day becomes night, and the air becomes stars, and down they fall, over and over again. I felt the endless beauty of someplace surrounded by wilderness. I felt the mystery of the wilderness inside me.

Once, at the planetarium in Los Angeles, I put my finger on a piece of moon rock. I remember how the rock felt, so different from anything I'd touched on Earth. A globe of mystery. A cannonball of celestial matter. Proof of other planets, evidence of space.

It made me cry, realizing in an instant that there is so much more out there than we can ever fathom. How relieving is that?

Entanglement takes us beyond the more ubiquitous understanding of interconnection and gestures toward our shared life, death, and future. The phrase *entangled futures* is employed in scholarship to signal a transdisciplinary experimentation that is interested in creating visions of futures to come. Such an endeavor is a harbinger of wild thinking for urgent times. Appropriate for the ones we are in. What if we can repattern what is coming next? How do we do that?

In Donna Haraway's *Staying with the Trouble*, she emphasizes the importance of making kin with other species as essential to reimagining what it is to be human. "We become-with each other or not at all," she warns.[2]

I looked out the window and saw a crack of reflected sunlight on the pond. Within this silvery strip were the shadows of plants, leaves, branches. I saw worlds upon worlds from where I sat. I was in the worlds I could imagine.

A duck flipped upside down to find its lunch. Tail feathers fanned into a cathedral as its turn sent concentric circles out into the pond. The duck burst through the surface with a mouthful of aquatic plants. I was happy for this creature. They were finding their way.

Last night, I saw a moose meander down to the same water's edge and drink. Today, too many birds to count took their fill. Ecosystems are multimodal confabulations. Communities. To see anything other than multiplicity misses the point.

I ached to be part of the feast. I am a species, and they are multispecies, and somehow, we are part of a flow. How do I "become-with" these creatures? How do I make kin with beings so different from me? I realized part of doing so is forgetting my humanness. To remember I, too, am a forest. I am not one animal. I am not static. My body is in process, in movement, with theirs. From where I sat, I could still see an American goldfinch land on the Cottonwood. I could still appreciate the gracious ripples on the water's surface. I could still decide to take my body down to the pond's edge and join them. I could still taste and see that our life—not *my* life—was good.

Entanglement heralds our ecological kinship. "Kin is a wild category," Haraway says, giving us courage to let go of our bloodlines and imagine other ways we share life. The community at the pond—me—the blazing sun—that's my kin, and in her words, our *oddkin*. Whether I believe it or not, it's a fact. Such a relationship "troubles important matters, like to whom one is actually responsible... What shape is this kinship, where and whom do its lines connect and disconnect, and so what?"[3]

When we find each other, in the compost heap, in the glistening pond, in the dripping glen, we become the circle of life in motion.

The incandescent mist was thick and syrupy, sliding down the mountain. The sun filtered through last night's rain on heavy branches, dazzling me with sparkles so bright and numerous I thought my own chest would explode. The chipmunks pirouetted in the lush grass. The birds' warble and trill was so brimful my cells darted awake—everything in my body said *More*. A forbidden fruit. This is the wild kinship we are part of. When I see this, I hear *Please don't forget that you are a forest.*

But we do forget. And there are reasons for our amnesia. So often our capacity to be present to our wild kin is stolen. Disembodied technological communication is an increasing feature of our everyday lives. Taken over an average adult life, we might literally spend years of our lives with our heads bowed—and not toward the Earth—but in front of a device. Excessive phone use blinds us to our entanglement with the living world. We lose our Earthly senses. It rips us from our roots.

Another feature of our lost sense of entanglement is the lack of equity within Earth's life processes. Vast and systemic imbalances within the web of life reinforce the eclipse of our sensory relations with the living world. We cannot hope to entangle with nature without tending to the cultural and societal worlds that we are part of.

Physicist Karen Barad tackles entanglement through a quantum physics and feminist lens and suggests that eco-justice requires getting rid of the nature-culture dualism. This split is a concept in anthropology, philosophy, and environmental studies that refers to the perceived division between nature (the natural world, including more-than-human life and ecosystems) and culture (human societies, their creations, and social practices). This dualism has been a foundational idea in Western thought and has implications for how the living world is understood and, consequently, protected or not.

Even within environmental movements, such a binary reduces the current climate crisis to a schism between humans and nature—which risks repeating colonial and imperial agendas through hegemonic climate discourse that does little to halt irreparable extraction and exploitation. For if we simply put human back in nature, human will continue to exploit the Earth unless the mind and soul of human, as well as their culture, society, and values (in all the intersections) radically change.

Instead, *entanglement* mixes this whole thing up and acknowledges the embodied confluence of humans, culture, and the more-than-human world. *We make each other.* Understanding that we co-create this world can inspire kinship care that stretches to every facet of socio-political structures. We need that torch as we travel through the wreckage toward multispecies eco-justice.

An example of the inseparability of nature and culture is inequitable greenspace. In the United States, colonialism and racism make access to nature rife with disparity and inequity. All sixty-three US national parks are on land that was originally stewarded by Native people, and most were established through the forced removal of these communities from their ancestral land. Many tribes are still fighting for their rights regarding sacred sites within park boundaries today.

For example, for the Blackfeet, the mountains of Glacier National Park are considered the backbone of the world. Yet they lost much of their access to these mountains after a controversial land transaction during the park's creation. In 1895, the US government pressured the Blackfeet into selling the land that makes up today's Glacier National Park. Accessing such lands for these communities is not merely a matter of enjoying greenspace, but rather a reclamation of thousands of years–long, deep kincentric relations.

For Black communities, Jim Crow–era laws, like city ordinances in Alabama and Louisiana, made greenspace access difficult at best and in some cases, illegal altogether. For example, in Atlanta, ordinances prohibited Black people from using public recreational facilities, and the parks that were designated for them were underfunded, poorly maintained, and fewer in number compared to those for white communities.

Today, greenspace access is still unequal. The Jim Crow–era laws led to permanently underdeveloped greenspaces in Black communities and systematic denial of park development and creation. A 2021 Trust for Public Land special report found that Black and Latino communities have 50 percent less park space per capita compared to white neighborhoods.[4] Additionally, about 77 percent of visitors to national parks are white, while only 7 percent are Black, according to a 2018 National Park Service survey. A 2021 report from the Outdoor Foundation found that Black people make up just 6 percent of outdoor activity participants.

There is a systemically racist reason for this. Natural places have been deeply intertwined with violent histories. In particular, trees were sites of racialized terror. The Equal Justice Initiative, a nonprofit committed to ending mass incarceration, documented 4,084 incidents of racial terror lynchings of Black people in the South between 1877 and 1950.[5] This is the first thorough examination of lynching in public history. Most were public hangings of victims on trees. These events were attended by large crowds of white people, turning them into family-friendly social spectacles by reinforcing racial hierarchy and white supremacy. White spectators would bring snacks and blankets and watch the vicious show. Lynchings were a horrific theater of death and dehumanization.

Trees, thus, became a symbol of racial terror and violence to Black communities. They have not had equal access to wild places in the United States and never have. Through an eco-centric lens, trees were unwilling accomplices to cruelty, forced to participate in the latest iteration of the elimination of Black lives. Reconciliation and healing are needed at these sites for both trees and people alike.

As the US national parks and greenspace inequity examples illustrate, there is no separating the living world from human societies and practices. Given that our reality is inextricably and undeniably tangled up with technology, sociopolitical systems, the natural world, and inequitable history, how can we remember we are a forest when not everyone is welcome? When the forest is dangerous?

Entanglement must reckon with both nature and culture. "Individuals do not preexist their interactions; rather, individuals emerge through and as part of their entangled intra-relating," writes Barad.[6] We must look at our relations. We must examine what lives there. We must understand we are processes, not bits of matter. We must give up the idea of a perfect utopian nature and instead understand nature is in us, around us, and between us. And thus, we must care for the mess and the beauty alike.

Barad argues we have a moral and ethical duty to notice how our interactions change the world. How our embodied relations contribute to or destroy equity for all. We are invited to fight for new worlds in which bodies—human, nature, animal, mineral—are valued equally—because that is a reflection of the imploded space we dwell within. Anything less is colonialism in another form. What if the world is not a noun, but an activity—a *worlding*? How can we participate in worlding other worlds—as in futures to come—ones full of protection, love, and joy?

We can look to ecological science to find numerous vivid examples that illustrate our entanglement. That can inspire our worlding. In the Pacific West Coast of British Columbia, salmon caught in fish traps built by people of the Heiltsuk Nation are eaten by grizzly bears and wolves. These predators take their prey to dry benches under mother trees, which grow along the banks. The bears then eat the salmon but leave the carcasses to decay.

The nutrients seep into the soil and the roots of the trees. The salmon nitrogen is then taken up by the mycorrhizal networks, fertilizing other mother trees and transmitting the salmon nitrogen from tree to tree through their fungal connections, all the way into the deepest parts of the forest. The trees then metabolize the nitrogen, helping them grow. They also store it in their tissues for centuries. Tree rings prove it's so.

In response, the forests shade and nurture salmon rivers, modulating water temperatures and creating a positive feedback loop that promotes the health of the fish. And in yet another step in the circle, the Northwest First Coast Nations, including the Tsimshian and Nuu-chah-nulth, make clothing and art out of the parts of the trees composed of that salmon nitrogen (the bark and the roots).[7] Fish to tree to human—one flowing circle of intrarelatings. The overall health of the forest is dependent on the health of the salmon, and the result is that everything thrives.

Another example of entanglement as a process of action, as *worlding*, is the Pando, the largest and oldest Aspen forest in the world. The Pando is one single organism of a massive colony of quaking Aspens and stands at more than eighty thousand years old. The forest spans approximately 106 acres in Oregon and is composed of more than forty-seven thousand tree stems. Even when one individual tree dies, the ancient root system continuously sprouts new ones, allowing the organism to live for millennia. Aspens live and breathe an entangled kinship family. They lack a self-contained existence. Their life is not an individual affair. It's myriad—and one—at once. When entangled, ecosystems can live a very, very, long time. Making kin with each other extends our futures. We can't even fathom the end of that. Kind of like space.

The galaxies we see in the night sky are also inside us. Since the atoms in our bodies, and in everything around us, were originally formed in the interior of stars, the sky is us, we are the Earth, and the Earth is the universe, formed in numberless relationships. As Harvey writes, an "epic poem of flowing verses."

Star V762 Cassiopeiae is about 16,308 light-years away from Earth, one of the farthest stars we can see with our naked eyes in the night sky. I like to wonder if, maybe, both the atom in the Aspen tree and the atom in my palm come from V762. That although my senses perceive space and betweenness, it's actually the same stuff. Nebulas, supernovas, dark matter. Black bears, wild roses, human skin. An exoplanet, an exoskeleton, an exosphere. This is us. Our fate, our future, our fabulous fractal fusion. Universe without beginning, and universe without end.

I was elated to visit Plum Village, a monastery in France, on one of the Days of Mindfulness, when it is open to the public. I felt the land immediately. The Plum trees, Umbrella Pines, and Weeping Willows felt exquisitely joyful. The Buddhist monk Thich Nhat Hanh, a renowned Zen master, poet, and founder of the Engaged Buddhism movement, started Plum Village, and his teachings pioneered the field of Buddhist deep ecology. He coined the term *interbeing*, which is informed by the Buddhist teaching on dependent arising, to express a perspective of reality in which everything is entangled. I'd always wanted to visit the land Nhat Hanh nurtured and loved.

"We have to change our whole relationship with the earth," writes Nhat Hanh in his *Love Letter to the Earth*.[8] He argues that to solve climate change, a mindfulness and spiritual revolution is the only path forward. A transformation, he believed, will occur once people recognize our kinship with the Earth. Notice that Nhat Hanh cited the relationship, or our kinship entanglement with the Earth, as the place from which we begin. Nhat Hanh's interbeing, Barad's entanglement, Bateson's continual process, and Indigenous peoples' reciprocity are all getting at a similar notion.

I joined the nuns and monks for a mindful, silent eating meditation. We carried our bowls to be served by kind hands, and then walked in procession into an immense meditation hall. In silence, we waited for everyone to arrive. Reverence grew for the food in my hands.

Five hundred people filed in and took their seats without words. The room was an ocean—sound distorted itself into undulating wispy rustles and then fell like a current dropping into the deep sea with low hums—the brothers gave the motion, and we began. As I ate, I could sense the sun that grew the beans, the hands that harvested them, the hearts that cooked them, and the bodies that served them. I was profoundly moved. This was, in essence, a meditation on interbeing.

There are sacred sites on Earth. Plum Village is one of them. This pocket of land had been watered with decades of such exquisite love from hearts dedicated to nonviolence, to embodying interbeing in lifelong vows, to demonstrating that one's cultivation of their mind and presence is indeed an important gift to the Earth, that the fruit rose up like a distinct aroma. The living world had been loved so well there that they welcomed me as one of their own. Years later I can still taste the tone of this place—tangible, sensuous proof that kinship makes flourishing equitable, bountiful, and possible.

To inter-be is to live in such a way that we "inter-are." Interbeing and entanglement are, therefore, a praxis, an ontology, and a cosmology. Disconnection creates harm. Entanglement creates love.

As Haraway says in *Staying with the Trouble*, every fiber of our beings is indeed interlaced, complicit even, in the webs that we get to repattern.[9] Our loving and caring *matter*, creating bridges through the ruins that have become our home *matters*. We are matter, *mattering*.

I've come to see healing as an ongoing process of loving, unfolding within and through the cycles of life. Healing unfurls from within our entanglement, an expression of interbeing in a never-ending process. As I moved through the stages of my chronic illness—denial, fight, despair, surrender, entanglement—I felt increasingly more "well" in direct proportion to the vibrancy and vitality of my kinship relations, not to any fix in my body. I am a flowing cycle in connection. The Earth has me, even if I can't hold myself. And new life, surprise, is always possible.

What better amazement than how nature regenerates itself in myriad ways? Nature never stops. Starfish, for example, can regrow any one of the five limbs that stem from their center. Amphibians can grow new tails. Fish can regrow their fins, birds replace lost feathers, and deer regrow their antlers. Rabbits and bats can regrow flesh to repair holes in their ears and wings, and when the human dermis is cut, the body rushes platelets to stop the bleeding. All life carries the ability to regenerate. If they can, can't we? May miracle never be abstract. It's happening. Every single day. It might not always seem plausible, but all biological life shares this potential. What if we can co-create new worlds? What if we can literally revivify, renew, restore? What if nothing is out of reach?

Entanglement can heal and spur new life, but what can it do to practically create ethical worlds? There are some true stories. Julia Butterfly Hill lived in a tree she named Luna for two whole years, without coming down. She was protesting the Pacific Lumber Company's destruction of old-growth forests. She climbed up a thousand-year-old California Redwood tree and stayed there for 738 days. Hill received support from a group of people who delivered food, fuel, mail, and batteries to her twice a week. She also sometimes allowed other protesters to join her in the tree. While some called her irrational and erratic, her civil disobedience, her oddkin dreaming of otherworlds, her entanglement, eventually led to an agreement with Pacific Lumber that protected Luna and a two-hundred-foot buffer zone around it. Pacific Lumber eventually went bankrupt. Luna still stands today.

When we believe, know, and sense the Earth is part of us, there is no limit to our loving. I was thinking about this while inside a summer snowstorm. White cotton moved sideways and landed on everything—the pond, the deck, my hair. The far edge of the tempest was clear air, but here, the nebulous haze of this wispy, white goodness filled every inch of space. I could have laid my head down in it and never gotten up.

In one giant burst, the Cottonwoods expel their seeds. Certain environmental factors, like hot and dry weather, create the right conditions for mast seeding every three to seven years. The Cottonwood seed, attached to the fluff, ensures it can travel far distances in the wind. Even though most of the seeds will never take root, each one sent into the air is still a little house of hope—glowing wombs in the midday sun.

These days, the sky was so thick with cotton that it looked like it was raining white. This was a mast seeding year. I knew because I was in a snow globe in July. The pond in front of the house was half-covered in white down. The ground, too. Out of the window, all day long, I watched seed after seed float like prayers through the air. The sun backlit the luminous and downy puffs. I placed my imagination in each one and let gravity, and wind, pull them every which way.

I realized I was a witness to ceremony, the ritual of life's kinship potential. Who was this theater for? The birds, the ducks, the other trees. Everyone was there. I wanted to open my mouth like a whale and swallow this air-bound plankton. To gestate these trees, too.

The Cottonwood forest is a community. Mast seeding is their oddkin celebration. In the form and emptiness, I could hear something. The sound of interbeing. The faint pulse of the tree's wild weave with the forest. The rhythm of gracious generosity most beautiful. Wouldn't most of these seeds go to waste? The ritual was bigger than that.

Forests are in the business of world building. They make universes and nurture them. With their mycelium, their salmon, their seeds. We should be worlding, too. They ask us, *What kind of world will you make?*

Let us build a world where salmon and mother trees can keep loving each other. Where every kind of body can access wild places without violence. Where every Luna and LiYan alike can be fully expressed as the trees that they are.

Three years after LiYan died, her husband, David, wrote to me and shared that he still sings the song she gifted us among the Redwoods. This ballad is entanglement in motion. He says he sings it as a meditation even though he remembers only fragments. He says he keeps it close to keep her close.

Her song made a world, one where we can find rest in the Earth, and the Earth finds rest in us. A song of continuous co-becoming. A spilling waterfall with one promise: not that things will work out, but that love will continue. Love never dies—it simply changes forms.

Snowpack.

Flowing stream.

Watersheds for every sensitive and intelligent being.

This is a law of nature.

Maybe the only one I want to remember.

Body Practice: Earth to Sun Breath

In this practice, you are invited to embody a sense of entanglement between your body and the Earth. By mindfully tracking your breath from its origin in the Earth, through your body, and back again, you can begin to taste the feeling of your woven nature.

Begin by bringing attention to the breath. Imagine that it begins deep inside the planet, moving up the rivers of the spine and out the top of your head toward the sun.

Then, imagine that your breath spills out from the sun,

back toward the Earth, and then up the roots of your body once again.

Breathe in this manner for at least five minutes, allowing a sense of widening to occur, relaxing the borders of the body. See if you can breathe toward your entangled kin and receive breath from them.

Once finished, return to an easeful breath. Notice if you feel any new sensations from practicing this Earth to sun breath. If you do not feel any different, that is completely fine. Try this again in the presence of your tree and see what opens or occurs by so doing.

Tree Practice: Entanglement with the Living World

For this tree practice, let this be a meditation on entanglement. To do so, tune in to the *process* of the tree, the unfolding motion of yourself, the variable and unending flow of becoming. In light of the exploration of entanglement in this chapter as a verb (to make), how are you, and the tree, in a process of becoming, *together*?

Begin by spending some time with your tree and take note of all the beings they are connected to. Imagine the fungi below the soil, the mycorrhizal world, the mycelium. See if you can notice and pay attention to the *forest* the tree is part of, not just the tree themself. Take note of the many beings connected to the tree's care.

Now, open your aperture of awareness. What is the motion occurring just below the soil, within the tree, through the veins of their leaves? What is the process of sunlight hitting their leaves and becoming food? What is the movement of water being pumped through their xylem? What does the suction feel like that pulls water upward from the roots? What systems, organic matter, and biological organisms does the tree experience moment by moment in order to keep marching onward in their growth?

Now, switch the lens. What is in motion right now within your body? What connects you to the tree's life, visible, invisible? What is the hidden life of air? Allow a sense of momentum to unfold between you two. Now stretch that understanding so there's not so much a betweenness as a fluid co-creation. Can you sense into the subtlety of your life's entanglement with the tree? With the forest?

Growing Deeper

1. When I breathe Earth to sun, I feel _____.
2. I can sense my wider wild kin through the sensation of _____.
3. What struck you when considering the tree's entangled world?
4. What relationships in your life do you consider kin, and why?
5. Who else, and what else, might you allow yourself to be entangled with?
6. When you dream from an entangled place, what do you see for the world?

IV
Feral Prayers for Liberation

II

Spirit, Magic, and Ceremony

And when you love, you let it go, you put it down, you show your shoulders what to do with sky, and love is how, and love is when, and love is why.
—Alexis Pauline Gumbs

The *Amanita muscaria* mushroom is the visible proof of other worlds. Bright red cap with white speckles, the amanita's emergence says summer's nearly over. The thunderstorms and fog, clapping in at promptly 3 p.m. every afternoon, wrap the valley in change. This week, the very first Aspen leaves turned yellow. Fall is coming.

    I walked up the road toward the light of a solar lamp. The late summer sky was clear, the wind rolled down the valley, and constellations shimmered with the precision of pinprick holes of light for stars. I arrived to the wide, warm bosom of an Aspen elder, holding court over the forest. The air was silent and cool. I could've sipped it through a bell jar. This tree's knots were so deep they were like eyelids, the rims folded linen curtains. Their gaze held back the night.

The Aspen leaves quivered. They were a river falling from the sky. The source was that patch of ground packed with life. Destination? Unknown.

As I pressed my face onto the tree, I could sense that I wasn't alone. The Aspen reminded me of my grandmother, somehow, the phantom cartography of her presence emerging through the bones of the tree.

In the summer, my grandmother used to take a tiny magnifying glass into the forest to find the wild orchids. The orchid family is the largest of all flowering plants in the world, including approximately thirty thousand species. Twenty-six of them call Colorado home. They bloom from May through September. Because orchid seeds are so minuscule, they have no food reserves and rely solely on fungus for nutrients. I pictured my grandmother, her face pressed to the glass, focusing on a wild royal orchid blown up ten times its size.

I crouched at the feet of the tree. *Oh yes*, a perfect purple orchid. Each petal was pressed together in pairs of prayer.

How could there be such unbearably rare beauty, right here, and so much destruction happening at that moment, somewhere? Unpredictable rainfall from climate change was already disrupting the orchid's habitats. I knew that worse was on its way.

Something stopped my rumination. My capillaries were flooded by signals, clearer than human words. *We are rooted in place. But you can move. Speak. There is enough for everything that lives.*

The tree's voice broke my cast of outdated thoughts. *Follow the way of the trees.*

The word *enough* landed in my body as an image, growing from the spine, blooming beyond time, enormous but not cavernous, soft but with structure. *Do not believe in ruin. If you share, there will indeed be enough for all.*

I opened my eyes. I was breathing heavily. The vision disappeared, and I leaned away from the grandmother tree, the echo of this wave still in me.

For many Indigenous communities, it is unfathomable to consider the Earth as anything other than animate, anything other than filled with spirit. In *Restoring the Kinship Worldview*, Mourning Dove is quoted as saying Indigenous children, from a very young age, are taught that the world is alive and is always speaking.[1] And though many in the overculture might have found spirit in nature when we were children, it has likely been stamped out as we've gotten older. However, we can rediscover the pulsing, animate aliveness within the living world again.

Where Western scholars once dismissed animism as "unscientific," recent research indicates that it is the very belief in the spiritual life and personhood of nature that drives care for them.[2] We love what lives. We are life recognizing life itself.

And so, kinship with the web of aliveness is essential for our protection of the Earth. There is an "anima mundi," or "soul spark," in every bear, bluebird, mountain lion, Aspen, and Redwood. Even stones have spirits. Even the wind can speak. Animals, trees, plants, everything is ensouled, as James Hillman writes, and so they are active, sentient, and alive.[3] All beings have faces. All beings speak. Everything is *alive*.

I know this because I can *feel* the animacy of the living world. When I pay attention. The agency, will, creativity, and *life* of the Earth are the field of simmering participation. What an immense intimacy. The wonder of recognizing the soul spark in everything that is turns the world from shapes and forms, processes, and interruptions, to a playful, unpredictable, beyond the beyond precious experience. Where there is a pulse, there can be love. And even in the most ancient of biological life, like the mountain, if we rebuke linearity, we can return to relationship within the endless circle. There is no limit to the depth of this nearness. When we are receptive through the land of our bodies, we can hear their wisdom. We can speak in the language of trees.

In fact, there has been a recent legal movement to formalize the animacy of the Earth by granting nature rights as persons. It's become clear that protection of nature is contingent on a vast reorientation of the human mind: a drastic shift from seeing the Earth as inert, soulless matter, to embracing the ensouled world as *alive*. Laws might facilitate that change.

The Māori tribe of Whanganui in the North Island of New Zealand fought for the recognition of their river—the third-largest in New Zealand—who is considered an ancestor, for 140 years. In 2017, New Zealand passed a groundbreaking law granting personhood status to the Whanganui River. This law declares that the river is a living being. And with that declaration comes certain protections. For example, this river could sue a human in a court of law if they are violated. The river has legal standing.

In 1972, Christopher Stone's article "Should Trees Have Standing?" first advanced the argument for nature to be granted the same rights as people.[4] Since the achievement of protecting the Whanganui River, other rivers, mountains, and ecosystems have been granted legal rights through rights of nature laws and declarations. In the United States, some of the most notable rights of nature initiatives have been established by tribal nations exercising their sovereign authority. While these represent important precedents, they apply only within tribal jurisdiction, highlighting the need for broader municipal and state-level ordinances to create more comprehensive legal protection. These have limited legal reach. We have work to do. Consider this: A corporation has more legal rights in the United States than any river, mountain, or ecosystem. A nonhuman entity possesses more personhood than the living world. What a tragedy.

If we cannot legally protect the Earth as animate, we can still, and we must, relate to the Earth as very much alive. In my PhD research, participants cited visions, nonlinear time, ceremony, and prayer as some of the forgotten ancestral technologies, or ancient "lifeways," that we can remember today to reconnect with the living Earth. All of these practices are rooted in the primacy and sacredness of animating spirit, which imbues everything with life.

From the ground of shared aliveness, we can relearn how to embody and practice the lifeways of our human and beyond-human ancestors. The cost of ignoring their animacy is simply far too great. "Yet if we no longer call out to the moon slipping between the clouds, or whisper to the spider setting the silken struts of her web," writes David Abram in his *Becoming Animal*, "well, then the numerous powers of this world will no longer address *us*—and if they still try, we will not likely hear them."[5] Let that never be. Do you experience the Earth's aliveness? Do you speak to the animals, the elements, the sky? Do you want to try? Let us listen through our sensuous terrain. Let us remember how to be together, so we can in turn *become together*, side by tree by side.

In my vision with the Aspen elder, I received the clear message that humans can advocate for trees, and through reciprocity, there is indeed enough for all. This transmission is guiding me into the next phase of my life.

Receiving messages like these from the animate world has been practiced in cultures throughout history. There is nothing unusual about it, except that it is odd many have stopped relying on these exchanges as meaningful sources of wisdom in our lives today. There is good reason some cultures value the sacredness of spiritual insight so much that they warn against reducing it by sharing it prematurely. Only when the wisdom has really grown its own synapses in the body and has started sprouting its fruit might it be mature enough to share. Sometimes, it's best to keep things in the inner, sacred sanctuary, until the wisdom ripens.

I offer it here because I believe that ecological wisdom is not meant for the person who receives it alone. I just happened to be the one who heard it that day. But like the *Amanita muscaria*, who forms symbiotic relationships with tree roots, their bright red fruiting body is just the visible part of their expansive self. Ecological wisdom is like that, too. We might see the mushroom, but really, there is an entire tangled mycelial underworld to which that wisdom is connected. We can practice being aware of both. And while the mushroom will grab our attention, the mycelium is where the wisdom really does its work, in a timeless place of ever-more aliveness.

The oldest Olive tree in the world showed me time outside of rational linearity. Instead of the line, the spiral. I visited this tree on Crete, an island in Greece. Known as the Vouves Olive Tree, they stood at somewhere around four thousand years old. The Vouves was bordered by a little stone fence, next to a quiet café, on an indiscriminate hill of olive groves. I felt silly driving hours out of the way to visit them, but I was set on it.

The tree was as ancient as the Egyptian Old Kingdom. They'd outlived every major human civilization, empire, epidemic, and war. And in their long life, they had not taken over the hillside or established a colony. The tree was simply rooted in the place they began, uninterested in domination. The tree was humble and holy. And incredibly, they still produced olives.

Hollow in the middle, the ancestor had no heartwood. Twirling like a spiraling galaxy around the sun, I realized the tree no longer needed a center, because they had become one.

But even without a middle, the spot had a central gravitational pull. They must have given their whole heart to all their living. This tree spent four thousand good years taking care of their neighbors, burying the dead, and welcoming new life. And by giving away everything they had, it's as if the tree's physical heart emptied out into a never-ending whirlpool of awareness without form. Spinning around and around and around. A dervish of time. Endless. Infinite. Here.

Yes, I thought, *this hollow howl is a clear picture of time.* The sound travels, but there is no final resting place. It may go forward or backward, upside down, or underland. All I know is the tree still stood.

I wanted to kiss them. In their presence, I did not sense that brute strength had won them all these years of life. No. This tree's life was a testament to gentle patience. Day after day of welcoming the sun. They knew in their bark and their bones that time was immemorial. They had nowhere else to be but the place they gave their heart to, and, in that surrender, they lasted forever.

The Vouves embodied nonlinear time. Time is a circle. Time happens in cycles, spirals, not linear lines of progress. What does this have to do with animacy? If we can unlearn linear time, we can more easily embrace talking to a tree. Positivist science and the Western industrial complex purport that time is linear, deployed without regard to context and culture. A product of or a driver of colonial epistemologies, it's an artifact of domination. The linear arrow of time ensnares Western societies in a monocultural hegemony.[6] Linear time makes sense for capitalism, but not the Earth. Linear time cannot fathom the polymorphous rhythms of people, societies, and more-than-human life. Linearity is a narrow sieve. Rigid boundaries of past, present, and future are too conceptually thin to hold the magnanimity and mystery of the Earth's confounding timescales. Eons, eras, fossil records, geologic time periods, radiometric and numerical dating. The best we can do is fragments, grasping at the hem of the universe, trying to make it make sense.

In the first law of thermodynamics, energy is neither created nor destroyed. There is no beginning, middle, or end of things. Instead, time is cyclical. In contrast to closed systems, the Earth, space, and the universe unfold in infinite and regenerative connections in an open system—one that is continuously expanding. We can't capture what is moving in ripples beyond conscious comprehension. The best we can do is try to pay attention.

Billions of years ago, the deaths of stars brought the elements together that eventually formed the Earth. Long after, the conditions became right for biological life. Seasons, lunar cycles, the inevitable birth-life-death rhythm all point to a cyclical model of biological life. If the flower, why not the human? If the sun, why not the Earth? As the Olive tree taught me, time is circular, and love is not just a human phenomenon.

If the evolutionary clock were fashioned into twelve hours, humans would appear on Earth just seconds before midnight. Humans are the newly arrived. Therefore, we are not the center of the universe. We are one tiny part of the fractal. And therefore, wisdom is held in Jupiter's moons, the salmon's DNA, and the Honey Fungus's very long life, not primarily in the minds of *Homo sapiens*. The time is ripe to relinquish our superiority and begin to learn from the animate world. Our ancestors. Our elders. Our kin.

Given that human communities that prioritize a harmonious, human-nature balance live by circular notions of time, we should follow their lead. For example, the Maya, Hopi, Cheyenne, Yawanawá, and many more are exemplars of cultures and societies built on alternative time conceptions. Two of the core threads between them all is a deep connection to the Earth as a sacred intelligence and to time having a "cyclic" or "circular" form.[7]

Such an ontology of time is ecological rather than abstracted to principles. Tyson Yunkaporta is of the Apalech Clan in far north Queensland and a senior lecturer on Indigenous knowledge. He explains how this works: "Kinship moves in cycles, the sky moves in stellar cycles, and time is so bound up in those things that it is not a separate concept from space... In our spheres of existence, time does not go in a straight line, and yet it is as tangible as the ground we stand on."[8]

We must move out of the default anthropocentric conception of time that supports disconnection with nature, and instead cultivate one that will encourage and nourish our connection to the Earth. This is a solid, primordial stone to stand on. For example, take "the Dreaming," the way Australian Aboriginal peoples understand time. "The Dreaming" is a kind of narrative to what has happened, a charter of things happening, and a logos of order transcending what is significant.[9] It is so much bigger than a sequence of bound events. It has power. Time, to Australian Aboriginal peoples, is existence itself, unbound by linearity, freed to spill out beyond categories. The Dreaming is a belief system and a philosophy that explains nature, humanity, and the creation of the universe. In the Dreaming, time is not separate from how one came to be here nor from the kinship of relations one is woven into. English fails to capture such a complex notion. The Australian anthropologist W. E. H. Stanner writes in his seminal 1956 essay that "We [non-Indigenous Australians] shall not understand The Dreaming fully except as a complex of meanings." Time is participatory, collective, and contextual. Time, even, can be a Dreaming.

If you aren't convinced yet, tell me, how do you know time is real? Have you ever had an experience where a moment seems to inflate like a balloon and become "longer," or another experience seems to be so tiny it disappears? This is not just about memory. We are talking about the nature of reality. Our experience of life, moment-to-moment, is not bound to a progressive sequence, even though it feels like that. The numbers on clocks tell us time is passing. But what's changed?

Tell me, that time when you gazed at the hawk and heard a shriek that opened your heart so wide you felt you'd vanished and then returned. Was that linear? Did you not travel backward to retrieve an ancestral gift of hearing and then emerge back in the present, tears on your face, and not know why? Time can expand, shrink, undulate, and explode. We can move in infinite directions, if not with our bodies, certainly within our imaginations, thoughts, feelings, stretching from the Cottonwood's hazy floating seed straight through to the iris of the orca, blinking through the diffused light in the Iberian Sea.

The implications of living by nonlinear time, the Dreaming, cycles, is that it unfashions human supremacy. By so doing, the myth of progress cracks under the weight of better stories. In this circle, harmony matters more than dominance, because we will return to each point on the circle again and again. And we know our lives depend on our kin. Deep time roots us in intergenerational, ecological connections across species and timescales. Deep time respects the sacred circularity in the living world. Instead of a twenty-four-hour clock, we could better mark the passage of things through the pillars of birth, death, decay, renewal. If you look closely, you will see these cycles are occurring constantly, through all things.

For anyone who has experienced chronic pain, we know these circles well. The agony of sickness broke the trajectory of linear time for me. My body cycled its sensations. The shore of arrival continued to drift further out of sight. A haiku of the human form. But this was the poem I lived within.

I live the circularity of time in my cells, in the spiral that whorls in my brain during a migraine. And yet, early in my healing journey I very much wanted time to be a line. I felt desperate to pin my story into some kind of sense. Without a destination, where would I end up? Without intelligibility, what would I become? Yet ironically, deep time holds out a promise that linear time cannot. Getting worse does not mean hope is lost, and feeling better does not ameliorate the possibility of pain. The mystery outstrips all notions of superiority, improvement, transcendence. By forgetting reformation, I am revived. And even if I am in pain, I can still be free. The cycle will always continue.

For those of us conditioned by the Western code, unwinding from notions of linear time that haunt and are entrenched in Western society is challenging. We must unlearn what has been. One solution might be practicing decolonized time, a term put forward by Indigenous scholar Leo Killsback, who argues that it subversively undermines the singular emphasis on technology and imperialism as measures of success, and instead privileges balance between humans and nature.[10] Let us begin to gently try this on.

How do we do that? Finding our solace, solidarity, and simplicity with the Earth. By *slowing down*. Scaling back our pace to move at the "pace of place" has been a theme throughout this book. It's an Earthly technology of circular time. As we slow down, our bodies will learn to dream just as they become fluent in the language of trees.

The geography and vocabulary of our bodies are our portals to deep time, our doorway in. May we be so slow and so attentive that we notice the brand-new inch of the lichen and the fresh line in the desert rock. May we become so geological that our bodies find intimacy with the rose quartz forged over millennia. May we relax out of linear time so completely that we simply become the stone we dream of. May we give up domination and seek harmony. Let us slow down and say feral prayers: *Dear Earth, make us free of linear time.*

In *How I Became a Tree*, Sumana Roy writes about how she wanted to live in "tree time." She puts it this way: "My need to become a tree, then, was my need to return to slow time."[11] Slowing into tree time is a revisioning of our participation in the natural world. Tree time frees us from linear time. Tree time can be our resting place.

Purposively resting is a choice to unsubscribe from productivity and helps us detox from linear time. "We must believe we are worthy of rest. We don't have to earn it. It is our birthright. It is one of our most ancient and primal needs," writes Tricia Hersey, author of *Rest Is Resistance*.[12] Hersey, also known as "the Nap Bishop," critiques the violent impact that grind culture has on Black and Brown communities specifically, a product of capitalism and linear time. It is time to rest. It is time for tree time. In rested, embodied states, we are much more likely to hear the Earth speak to us.

If I am rested, if I move slowly, it's not a leap to see the world differently. This wild orchid might be my grandmother. This tree is certainly someone's ancestor. This river has wisdom that humans could never dream of knowing. But they draw us near. They draw us close. They let us taste the rapture of falling out of time and into theirs. To inhaling the luminosity of a world that is *alive*.

Another ancestral technology of reconnecting with the living world is ceremony. Right after my first chronic health symptoms began, I found myself in an unusual one.

I was sitting in a circle with nine strangers, holding a little cup filled with blue liquid. The vessel held a truffle tea containing psilocybin. Although a mentor of mine had warned that psychedelics could be a "spiritual shortcut," clinical psychologist William Richards says in his book *Sacred Knowledge*, "When approached with respect and care, psychedelics can be valuable tools for spiritual exploration, psychological healing, and personal transformation."[13] I was curious what I could learn from plant consciousness in this way.

The popular Western use of psilocybin can be traced to a little town in Oaxaca, Mexico, and a Mazatecan woman named María Sabina. Although psilocybin-containing mushrooms, or truffles, grow freely on every continent on Earth, their infamy began in Mexico, and unfortunately, the appropriative Eurocentric process was replicated.

Sabina was a Mazatec shaman and poet known as the "priestess of mushrooms." She became well-regarded globally when the American writer Robert Wasson, who wanted to experience a ceremony with "los Niños Santos," or sacred little children, as Sabina affectionately called the mushrooms, published an article in 1957 in *Life* magazine, as well as a string of books in the 1960s about his experience. These works popularized psilocybin and created a mystique around their use. Tragically, Sabina didn't get to share her relationship with los Niños Santos from her point of view, and her town was overrun with enthusiasts looking for healing, which created economic issues. Colonialism knows no bounds. As the use of psilocybin for all kinds of healing grew in the West, their original use for connecting with nature and finding missing loved ones became more obscured.

Sixty years later, I found myself in a psilocybin ceremony at a legal psychedelic retreat center in the Netherlands. This particular one offered mostly a Western scientific and therapeutic approach to psychedelics. As an adult child of an alcoholic, I grew up scared of drugs. I'd attended hundreds of AA meetings to support my father. I viscerally knew that drugs could ruin lives. I surprised myself by sitting in that room. Psilocybin, though, is a fungi, which is technically neither a plant nor an animal, and it isn't addictive. Psychedelics always hold a risk, though, even if it is mostly an existential one. At that time, I was unaware of their history, had never heard of Maria Sabina, and certainly did not understand the complexities of the world I was stepping into. But I was there because I wondered if psychedelics could help my body.

We were in ceremony, which meant gathering in community to learn from the mushrooms together. We had shared our intentions and made offerings. The ten of us were from various backgrounds and held diverse desires for ceremony. What stitched them together into the fabric that created the ceremonial space was a willingness to be touched—changed, somehow—by the wisdom of the mushroom. Together, we partook in the ritual of drinking the fungi tea. The atmosphere was reverent and spacious, and trained facilitators created a circle around us. They sang songs and shared the scents of sage, Palo Santo, and lavender. I felt held in by their care.

The experience flowed in a spiral, not a line. But these are the moments I recall now. There was a loud noise and the feeling of pressure in my brain. Next, a sensation that I was sideways, upside down, and to the left. The whoosh of a plane seemed to come from my belly. A flicker of a candle waffled and then bloomed, enormous as a city. I felt confused why the woman next to me was crying so much, and why I wasn't, when all of a sudden my consciousness disappeared from me, taken up into a state of simultaneous dissolution and clarity. I could no longer feel "me" as a discrete entity, but I also wasn't outside myself looking in. I was beyond form.

In that emptiness, or sunyata, the spirit of my grandmother came to me. Her presence was imminent and immediate, and there was no questioning if it was her. I felt ensconced in thermal waters, and my entire body radiated with heat. What I can only call love both filled and poured out of every cell at the same time. A trembling ache rippled through my nerves. My physical heart felt like it actually tore open, then, a fault line in the Earth shaken loose in seismic euphoria. I breathed in. The inhale felt like my very first breath of life. A defibrillation of my heart. All I could see, feel, and taste in every direction was love. Tears seemed to leak out of my body without crying them. My grandmother's spirit was a spectral apparition that had become present to my consciousness.

"What do I do with my life?" I asked her.

The magnitude of love was so enormous that I laughed at myself for asking something so banal. I stayed in that place with her for what felt like eons, but was likely just minutes. There was little thought; it was embodied sensations of goodness in timeless loops.

In the closing circle, seven hours later, I was mostly speechless. As the Sufi poet Rumi says, "Your task is not to seek for love, but merely to seek and find all the barriers within yourself that you have built against it."[14] This is what had happened. The mushroom seemingly punctured my defenses, one by one. I don't know what they are, and it doesn't really matter. But as a result, I experienced love more directly, which, I realized, was simply the capacity to recognize the infinite expanse of love that was already there.

* * *

The ritual wove the container for this experience of direct, embodied love to find me. A ceremony can have roots in a particular tradition, or it can also be a series of acts, gestures, offerings, done in contemplation and reverence. This is also called the set and the setting of a psychedelic ceremony. But the substance is more than the environment, the intentions we held, the facilitators, the music, the flowers, or the mandala in the center of the room. Ceremony should bring us to the edge of our knowing—and beyond it.

Western people are starved for this. I felt that deeply. And I sensed that such practices—nonreligious, prayerful, mindful sequences that stir us profoundly—can shake loose the scales of trance that obscure our right seeing. These are essential for remembering our connection to the Earth. Looking back, I see that psilocybin ceremony as an essential foundation for my eventual eco-erotic connection to the Earth. The blue tea–invoked experience had no content, not really, that related to nature. And at the time, I did not really understand how it helped my body's symptoms. But now, I can trace how it awakened a capacity for embodied presence, enlivened an openhearted awareness, and nurtured a growing connection to our entangled life, which surely set the process in motion.

I was also deeply moved by the transformation I saw in the rest of the group. Such a profound shared vulnerability in communal co-presence reminds our bodies that we are part of each other's undoings and becomings. That we are wholly and hopelessly holding reality together. That we are part and parcel of the great pattern. We transform together while also maintaining our own solitude. I wanted to learn how to support other people to experience such rarity. I could taste how thirsty we were for real connection. I decided to train to be a psychedelic facilitator at the same retreat center, went through their certification program, and eventually worked there, co-facilitating psilocybin ceremonies for others.

While there is copious research into the benefits of psychedelics for mental health challenges, I am most interested in their efficacy to help us remember our embodied entanglement with the Earth. To motivate care of our webbed existence. There is a term to capture this: ecodelia, which is the fostering of ecological awareness through altered states of consciousness. Psilocybin, in particular, has been found to increase people's nature connectedness over time.[15] From egoism to ecoism, psilocybin can elevate a sense of ecological intimacy. How does that work?

I intuit that it has much to do with the qualities of being that these experiences can open for people. When we can be in our bodies and experience what is here, we are also able to touch, and be touched, by the living world. We can feel awe, gratitude, and compassion. Moving toward, through, and beyond us. For a moment, these altered states can facilitate the nonduality and nonseparateness between humans and nature that is our original design. Once you *know* you are not other than the living world, transformation of values and worldview often follows. Such an experience can change someone's entire life in a toppling of the human-centric delusion of Western society. Of course, psychedelics are not needed to bring about this momentous shift. But they can be potent catalysts of it.

The physicist and deep ecologist Fritjof Capra underscores the importance of this change: "The Western version of mystical awareness, our version of Buddhism or Taoisim, will be ecological awareness."[16] But just like working with psychedelics for mental health or other reasons, their use demands maturity and cultural contextualization. Applied ethics, field of practice accountability, long-term integration support, and equity-focused and community-held models are essential.

Indigenous practitioners in the Amazon like the Shipibo or the Huni Kuin, who work with Ayahuasca, a brew made from the leaves of the *Psychotria viridis* shrub along with the stalks of the *Banisteriopsis caapi* vine, are known to refuse psychedelics to people unless they are deemed "ready." What do people need to be ready for?

There is a great responsibility that comes with experiencing the interconnectedness of all life. Maturity is necessary to honor and wield that wisdom. One indication of it is the capacity to grow spiritually without dependency on psychedelics. Another is integrating psychedelic experiences in service of social justice and collective transformation, not just individual well-being. To use the developmental framing of integral philosopher and theorist Ken Wilber, growth means growing up, cleaning up, waking up, and then showing up differently to the world. Sometimes people can get stuck in the waking up part. But that's not the end of the story.

These plant teachers are special and deserve respect and humility. Altered states of beyond ordinary consciousness offer a chance to let go of the rational mind. To experience the in-between, the felt, and the mysterious. To encounter other ways of being and knowing. Such a gift is particularly potent for those from the dominant overculture, whose allegiance to empirical rationality is fossilized and bone-deep. If health is built on right relations with every living thing, the healing nature of a ceremony is due in part to how it mends the connection between people and the rest of the world. Ceremony taps an ancient capacity to gather in ritual, to become porous in our bodies to wisdom that is mythic and mysterious, and to support each other, come what may.

After years of working with people in ceremonial psychedelic containers, my reverence for sacred plant allies and teachers has only increased. Simultaneously, my reticence about the emerging psychedelic industry and the so-called psychedelic renaissance has also increased. The same psychedelic center where I had my first experience and later worked ended up being an unfortunate prime example of the capitalist wellness complex. When I left, I became increasingly troubled at what I saw as a wider pattern within the psychedelic industry of conflating capitalism and healing, often while culturally appropriating Indigenous knowledge and ways of life. Psychedelics are nonspecific amplifiers, and I have found they reliably amplify the mess within organizations, cultures, and systems, too.

The potential efficacy of psychedelics to engender experiential, deep entanglement with the natural world and impact collective justice is getting hijacked. And what is wellness if not for the benefit of the collective? Additionally, there are critical conservation issues and Indigenous rights at risk in the commercialization of psychedelics that should not be ignored. Psychedelics have already fallen prey to the same hegemonic capitalist extractivism that has infected Western medicine. Baked into this system is the psychologization of psychedelics, which means the prioritization of their use solely for psychological means, disregarding their spiritual, numinous, ancestral, and ecological purposes. What is ultimately from the Earth has been rapidly commodified. Humans are quick to exploit whatever we can, given the systems we are living in. Furthermore, although psychedelics reliably lead us toward the medicine within the Earth, when they are then bought and sold *as* the medicine, we can miss the medicine under our feet. *We* also get off the hook from asking ourselves how we can be medicine to the Earth. Is there ever a limit to our taking?

Yes, psychedelics can be genuinely life-changing, facilitating reductions in depression and anxiety, breaking addiction cycles, easing end-of-life suffering, and opening new ways of being and seeing. Research continues to expand into their potential efficacy for bulimia, migraine headaches, traumatic brain injuries, and so much more. Yet if this remarkable therapeutic potential does not translate to better care for marginalized communities and our wider planet, it is not going far enough. Additionally, in the hype around these compounds, there is risk for misuse and harm. Psychedelics are not for everyone, and they are not a panacea. Let me say that again: Psychedelics are not for everyone, and they are not a panacea.

This book so far has been an exploration of connecting to the Earth without the use of psychoactive plants. Everything alive can teach us through their animacy. The multi-voiced world is always speaking. Even illness, in its cacophony of symptoms and sensory-warping faculties, is certainly an altered state. My migraines shift and change my senses in ways psychedelics do, but in experiences I am not choosing.

Both plants and illness are my teachers. Sickness has brought me straight to the altar of ceremony. So yes, the psilocybin in mushrooms, or the mescaline inside a peyote cactus, might be particularly potent, but everything alive has a spirit, so everything alive can speak. The Redwood, the Rocky Mountain iris, the red fox, the rock wren, the Colorado River. Our glitchy bodies, unpredictable nerves, kaleidoscopic brains and veins. All of it can be our teacher.

I see how psychedelics could help disrupt Western notions of health, opening pathways to remembering sacred, collective rituals and enacting communal healing instead of individual wellness. But there are also ceremonies that can be created without them. "Ceremony is a vehicle for belonging—to a family, to a people, and to the land," writes Robin Wall Kimmerer in *Braiding Sweetgrass*. Ceremony helps us to remember our innate belonging. Ceremony is meant to open us to mysteries and the numinous.

In the early-May mornings in the Rocky Mountains, the freshly bloomed dandelions are little closed palms. They wind themselves up tight during the night. As soon as sunshine hits them, they fold open. This is effortless, instinctual, and remarkable. I tried to be there the very moment their yellow petals stretched to the sun. I never caught it, but I felt a shock of awe anyway. These flowers, unfolding their own ceremonial prayers in pace with the rotation of the Earth, were an exquisite rendering of opening and closing the heart. I suppose all life is a ceremony. And we might just notice, if we pay attention.

According to Four Arrows, ceremony is a crucial tool to awaken the capacity to give thanks to the Earth. To live within a spirit of gratitude. Ceremony also helps us surrender to the Earth. They are our *first teacher*. Rituals are essential practices for intimacy with the living world. Weave your own ceremonies with the Earth, remembering rituals inside you just waiting to be expressed. See how these experiences infuse your being with a deeper sense of homecoming, awe, and belonging.

The magic of animating spirit, of embodying our entanglement, of listening to our beyond-human ancestors, is made possible through ceremonial ways of living. Messages, divinations, the magic, or the otherwise—meaning that which is outside of the dominant paradigmatic ways of seeing, thinking, feeling—can come to us. Ceremony opens us to other ways of knowing, to letting go of reductionist ways of looking, to connecting us to experiences and wisdom that defy our preconceptions. Can we release our grip on rationality and open to the unknown? Can we trust the interstitial to meet our hearts, even without understanding it?

In my PhD research, every participant recounted a life-altering message they received from the Earth—without psychedelics. Life advice from a Redwood, life direction from the Datura plant, life purpose from a horse. All of this wisdom arrived in its own perfect timing through co-presence, agency, and curiosity. Such Earthly medicine is everywhere. I was wildly inspired by these stories, reminders that my whole life could change in a flash.

On a recent visit to Utah to flee the smoke from Colorado wildfires, I received a lesson in how possible and fragile this is. The red slickrock cliffs stretched up above me, shooting out of the Colorado River winding through Castle Valley. The river was glassy, lazy, primeval forest green. Soft, somehow, even though I knew they'd carved this desert clear out. Water had made this place. The rocks, tall, regal giants, were millions of years old. I could feel the weight of those years come and gone, down, down, down, all the way to the river and below it, their polished bodies descended through geologic time.

I studied the shadowy face of the stone. If I softened my gaze, I could feel their shapes start to warp. Beings, not stones. Creatures, not rock. Suddenly, I felt bombarded with images that I knew were old. I couldn't make them out, but I had the interior sense it was a story about a people who loved this land. I got scared and diverted my awareness. The images, floating just above the rocks, disappeared. But the feeling has never left me.

"How are we to ward off the immorality of ignorance and greed, the disease of indifference to the Earth?" asks N. Scott Momaday in his *Earth Keeper*.[17] "Perhaps the answer lies in the expression of the spirit, in words of a sacred nature."

When we are present with the living world, they can speak to us. New possibilities open at the sites of such unfurlings, ones I am longing to see. Next time, I want to be ready.

I have also received ecological wisdom even in the midst of my sickness. And, perhaps, because of it. I wonder, can sickness itself be a ceremony?

The ceremony of my body's confusion, complexity, and curiosity has been a crucible. I have had to unlearn all that I had known. About the illusion of separation between my mind, body, and heart and how to bring them into coherence, about the delusion of difference between me and the Earth, and how to return to coherence. The theater of ceremony suspended time and categorical frameworks so that I could see, dream, breathe anew. A hypnagogic death and rebirth. This conceptual clearing opened trapdoors, portals, and thresholds. Sickness is certainly an "altered state," and in it, I have witnessed the oracular, metaphysical, and unspeakable arrive. I have been able to think from within a tree, or a river, or a lark. And it's changed what I understand about animacy, intelligence, and individuality. I'm more animal because of it.

Or maybe, I've finally started to see with more sobriety what the sickness of systems really does, what cunning destruction they wield. I suppose I am grateful for the lift out of my preconditioned thinking so I could see from the perspective of the trees, the animals, and the plants. Even if it came with great pain.

The infinite spectral color story, the sunlight and moon shadow, the Aspen forest, and the pulsing change of seasons architect the ceremony unfolding all around us. The grand ritual of life is always in process and forever in motion. May we never lose touch with it.

May ceremonies be some other kind of sun for our thirsty Earth. May they join the light already shining out of the compost pile, the ruin, the dead trees. May they amplify the life long past and yet to be lived. May these rituals help us see sideways, diagonally—a looping, swooping, revolving orbit—the light refracting off corners to illuminate truths that are hard to bear but must be faced. Ceremonies might be a way to tilt away from climate collapse, to plunge toward eco-species justice. They are not the answer; nothing is in singularity. But they might help.

I see ceremony everywhere I look. Rainbow trout meandered effortlessly, immersed in jeweled waters. The shades of emerald, seafoam, jade, and shamrock green swirled into glassy reflections, warping the green lining the shore. And then there was the trout, oblivious to all that.

They were iridescent—silvery blues, pale yellows, metallic speckled blacks. Could they see the beauty of the home they lived in? Could they feel the radiance of their own miraculous skin? Winding like wind, the light changed their mirrored forms as smoothly as the shape their body made in the water as they swam. Arc. Circle. Storm.

What can a rainbow trout say about magic? Or the otherwise? The rhythmic seasonal ripples unfurled in the water around their body feel like a call for freedom's pheromone, a palette of sonic, visual, and imaginal sense tales. This was certainly psychedelic. I felt the rainbow trout's effervescent movements as timeless. Everything rises, and everything dies.

I don't know what magic is, not exactly, but I do know this: When the rain comes in the middle of summer's heat, the Earth drinks it with gratitude. When we widen our hearts, we can feel the praise of the dry soil, the delight of hungry flowers, and the gratitude of thirsty trees. I imagine a purple orchid opening their body to the rain, to my grandmother's eyes, to me. These movements make up our liveliness. We are stitched into intimacies. Magic is witnessing the life that is here.

The entangled soulful life is not something we can find on our own. We do so with our kin. The timeless Olive tree, the infinite creativity of the fungi, the rainbow trout. They are always beckoning to us: *Come closer.*

We share. We participate. We are held together by simple gestures of love. Is this not ceremony?

I can still hear the echo of the Aspen elder and their generous divination so long after. *There is enough for everything that lives.* Let us follow the way of the trees. For what if that were true?

Body Practice: Trusting the Body

For this practice, you are invited to root into the simple magic of your own body. In the spectrum of body awareness, trusting the body is the result of the more subtle earlier steps of listening, noticing, and sensing. When we can trust what our body is communicating, we have at our fingertips so many more opportunities to listen to and connect with the aliveness of everything else. When we listen to our bodies, we build trust. As we extend trust to our bodies, they invariably want to open more. Dissociation does not feel good. Not really. We are robbed of presence, and if we are not present, we can't experience the living world.

To begin, find a quiet, comfortable place for this practice, whether that's sitting, standing, or lying down. Bring your awareness to your sense of the body. What is present right now? There is no need to shift or change anything; just notice what's here.

Next, bring your attention to a decision you need to make. There are many ways we make decisions about important things in our lives. Are you the type to listen to your body for insight to gauge if a choice is right for you, if it's in alignment and feels good? How do you do that? Whether or not this is something you're adept at, let's practice this method with something simple.

Pick a decision or choice that you need to make today. It can be very small, like what to have for dinner or whether to do a certain activity or spend time with someone.

Now, bring the various choices into your awareness and, at the same time, tune in to your body's sensations. Is there a clue as to which decision would bring the most alignment, ease, and coherence based on the signals your body is giving? If you don't notice anything or if you're feeling frustrated, don't worry. This is a skill to practice, and it builds over time.

Now, as an easy experiment, bring to mind an activity that you know you enjoy doing. Take note of what sensations occur in your body at the thought of it. Perhaps you feel a lightness within you, tingles throughout your body, or something else. This could be a clue to which sensations your body already associates with pleasure and good things. These sensations are always particular to each person, and no two people are the same.

Once you've completed this practice, take this same awareness of alignment and inner coherency into your relationship with the living world. As you open to your own body, you can begin to open to the world around you.

Tree Practice: Ceremony Walk

A ceremony walk is a ritual that allows you to slow down and receive the medicine you need, like a tryst with the Earth. The origin of this practice is a modern form of a rite of passage found in many cultures around the world. You can think of this as a ceremony. The purpose of this practice is to ask questions that are alive in your heart and then to open and receive wisdom from the more-than-human world. By so doing, you will become more intimate with both yourself and the Earth.

Set aside about an hour to complete this practice.[18] If walking is not available to you, you may be able to use a mobility device, or feel free to follow the prompts but do so indoors lying down, or you can imagine a walk instead. There are three parts to this practice: intention setting, wandering, and listening. Feel free to engage with each part for as long as you'd like.

Intention Setting

Create an intention for your walk. What would you like to bring into this practice and receive an answer for? Here are some helpful prompts for consideration:

- What question are you holding in your heart?
- What important commitment or transition would you like to mark?
- What do you desire to let go of or be thankful for?
- What do you need wisdom or guidance for in your life right now?

If you do not feel clear about an intention, you can set an intention to be open to what comes during your walk.

Wandering

Please complete this practice without the aid of music or a podcast. Be fully present.

Find a place that you can have some access to the sky, Earth, plants, and other beings. Bring along an offering. I like to bring something I have found outside before I begin.

As you arrive in the area where you will do your ceremony walk, find a natural threshold where you can start. This could be the beginning of a path or a particular grouping of trees.

Pause here. Take a moment to acknowledge the unceded land you are on. Honor the creatures and critters who live there, the elements, the cardinal directions, the moon, whatever feels right. Thank the land for being here for you.

Review your intention and share your question out loud to the Earth.

Once spoken, offer a gesture to your body to honor that intention, and then mindfully release it. You do not need to hold on to it from here on out. Trust that the Earth has heard it and you can let go.

Ask the land for permission to enter. Listen for a reply of welcome and give your offering if you have one. Take a moment to breathe in the reality that your body is an extension of the Earth. Notice if any gratitude grows as you do.

When you are ready to start, cross the threshold, and your ceremonial walk will begin. Pass over this threshold as if you are moving into a magical and liminal space between worlds.

Take your walk, moving slowly and mindfully. Really allow yourself to be drawn by what interests you. Pay attention to what is around you, periodically pausing to listen to the birds, the ocean, or whatever is there. Let yourself be attracted, drawn in, turned on. Linger where you intuitively want to and pause when it feels right. This walk is less about traversing distance than being mindful of each step, sensation, color, and smell that arises before you. As you allow the wandering to unfold, take a beginner's mind approach and witness what opens in you, between you and the Earth, and around your original question.

Listening

Once you have walked until you feel "complete," pause somewhere specific to be with that particular spot and listen. Let yourself be moved by what draws or interests you. Perhaps you will be inspired to lie down and listen to the leaves, or maybe you'll want to sit on a rock, study the bark on a tree, or hold a tender flower in your palms.

What can you feel, learn, hear, and be nourished by in these interactions with various elements in the more-than-human world? Keep yourself open to what attracts you. Perhaps you want to explore a conversation with a living being. What is it like to have a dialogue with a rock or a tree? Perhaps this is felt, and no words are used. Perhaps you use the language of trees.

Close

Once you have a sense of an "answer" to your question or intention, even subtly, you have reached the end of your ceremonial walk. Lightly bring awareness to how your intention was answered, however mysteriously, and allow that gratitude to permeate until you can sense it.

Before you depart, thank the land for the gifts you have received and the time you were given to learn from your Earth kin.

Take some time to write down what occurred in your walk, if that feels right. If you received what might be considered ecological wisdom, consider how to integrate that. Who might you want to share this experience with? How might this wisdom influence your life?

Growing Deeper

1. What do decisions feel like in your body?
2. Do you trust your body? How do you know?
3. Have you ever had a transmission or wisdom come through plants, trees, or the Earth?
4. The question or intention I had for my ceremony walk was _____.
5. What did you sense, experience, and learn through your ceremonial walk?
6. How can you deeply sense the animacy of the living world? What tells you the Earth is alive?
7. What is your experience of deep time? How might that notion change your sense of the animacy of the living world?
8. What is a ceremony you would like to practice with the Earth?

12

Intersectional Wild Weave of Justice

Love and justice are not two.
Without inner change, there can be no outer change.
Without outer change, no change matters.
—Rev. angel Kyodo williams

I'd hoped the Roaring Fork Valley was protected from ecological destruction. Here is a bastion of environmental awareness where myriad organizations and decades-long efforts have fiercely protected wild places. But that day, the river ran orange. And I was reminded—there is no place on Earth safe from human carelessness.

Sediment from Grizzly Reservoir was released from the dam upriver, which spilled into the Roaring Fork. Hovering over the water on the Rio Grande Trail, I stood stunned. Below me, the crystal-clear waters were now an opaque milky rust. An oxidized chestnut scar tore through the valley.

I knew the spillage would harm everything it touched. The orange color meant the water was now packed with high loads of copper, aluminum, iron, and other minerals. This would cause acute and chronic toxicity to the fish, smother their habitats, and harm the aquatic plants, reducing the availability of food for other organisms. And then there's the wildlife—the countless lives of the moose, deer, and the 240-plus bird species who call this river home. They would likely experience organ damage if they drank the decay. How unjust for a reliably safe wild river to become deadly on a whim. I looked anxiously from tree to plant to water, scanning the brush for those who might be approaching. But there was no way to warn them.

My heart squeezed as I took it in. This hurt. These once pellucid waters, where light had plunged unhindered to illumine every stone—a clear river of high alpine pure snow melt—now ran turbid with ferrous silt. I saw not the minerals obstructing the water's clarity, but human hands and actions. I saw a river choked by people.

Is nowhere safe from human ruin? The question haunts me. Another wildfire erupts. And another. More smoke settles on tree leaves and deep inside human lungs. What have we done? Can we ever make it right?

The Earth is not a passive victim. They are endlessly creative in their capacity to resist and adapt to rising global temperatures, and deeper than that, they still reach for us. Even though we are the perpetrators of their pain.

I can sense them asking us to join them in weaving a flourishing world for all beings. I can hear the Earth beckoning us to create a more loving, *just* world, for all of life. A true ceremony. One where those who've been oppressed, marginalized, and endured violence are included. One where the whole Earth benefits.

I am attracted to Engaged Buddhism because it's a philosophy and set of practices with a clear focus on intersectional environmental justice, not just individual enlightenment. It's rooted in a commitment to expand in compassion for *all that is alive*. From the qualities of equanimity and inner radiance. From the river to the tree.

In this path of reciprocal compassion with the living world, repair, renewal, revival, and restoration are possible. What a joyful invitation. Perhaps the greatest honor of our lives.

The very first step in the eightfold path of Buddhism is *right seeing*. We must see reality as it is. The Earth is suffering. We are suffering, too. We must see how various threads of injustice tie together and then set upon the lifelong task of untangling them. For example, we can't ethically pursue kinship with the Earth without also facing Indigenous erasure. Without working toward their inclusion, self-determination, and sovereignty. The promise of this work is true liberation—ecological healing that includes all beings and communities. I am not free unless the whole Earth is.

Right action and *right effort* follow suit. We can love profoundly. We can navigate ourselves out of the turbid current. We can nurture co-creation, re-creation. Here. Now. We can stand clear and tall in the truth of our hearts.

What is the wild weave of justice for the river? What is their ancient, primordial form? Boundless animal life, an unimpeded course, equitable clean drinking water for all, agency, and self-determination from snowmelt to sea. When we start to see it, the intersections are everywhere. Layer upon layer we travel. Tributaries braid themselves into the flow. The ceremony has begun.

A moth flew straight into the window, bouncing off the three-layered stretched acrylic, and fell onto my lap. I gasped. I was in a plane, and we'd just landed in Chicago. What were they doing here? The moth must've flown inside on the tarmac in Colorado just before takeoff. Now, they were trapped, a thousand miles from home. They flopped on my legs, trying to catch air that wasn't there. I wanted to weep. This creature would not survive, stolen from its Rocky Mountain home.

Maybe it was a Rocky Mountain clearwing moth. Their wings are transparent windows, bordered by the shade of rust. When I looked through their rapid wing beats, I thought about how inextricable land and justice really are in the so-called United States. For this is all stolen land. The critters, creatures, and people were taken from their homes and forced to survive so far away from the places they knew by heart.

Here begins the story of the climate crisis. For it's a long-tailed result of a few trying to exploit what actually belongs to all. The environmental impacts of that time put the process in motion. Often people ask, wide-eyed at the latest extreme weather event: *Why? Why now?* There is an origin.

The arrival of European settlers and colonization brought disease, war, and slavery to Turtle Island,[1] which killed around 56 million people, or 90 percent of the Indigenous population. Generations of land-based trauma was enacted from the violence. This incalculable loss also caused immense climate change impacts.

In a recent study,[2] it was shown that the ramifications of the Great Dying, the decimation of Indigenous peoples by European settlers, were so significant that they even altered the Earth's temperatures.[3] It's as if the whole planet grieved. When the agricultural land belonging to the now disappeared Indigenous peoples fell into disarray, carbon was trapped in the ground, initiating what historians call the Little Ice Age. It got much colder than usual. The mass genocide of Indigenous peoples was so catastrophic, it literally transfigured the weather.

Another climate impact is the link between mass deforestation during that time and increased carbon emissions that continue today. When European settlers arrived, it is estimated there were around 1 billion acres of forested land. Today, the US Forest

Service estimates that about 766 million acres remain, meaning that 25 percent of forested land was lost to the extensive logging, agriculture, and urban development of that time.[4] The University of Michigan found that 90 percent of indigenous forests (those native to a given area) have been removed since 1600.[5] That's nearly all of them. Colonization was a rampant, unmitigated plunder of people and trees. What would these old-growth forests have looked like today? What stories would they tell? What wildfires would have been prevented if these lands were tended to by their original stewards? What have we lost? Will we ever really know?

Telling the truth about this time is an important part of healing the past and protecting the future. For the first time, a seven-year study published in *Science* found that Indigenous land loss from colonization was near total, at 98.9 percent of their historical land base.[6] The study also revealed that tribes' present-day lands are on average more exposed to climate change risks and hazards, including more extreme heat and less precipitation. Nearly half of the tribes are at risk of increased wildfires. They did not cause this, and yet they will suffer more because of it. There is no separating Indigenous rights, climate change, and the future of our planet.

Today, the Indigenous peoples of the world protect the planet's biodiversity and yet experience the most environmental racism, environmental toxicity, disproportionate effects of climate change, and arrests for their land-protection efforts. When Indigenous peoples do have land rights, deforestation drops by two to three times less, biodiversity increases, and carbon emissions drop.[7] It's quite clear they should be at the helm. Yet they still face many systemic obstacles to their rightful self-determination.

I am thinking about how the trees are an invisible carnage of colonization. How the forests were victims too. And what that's done to speed up global warming. For example, the decimation of trees during those five hundred years of colonization caused an immense loss in carbon sequestration capacity of about 250 billion metric tons of CO_2.[8] This extra carbon has gone straight into heating the planet.

Forests, soil, oceans, and microalgae are some of our most important carbon capture natural systems. But even that is changing. An alarming new study by the US Department of Agriculture found that forests are rapidly losing their ability to store carbon at all. We can't plant more trees at the pace needed to counteract this trend. The report says that after 2025, it will plummet, and that by 2070, forests will start emitting carbon.[9] Trees' very way of being is falling apart. There is no other way to say it: Theft, greed, and domination did this. The trees, and the people, suffer.

At the current pace of carbon emissions, trees may transform from climate change solvers to a driver of the imbalance itself. Our trees are weeping. I want to pound my fists and scream.

Let's pause here. The very lungs of our Earth, essential for a livable planet, are breaking. By the time this is obvious, it will be more than too late.

But today, right now, there is still time to come alongside them and take right action. *We have never needed the trees more. We have never been so far from treating them as kin.*

I know digesting these things is heavy, hard, and horrible. We have much unlearning to do to make colonial ways of living unthinkable. I know that complex forms of uncertainty, exhaustion, and stress can surface as we open to these historical ills. And perhaps, to our role in them or to our suffering underneath them.

But through our bodies, speaking the language of sensation, in communion with the Earth, we can face the truth. From there, right action will come. The Earth is here to hold us through the precarity.

I knelt in the Colorado River and held up a handful of water to practice how to see. The wildfire smoke from the Lee fire, the fifth largest in Colorado's history at the time of this writing, burned nearby.

The smoke was so thick, I had left the Roaring Fork Valley to find clean air. Because I have a vulnerable body, the acute effects of the particulate matter were immediate and obvious. I wished the valley I loved was spared from climate change, but, of course, I knew it couldn't be. Nowhere is.

I couldn't breathe because I was breathing dead trees. That's what made me sick. I choked on their dying kin, their beloved home, their forest, their grief. This was not a metaphor. It's called particulate matter with a diameter of 2.5 micrometers or less. But I knew what it was. I carried the dying trees in my lungs now. I felt so much fear.

But in the water cupped in my hands, looking very, very close, there was crystalline clarity. Not even a lick of sediment. The waters had wound their way through hundreds of miles of smoke to find me. The sight made my whole body breathe.

I cannot outrun climate change. I want to. I don't want to be in the center of it. But I have no choice. I cry. I hug a Cottonwood tree. I grip their knobby old skin and hang on tight. I watch a dragonfly, wings of clear tears, shimmy and skim the river's smooth belly. I summon the courage to trust the circle is moving, is motion, is tumbling onward. Somewhere, I know that's true.

We can learn something from the river, as we stand at their edge, looking in. They are not one form, shape, or container, but rather, infinite gestures. Branching veins. Roots on the surface.

The Colorado River has over twenty-five tributaries. The river basin started forming over 7 million years ago. Numberless trees depend on them. Over 40 million people do, too. Yet they've been mutilated by over fifteen dams and no longer have enough flow to complete their ancestral journey to the sea. The Colorado is a river in captivity.

This river teaches me the cost of being tamed. I am thinking of the Vishnu Schist, the oldest rocks in the Grand Canyon, cut by the Colorado. They are 1.742 billion years old. This water cradles the tectonic history of the land. And we have the hubris to attempt to contain them? The river will win. What if we let the sometimes still, sometimes raging waters carry us to someplace else? What if we forget the well-worn grooves of exploitation and, like the endless creativity of this water, take a leap? What if we could be wild again? Behold the bear and their will. Look how the eagle carves an arc in the bright blue sky. The Earth is active in their self-protective sovereignty. They can show us what we cannot see.

The blooming moon slips above the rock's face. The river spills with their light, cascading down the canyon. Silvery curls amid endless, deepest blackness.

Come, Earthly wisdom. Come, great mystery. Trouble, disrupt, and reconfigure our assumptions about the living world so we may be in service of collective justice.[10] Roam and haunt new spaces in us, fortifying our commitment to the web of life, to make eco-species justice reachable. Terry Tempest Williams writes in her book *Red* about the desert:

Hand on stone—patience.
Hand on water—music.
Hand raised to the wind—Is this the birthplace of inspiration?[11]

For love of all the poisoned rivers, oceans, and streams. For love of all the biodiversity under threat. For love of all the beings, human and beyond human, who must figure it out together. The forests we will never get back. The people who will never live on their original land. The fires yet to begin.

Earth relationship *could be* an act of justice. Earth kinship *could be* good fruit for the world. Earth belovedness *could be* a deep resting place for all. May it be so.

I am thinking about the White River National Forest in Colorado, where my Aspen family lives. How this land was originally tended to by the Ute people. They called themselves the Nuche, which means a people of heart. Every year, as winter ended, they would perform their Bear Dance to announce the coming of spring. When they were forcibly displaced throughout the 1800s, their knowledge of plants and animals, reflected in their specific vocabulary, was lost as elders passed.[12] Reparations, including returning land back, have not happened. They still perform the Bear Dance, even though they've been ripped from their land. From this very valley.[13] It's painful to face this.

I want to ask my Aspen family: What do you remember about the people of great heart? What was it like to lose your kin? If history lives in our bodies, as Resmaa Menakem the somatic abolitionist suggests, then the trees carry this memory. How can I honor what they've loved and lost?

"There's a way out of this mess," suggests Resmaa Menakem in his book *My Grandmother's Hands*, "and it requires each of us to begin with our own body. You and your body are parts of the solution."[14] What does that mean? Like the polluted rivers, these wounds run deep.

How can we clean out the wreckage of the past and how it unconsciously warps and wrecks our right seeing today? For if we are the Earth, what harms them harms us. And what frees the Earth is medicine for us, too. Just as healing a poisoned river is good for all who depend on it.

There is much to absorb. The vision of Frantz Fanon is illuminating to this quest, the Black Martinican clinician and philosopher whose revolutionary writing was central to postcolonial studies in the 1950s. He first pointed out that the colonial wound is embodied. Looking at the wound as a body helps me see it in the Earth. Coal mine. Oil pipeline. Polluted air. Enormous dam. These are the wounds of industrial, imperial empire. But someone, some*body* cut those gashes in the Earth, tore into the flesh of that mountain, ripped open the sky.

How can we heal? According to Leanne Betasamosake Simpson, a Michi Saagiig Nishnaabeg scholar, writer, and activist, we begin by refusing the norms and values of white supremacy, anti-Blackness, and settler colonialism. Such systems have taken root in us. And we can shed them.

Oh, running river.

Oh, clear stream.

Unearth these wounds within our bodies, communities, and ecologies.

When the sun hits at twilight, the river is a ribbon of ecstatic mirrors. A winding wall of gleaming brightness. When I look at them it's as if my face is next to a shooting star. Just like that. I have to hope that the exploding folding light can carry us. Robert Macfarlane writes in his astonishing book *Is a River Alive?*, "Rivers are easily wounded, but given a chance they heal themselves with remarkable speed. Their life pours back."[15]

May it be the same with the whole living world.

We can move closer to protecting the Earth, to embodying the wild weave of justice. But as Audre Lorde implores in one of her most famous essays, "the master's tools will never dismantle the master's house."[16]

So, we need to rip out the roots. Repot. Replant. Melt and compost. For those of us quite heavily conditioned to think in linear lines and value growth at all costs, this will take some work. But it's worthy and worth it. If we can do so, our entangled bonds might find each other, mycorrhizal wisdom of immense strength, vibrating with the potential to catalyze a radical shift toward collective care and compassion.

If we look honestly and bravely within, what kind of relationship do we have with the Earth? What values and assumptions drive that bond? Is it good for the Earth? How do we know? Is it dewy and damp? Does it smell of soil? Or does it stink of human greed?

"Theory can be a dew that rises from the earth and collects in the rain cloud and returns to earth over and over," writes the feminist poet Adrienne Rich. "But if it doesn't smell of the Earth, it isn't good for the earth."[17] So let us hold up our bonds with the Earth to piercing clarity as transparent as the dragonfly's wing. Is it good for the living world? Are we?

How do we move closer to right relationship? Queer and feminist science studies suggest starting with power and privilege. From there, invariably, we will see how a right relationship with the Earth is coterminous with racial and environmental justice, Indigenous sovereignty, disability rights, gender and class justice, and LGBTQIA+ rights. Many have been ringing this bell for years, differentiating this message from environmental movements and efforts that exclude these intersections. By trying to make environmentalism palatable, in many respects, it's not gone nearly far enough.

We can envision skillful actions that do not cause more harm, through a wholesome heart. We can give birth to deep change. We can tend to the riverbank, the fish, the air. We can recognize that the Earth is endless layers, whirling and spinning into a whole. We can be fierce and soft at once. The wild weave of justice is just that.

As I reflect on my own power and privilege, I see my ancestry has a thread woven throughout it: searching for belonging to a place, and a knowing that the wisdom of the Earth is baked into our blood and bones. I sense I have long been in a conversation with the more-than-human world—through my dreams and imagination, and now, in the flesh of my material body.

As a descendant of settler colonialists, this is a form of privilege—*Earth-relationship privilege*. In many ways, I am free to attach to the Earth without the burden of violent histories. I do not carry land dispossession trauma. In fact, I have the opposite. An internalized entitlement to place. I know this can cloud my heart.

What do I do with this uneven, unearned privilege? Since it's the impulse and tendency of my settler ancestors to own, possess, and dominate, I don't want to repeat that. Thinking deeply about right seeing and right action for the entire web of life helps keep this in check. Being honest about my own impulses and letting myself be humbled and taught by a value system in nature that is antithetical to my inherited norms is a lifelong endeavor. I fall short. But I will keep asking: Is my Earth kinship good for the collective? How do I know?

We can tend to the colonial embodied wound. We can see to the bottom of the river and beyond it.

I implore you, dear reader, to not give up on this quest. Equity and liberty is not too big a dream.[18]

What do we know? How do we know it? What questions are the most fertile, messy, Earthy? This is a deep inquiry for me having been trained as a scientist. Historically, those who control the "knowledge" control the resources. But there are other ways of knowing. Who is asking the questions? Who does it benefit? If we can grow a fissure in what seems like the impenetrable fortress of Western certainty, perhaps more equitable kinds of knowledge could gain value.

As a poignant example, Indigenous knowledge about land management was dismissed as "unscientific" for centuries. Yet Western approaches have led to rampant forest fires and ecosystem collapse. In a stunning turn of events, some states are finally recognizing Indigenous cultural burn practices with recent legislation aiming to support tribal fire stewardship. In California, the Prescribed Fire: Civil Liability and Cultural Burns Bill (SB 310) passed in 2024. The result is that burnable fuel load is reduced to prevent out-of-control mega wildfires, ecosystem health improves, and Indigenous communities can reclaim what is a cherished, sacred practice. This is intersectional climate justice in action. This is how knowledge can be healing for the Earth.

The world is burning, and we must try everything differently. Our north star is multispecies eco-justice. It will take all of us in our prophetic imagining to reach toward such a horizon.

Part of that will certainly include Indigenous sovereignty. Decolonization is an empty virtue signal, points out Indigenous scholar Linda Tuhiwai Smith, unless it practically protects and preserves Indigenous lives and land.[19] For example, returning land to Indigenous communities requires sacrifice and fleshy actions that can rebalance what has been stolen. These efforts, being led by organizations like Tenure Facility, Life Comes from It, and NDN Collective, are examples of Indigenous alternatives to the settler-colonial state. Indigenous people are at the epicenter of protecting the planet we all share. Supporting this work is part of how we can heal the colonial embodied wound.

I am imagining how healing that gaping scar that tears through this land is connected to the river. Rivers are always finding new tributaries, circling, cleaning the sediment, forging downstream beauty that is a gift to the whole entire Earth. They do so with ease and grace, matched only by their power and eternal age, undiscernible in their origin. Maybe healing is like that. A living, spilling prayer.

Our fate is bound together. And what good news this is. We are not alone. "As we work to heal the earth, the earth heals us," writes Joanna Macy.[20] Let us listen to the Earth so that we may participate in their healing and justice, too.

What have they survived? Where are they hurting? How can we participate in the repair of wounded lands, waters, and animals? How can we pay such close attention that we are responsive to their needs?

In my PhD research, one participant endeavored to do just this. Ekua Adisa is a gender expansive liberationist medicine person who has been facilitating personal and collective healing for over fifteen years.[21] They make medicines with plants under the guidance of their ancestors to support others to release grief. Ekua's apprenticeship with plants to help people heal is inspiring, but what deeply struck me was how they do the same with wounded lands.

Ekua finds specific sites in the American South that have experienced the pain of witnessing violence against Black people and creates ceremonial containers to excise these wounds. They sense when the land is wounded. They know when it's time to heal. Through the nurturing attention of people and plants, Ekua guides a ceremony so the land can experience renewal.

They invite people to gather, listen to the land, and participate in repair. Ekua says that afterward, the land opens and they can sense in their body that something has shifted, and something else has lifted. The intention and care at the center of such a ritual is profoundly reciprocal and liberationist. This is a striking example of how human bodies and the Earth body are implicated in one another's pain and in one another's freedom.

What would change if we moved through the Earth looking and listening for ways to show care? What if we were oriented to the Earth's needs instead of our own? What if we could be the Earth's medicine, as they are surely ours?

As this book has explored, healing is not fixing, ending, or solving an individual embodied ill. Healing is an emergent collective process that opens more space for pleasure, joy, and connection. This means that "healing" happens in step with our participation in relationship with all of life. Healing through this lens is decolonial in that it centers the Earth's needs and the Earth's wellness, too. This, to me, is justice. This, to me, is the world that is waiting for us to join them. Ekua has certainly been weaving the strands of justice together. Thread by tender thread. And what is dawning is stunning to behold.

I am thinking about how Ekua did not say they were confident these ceremonies would upend or rectify hundreds of years of oppression. But that did not dim their devotion. Holding no cherished outcomes, even from the results of our actions, is not apathy. Rather, such equanimity is a wellspring to continue loving simply because it is right to do so.

When I get very still and listen to my heart, I know this is the kind of life I want to live. Even if I cannot save all I want to save. Even if I fail.

Our greatest teacher in intersectional environmental justice is, of course, the Earth. We don't have to look any further than the living world to see what equality, power sharing, and mutual care look like. The infinite ecosystems of the planet are inherently equanimous. In fact, the Earth is already decolonized, meaning that they do not conquer, conquest, wield power, or steal land and bodies like humans do.

In fact, biological life engages in interactions that could be interpreted as sharing power or conceding territory for mutual benefit. For example: mycorrhizal fungi and plants, Acacia trees and ants, barnacles on whales, and beavers and wetland ecosystems. These relationships fall under the categories of mutualism, commensalism, and facilitation. Each of these exchanges illustrates how species share resources and engage in behaviors for mutual benefit. For example, a beaver furiously builds their lodge. But it's not just for them. Their generous engineering is so essential for the health of wetland ecosystems that they are a keystone species. Nature reciprocates.

May we become more like a barnacle and a whale, a beaver and an Acacia tree. May we seek to give power away instead of wield it. May we lose interest in ownership and possession. May we become the ancestors we need. There are beautiful examples of this.

One of the most enduring and inspiring illustrations of being a good ancestor to me, a lighthouse of climate justice, is the women-led Chipko movement in India during the 1970s. Rural women formed a nonviolent and peaceful response to protect their trees from deforestation. At the time, there was an upsurge in commercial logging in the Garhwal Himalayan region of

Uttarakhand. These women knew their livelihoods and futures were inseparable from the forests.

The folk songs of that period said:

> *These beautiful oaks and rhododendrons,*
> *They give us cool water.*
> *Don't cut these trees,*
> *We have to keep them alive.*[22]

The women formed human chains around old-growth trees. *Chipko* means to hug, and hug those trees they did. They knew in their bodies that the trees were part of them, that their mutual well-being was interlinked with ecological protection. Diversity, harmony, and the self-sustaining nature of the forest were so valuable to these women that they sacrificed and risked themselves to show the world what they were really worth.

I adore the black-and-white photos of the women from that time. In these images, with their backs pressed to their beloved trees, they face outward, their hands gently resting on the bark while they stare straight ahead. I see white-hot flames. Tree hugging was never sentimentality; it was radical political and ecological protest. In their love lives real power.

In 1981, the Indian government recognized that the women were right. Logging was banned above one thousand kilometers in the Garhwal Himalaya. I can only imagine their euphoria. Their love had won. Their legacy of tree hugging continues today.

How can we participate practically in intersectional climate justice like the Chipko movement? What right action can we take? Here are a few ideas. But there is no end to the creativity of right loving. Hold ceremonies for wounded lands; become attuned to relevant bioregional food, water, and animal justice issues; advocate for equitable access to greenspace; become educated about how climate and other strains of injustice intersect; support projects and organizations that are mindful of these intersections; engage in rituals that honor the wounds of colonialism and move toward repair; support regenerative farming practices and reforestation; and uplift and champion Indigenous-led organizations, coalitions, and movements.[23] And, of course, return, again and again, to the reciprocal, embodied kinship we have with the living world. This is the soil and seawater of our shared heartwood.

Thimbleberries grow in late August in the Rocky Mountains. There is seldom a sweeter delight. Thimbleberry is like a peach-berry jam. I foraged them on every walk, a delicious gift found between the Aspen trees. They are called thimbleberry because you should wear them like jewels on your fingertips. I put them on my ring fingers and played the imaginal piano with its deep red, jammy hues.

Let us appreciate the Earth with everything in our bodies. Let us taste what the wild gives us. Let us continue to reckon with our human power and open ourselves to revision and restraint. Let us ask beautiful questions to uncover the organic intelligence that is good for nature. Let us unsubscribe from a relationship with nature that is just individualism in another form. Let us water the garden until the whole Earth thrives again in mutualism, communal care, and symbiosis. This is the way of the trees. This can be our way too.

How we tend to our ecological attachments, how we lovingly heal the colonial embodied wound, will tell us what kind of world and future we will share. We are each responsible for our piece in the web of life. Let us take such good care.

Shapes rose up from the Maroon Creek river valley. Slow moving but steady. Opaque mists bloomed from the chemical contact of the morning sun hitting the dewy grass. Ghosts. The apparitions—proof of rain after such a long dry spell—soaked me in hope.

Near the soil, the coiled newborn leaves were starting to gently open, without fear of falling. Barely beginning, they were already a shade of bioluminescent green. How do we bear to open our hearts like this? But like the leaf, we must catch our breath in the sun's yawn, and try.

I want to stretch my body to imagine that the river could be wild again, and free. I want to widen my heart to envision that, despite what the land has suffered, healing is possible. I want to expand my spirit to dream beyond what history tells us we will repeat.

Old-growth forest.

Colorado River.

Setting sun.

I see a loving Earth tended to by loving people. Can it be?

A few weeks after that day of pollution, the Roaring Fork River, where the water ran orange, eventually cleared itself out completely of all the rot. The waters tumbled on. They didn't stop. They washed and washed and washed, until they were good again for all who needed them. I think of myself, holding a handful of river water to remember how to see.

The Earth knows repair.

Can we join them?

Body Practice: Honoring Our Ancestors

This practice is a set of writing prompts to help you consider how your ancestry lives within your body. This may bring up all kinds of emotions, so please be gentle with yourself, and if needed, resource yourself with the rhythmic tapping from chapter 7. You can always start and return when you have capacity.

- What is your ancestral history? What lands and waters are you from? If you do not know your ancestral history and cannot ask anyone in your family to find out more, complete this exercise within the limitations of your knowledge.
- Where does colonialism live in your ancestral history? Regardless of whether your ancestors were settlers or those affected by settler colonialism, this history has affected all of us.
- What values or norms informed by colonialism are still alive in you today (e.g., ownership, individualism, power)?
- What emotions come up as you consider the impact colonialism has had on you? What are three sources of resilience and support that you can resource as you continue this exploration?
- What is your ancestral connection to land and place? Are there threads of this you want to either shed or carry forward?
- If the colonialism wound is embodied, what is one way you can tend to this fissure in yourself?

Once you've taken time to answer these questions, spend time with the Earth to process what you've uncovered. Take note of any shifts that occur within you in so doing.

Tree Practice: What Does the Tree Need?

In this practice, you are invited to listen to a tree's story and history. Spend twenty minutes with your tree, ask them the following questions, and listen deeply for answers in your body:

- What have you survived that you would like me to understand?
- What wounds do you carry that you would like me to see?
- How has climate change affected you?
- What have you witnessed here?
- Who are the original stewards of the land you live on, and what was your relationship with them like?
- What do you need to heal the embodied colonial wound?

By practicing listening to the trees, you are decentering your own experience and deepening into an eco-centric way of living and participating. This is a way to open yourself to intersectional justice, understanding that Indigenous rights is connected to land is connected to climate change is connected to your own relationship to place. Once you have felt that you've learned about the tree's wounds and experiences, take note of what it feels like to be a witness to the tree. How does this awareness open your body and heart? How does this deepen your intimacy with your true kin?

Growing Deeper

1. How do you knowingly or unknowingly embody, experience, or understand the colonial wound?
2. What is your identity and positionality? How has that shaped your connection to the Earth? What do you notice as you attend to these intersecting domains?

3. Have you been severed from land? Or your ancestors? How do you know this wound exists?
4. How does intersectional justice challenge or complicate your connection to the Earth?
5. What is your relationship between ecological care and buying animal products? Can you be mindful of humane animal practices and buy accordingly?
6. What did you hear when you listened to the tree's wounds?
7. How might you begin to, or continue to, decolonize yourself?
8. What Indigenous-led organizations would you like to learn about and support?

13

Queer Ecology and Making Vows

If we surrendered to the earth's intelligence we could rise up rooted like trees.

—Rainer Maria Rilke

Pyramid Peak reached for the sun at the end of the valley like a luminous temple. Aspen trees rose beside me in rapt attention. But I was not ascending. Lately, I felt like I had so many paradoxical desires inside my body, all vying for their own stage, song, and spotlight. Some of these conflicting selves were difficult to reconcile. Some of these parts had given me much grief. I offered the fragments to the mountain: *What do I do with this?*

I looked up into the chimeric sky. It tumbled over itself, the light scattering this way and that. And then, all of a sudden, the clouds parted ever so slightly. Two lips readied for their kiss, revealing a perfectly faint little rainbow. A breath of polychromatic color.

Does nature not embody every variation? Are there not colors yet to be discovered? Is the infinite creative expression of the

Earth not the remarkable proof that difference is an essential cornerstone to life? Nature is paradox. Nature is strange. We are all myriad.

You do not have to reconcile it all, I felt the Earth say. *We don't.*

I am bending the light both inside my being and on the surface of a drop of water. I am refracting myself again and again into component colors. I am the dispersion of light. I am a spectrum. I am a multicolored circular arc. Beyond the beyond. Shades without name, without form, without end.

There is no barrier between humans and nature. There is fluidity, not fixed categories, interstitial spaces where humans and more-than-human kin can meet, overlap, and communicate. Dissolving the binaries, dichotomies, and separations, wherever we find them, with our creative, loving relationships, is such an essential pathway to freedom. Feminist and anthropologist Donna Haraway[1] calls the refusal to snap into binaries a way to *stay with the trouble*. She continues, "We need to understand how our entanglements with the natural world are inherently queer, marked by fluidity and multiplicity."[2]

The ever-changing, dynamic nature of the human and more-than-human experience invites us to question dominant narratives and make room for life-affirming ones to germinate. To be queer, ecologically speaking, is to affirm and confirm the weird, wonderful, and possible, and to never, ever look to constrain biological life into any fiction of "normalcy." Normal, life never was.

What if we could experience difference as the essential, beautiful necessity it is to foster such a diverse universe? What if diversity was indeed a biological essential for life to exist at all? And what if the Earth's fluidity could help us both become more free?

Softening the separations—between our minds and bodies, bodies and the living world, and the living world and the culture of our world—is one of the greatest and most essential works we can take up in our pursuit of loving entanglement, in our commitment to equitable and just futures. Eroding the edges, through river-washing rigid categories, is a radical act. Together, throughout these pages, we have sought to learn to listen to the language of trees, embrace tree time, and enter their kinship. Now, let us *queer* it, meaning let us unseal even more possibilities, fling open more windows, welcome even more radiant colors into our bodies, breath, and bones.

Queer ecological theory, coined by environmental humanities scholar Catriona Sandilands, affirms difference, celebrates it, and provides a model beyond the dominant and oppressive cultural norms. Queer ecology acknowledges how biological life defies boundaries already. In nature, difference is multiplied as a stratagem to proliferate life, not reduce it.

As Sophie Strand writes in *The Flowering Wand*, "The opposite of our current predicament—climate collapse, social unrest, extinction, mass migrations, solastalgia, genocide—is, in fact, the disintegration of opposites altogether." Queerness is not just about being different for the sake of it, nor is it only about sexual orientation; it's a solid touchstone that celebrates how queerness promotes life. Strand continues: "Everything is both. And more."[3]

In the fall, the Aspen leaves dazzle. The gold, crimson, orange, and red become palettes of such remarkable color, of such exquisite clarity, that the Roaring Fork Valley is suddenly a cauldron of alchemy. Greens are gone, and the liquidity of autumn soaks the land with a sublime regality. I've always wondered why some leaves turn gold and others red, how and what the logic behind such flamboyance might be. I discovered that the shorter days bring a reduction in sunlight, which drains the chlorophyll from the leaves that gives them their green color. As the verdant greenness dissolves, the myriad colors waiting patiently within are revealed without. Every leaf already contains every bit of color. The rainbow emerges from the deep as the season lets go. Nature is *more*.

The infinite colors held within every single leaf remind me of the term *diffraction* as used by physicist Karen Barad: a method of thinking that helps us understand how difference might enhance our entangled relations. Simple refractions, or reflections, just show us what we can already see. Which, in most cases, is division. Instead of the surface of things, go deeper. Look for what is under, sideways, behind, beyond. Look outside of the status quo. We might see complex patterns surface. We might see relationship. We might visualize the living world. Paradox. Multiple. Matrix. What do we see? How might that change how we love ourselves? How we love the Earth?

Let us look into the spectral prismatic light bouncing off the surface of the pond. Let us peer into the mycorrhizal underground universe. Let us look into cracks and crevices. The glowing orbs of the eyes of the red fox, the tumult of a thrashing sea. The surface is but one version of what we call reality. There is more.

Queer ecology is a gorgeous way to compost categories. According to queer ecological theory, we do not seek to find the mirror reflection of the established way, to perpetuate the norms that have caused incalculable harms to anyone and anything considered "abnormal." This includes race, sexual orientation, ability, gender identity, neurotype, and more. In contrast, queerness, indeed, is integral to nature. About 90 percent of flowering plants produce bisexual flowers, with both male and female reproductive organs. Many species of fish are sequential hermaphrodites, meaning they begin as one sex but switch to the other later in life. Biologist Patricia Kaishian points out how fungi, who are beings that exist beyond the categories of plant or animal, have been largely left out of conservation efforts. They do not conform to taxonomic boxes.

I am uninterested in whatever dead, vapid, blank categories our capitalist and colonial culture has deemed normal. Instead, give me aberration, outlier, rarity, oddity, weird, and variant. For those beings who take up the in-between, who haunt the marginal and transitional, are sacred seers; they can straddle worlds. Here, you have our world's oracles, visionaries, sages, and clairvoyants. Wisdom, life-transforming insight, is not ever found in the center of social and cultural consciousness, but at the edges. Heartwood embodies such strangeness. The center of the tree is made up of dead cells. How can life be held together by death? And yet, nature does not resist dying. Nature fights for life, always, but also embodies mystery, absolute. Queerness is an affirmation of the holiness of the fringe.

But it's because of these margins that queer and transgender people are the most vulnerable. They are targeted because they are different, a historically and culturally entrenched phenomenon. For example, the number of reported violent deaths of transgender people, particularly transgender women of color, has been alarmingly high in recent years, according to the Human Rights Campaign. LGBTQIA+ people are also a significant target for hate crimes, discrimination, harassment, and violence.

Gender nonconforming, transgender, and LGBTQIA+ people are feared for being different, enough to be killed. But as Alok Vaid-Menon, poet, activist, and advocate for transgender and nonbinary rights, admonishes, it is their very embodiment of difference that confronts those who cannot accept the "difference" in themselves. Alok says, "We have been taught to fear the very things that have the potential to set us free."[4] What do we fear in ourselves? What do we fear in nature? Could this be the exact seed for our mutual liberation? May we embrace the full diversity of ourselves, *all of our selves*. For we all contain every possible color, anyway, just like the leaves.

Through this lens, we can puncture wounds in the veil of imperialism and colonialism. We can cast light into what's been discarded and refuse to be pawns of the nightmare of domination. When I think of queerness, of diffraction, I am set free to embrace the infinite possibilities of polymorphous relations. I can submit to the mentorship of the rose teacher, I can envision the Aspens' and the Cottonwoods' shared roots, I can surrender to the bear's eyes in the woods, and I can receive the sorrow of the moth trapped in the plane so far from home. I am also river, tree, mountain. So how can I reject myself when my body is everywhere?

I am willing to be changed by what is different from me, and I am willing to embrace the many differences in myself. As a person living with various levels of ability, my body feels inherently queered. My chronic health journey has, in many ways, been an unending invitation to embrace the strange. My brain does not behave. My symptoms warp my senses. Sometimes I am the echo of some other place. Chronic migraine headaches create abnormalities in every cell. I've had to make a choice.

Do I set my energy toward rejecting what I deem aberrant in myself? What does not reflect "normalcy"? Or do I slough off my normal snakeskin and let myself grow new eyes, scales, teeth? Can I accept this queer body? Can it not be a portal to perspectives, experiences, senses that, yes, are different but, maybe, can teach me how to truly see? I think so. In the end, I either choose to love my glitchy body or not. I choose love. Or maybe it's choosing me.

Love not as a saccharine sentimentality, but as radical acceptance. Love as an erotic ecological phenomenon. The postcolonial theorist Chela Sandoval built such a theory of love. Inspired by the manifestos for freedom prevalent in the works of Donna Haraway, Michel Foucault, Jacques Derrida, Frantz Fanon, Gloria Anzaldúa, Audre Lorde, Roland Barthes, and others, she argues—love is a revolutionary political force that can enact social change in the world.[5] How might our Earthly loving become sites of social change where just futures can be remade? How can we co-constitute each other?

If love is so emancipatory—which it must be, which it can be—then affective bonds of love between humans and the Earth could be technologies for such liberation. If I can learn to accept myself, I can embrace the difference in another—plant, animal, and human alike. A love technology, then, manifested through queered experiences with the Earth, could alter our collective trajectory. Queered kinship. Deep intimacy inherent in our eco-erotic connections could carve new cracks into our collective imaginings and embodied pursuits. A queered love technology might just be a shrewd tool of resistance to the structures and systems that are hell-bent on destroying life. Could love topple empire? I ask this as an ecological possibility, not fantasy.

When I consider the foolishness of climate collapse and the grief that marks our travel through these times, perhaps a queer ecological love technology contains the power necessary to topple dominant structures and plant the seeds of a wonderful life for a more wonderful world. Joy, pleasure, ecstasy. Maybe it's folly to bet it all on love, but what other choice do we have?

There is a secret forest in Los Angeles, and it's right by my house. A grove of Cedar trees forms a womb on a hill. I say *womb* because it's a heavenly cave both within the city and yet completely removed from it. Even after living in the neighborhood for an entire year, I'd never spotted it. But after a friend showed it to me, and once inside its atmosphere, I felt I'd been invited to an otherworld. Cool air, blue-toned conifers, and a bed of squishy needles underfoot. This was an arboreal oasis inside a city of cars, smog, and sunshine. It became a daily ritual to visit the cave, to sit inside its stone-cold walls and find something in the quiet that needed seeing.

I was sitting on my usual chosen rock in the center of the Cedar grove, thinking about *vows*. The Buddhist environmental scholar and activist Joanna Macy had made her own vows as a prayerful set of intentions to live in a compassionate commitment to the Earth. These simple devotional rites felt alive, rooted to the living world in a manner necessary for growth for both of them. I was inspired.

I closed my eyes to meditate. I started to sense something in the soil. My mind was in the Earth, then, and I could "hear" the trees whispering to each other down there, entangled in mycorrhizal mischief. I wanted to make my own vows, something to mark what the trees had taught me, how the Earth had become medicine for me, something to bind me in sacred commitment to their care. I waited.

Wisdom unveiled itself—from the ground of me—which is to say, from inside the body of the Earth. From those that give us breath, I heard this: *Help others to hear the language of the Earth, so that they might have a relationship with us, and therefore care for us in return.*

The invitation emerged simultaneously with my request for it, collapsing into a single moment, so there's no way to know where it came from. The energy of the turning reverberated in my body and began to move in a counterclockwise direction around me in a spiral. Within that swirl, what Joanna Macy calls the Council of All Beings appeared—my Aspen family, the dead mother Redwood tree, the Colorado River, the beautiful big bear. Everyone was there. They formed a circle around me, holding my gaze.

In such an interstitial and interspecies gathering, I felt the weight of it. To make a promise with this community as my witness would bind me to honor it. I immediately felt my body contract with inferiority.

I'm not good enough, I reasoned.

The Council of All Beings responded with the words of poet Mary Oliver's "Wild Geese." The sounds echoed through my inner chambers.

This animal loves the animate Earth, I thought in response.

And that love is good.

The extraordinary reciprocity in the Council of All Beings around me was a gentle tug to keep giving the gift in motion. To not thwart the self-perpetuating cycle of reciprocity that is at the heart of the more-than-human world.

I could see in that moment how my illness was a snakeskin. It had forced me to slither on my belly on the ground, and that's how I'd come to rest at the heart of the trees. I'd never have been so receptive to the Earth without this reptilian underworld descent. I do not wish pain on anyone, but I have come to see that mine had, and continues to have, its purpose.

I will shed my snakeskin again and again. This cycle is its own offering. The skin decomposes, a nutrient-rich gift to the forest. And each new one is more vibrant than the last, a gleaming, patterned set of scales. But whether I am an old one tied in a knot, dull and crumpled, or fresh and shiny, embracing my own cycle of giving and receiving, is the exact doorway for my understanding of the reciprocity of the Earth. The healing I seek—and the relationships I am in with my beyond-human kin—is on a continuous loop. There is no beginning, and there is no end. I'm part of one long homecoming into sacred relationship with the living world.

The Council of All Beings was still waiting. The wind whistled through the Cedar boughs, weepy over my head. Would I accept the invitation? I felt into my snakeskin, my scaly, smooth spirit, and I could sense something very sound and deep in the seat of me. *It was all yes.*

So, I made my vow:

> *I vow to hear the language of the Earth,*
> *I vow to create a relationship with the Earth,*
> *I vow to care for the Earth.*
> *I vow to help others hear the language of the Earth,*
> *I vow to help others build a relationship with the Earth,*
> *I vow to help others care for the Earth in return.*

Time is an ascending spiral, and we have no idea where we really are on it. So, when I made that vow, it seemingly initiated something brand new that's never happened before, while consummating something very ancient all at once. I felt the energy of loving present awareness swing this way and that. When truth, love, and beauty unite, something dies and something else is born.

The only vows that make sense to take are the ones that grow in all directions like fungi, beyond the center and the edges of our embodied, animal ecologies. As we slow down, listen to the Earth, speak in the language of sensation, and foster our secure attachment to the natural world, the promises that are ours and ours alone to make will come to light. The Earth is always speaking, endlessly asking for our companionship in their odyssey to love the world and the whole of it.

It's a matter of ethics to identify the commitments we are willing to make in response to the love we've been given. Vows are a onetime decision made in ceremony in the witness of community and are also lived out in a million small and large ways every day. Reciprocity and participation must be enacted. And this is exactly the kind of wide ecological consciousness we are invited to be a part of. The Council of All Beings that gathered in the Cedar grove that day wove no ordinary ritual. That was a marriage ceremony. The promise I made on that hill gently guides my life today, and always will. For it was the day I married the Earth.

Cedar trees are unusual in Los Angeles. Someone intentionally planted them there. Even the experts on the city's botanical history say that the mini grove in Griffith Park is something of a mystery. Native conifers are generally found high up in the mountains, above five thousand feet. Yet, despite that fact, here the grove stands at nearly sea level. It's magic, how our beyond-human kin can confound us with their resilience. It's wonderful that someone, or maybe someones, had the gall to plant them there.

We do not know all that will become of our little acts of defiance to capitalism, our gestures to try something queer and weird just because we want to. I like to imagine that these Cedars were planted in the middle of the night, so no one would ever know why or how they got there. I like to dream that they are the fruit of someone else's vow. I like to "reverie" that someone else's creative heart for trees would one day become the venue for my own wedding to the Earth.[6] We just don't know all the ways we touch each other. Time. It's funny. And yet, when I consider all that happened to make that moment possible, the only words I can utter are *thank you*.

Body Practice: In Devotion to the Body

Sometimes the pain of not being able to decipher how to meet my body's needs has felt unlivable. When in pain, all I want to do is respond correctly. But I've learned over time that being present to conflicting and contrasting sensations widens my capacity to metabolize difference. Nonverbal, nonrational, noncognitive dialogue can be a resting place. The urge to cognitively rationalize pain is so understandable. But the body is where we are feeling the sensations, and so the mind can join the body in being present to what is already unfolding. All are welcome.

What is your relationship like with your body right now? How could you begin to accept and honor more of the differences you contain? These "abnormalities" could be sensations, or they might be identities, parts, aspects of yourself that have been challenging to reconcile.

In this practice, take some time to write a love letter, a letter of lament, a poem, a haiku, or an unedited stream of consciousness to acknowledge the shape and contours of your relationship with your body. And to honor the differences you contain. This relationship is, after all, the core bond of our lives. Just like it is good practice to take inventory of our relationships with beloved ones, so, too, it is with our bodies. This letter and self-inquiry is a devotional practice, meaning that it's meant to foster a sense of continuous respect, awe, and reverence toward your body. This is a foundation for holding difference.

Here are a few questions you can ask yourself to support your exploration:

- What is my body holding right now that I could pay more attention to?
- What conflict or friction is asking for my care?
- How does my body respond to these paradoxes?
- When I feel into these places, what is the sensational instinctual response in my body? (Tightness, fear, avoidance, sadness, rumination, etc.)
- How do I spend time with my body? What does that look like?
- Is there intimacy? Am I experiencing play and freedom?
- Does this relationship feel expansive or constricting?
- Do I feel a sense of devotion to my body? What would devotion to my body look like?

Devotion often gets sidelined because of how religion has contorted and polluted it for radical agendas. But at its heart, all it means is that you care—a whole lot. Devotion is a sacred commitment to keep showing up to the mostly invisible work of love. Devotion pulls you to the tree's side daily to listen to their wisdom. Devotion sits you on your meditation cushion to attempt relaxing back into loving awareness once again, despite your "monkey mind." Devotion draws hot water for tea to offer your neighbor, even when you're tired. Devotion is the art of loving.

When you have finished reflecting on what your devotion looks like to your body, turn your attention to your devotion to the Earth. Are you devoted? How do you know? After a few moments, let the inquiry go. Perhaps this is a question you would like to return to from time to time.

Tree Practice: Taking a Vow

For this practice, you are invited to consider what you might desire to offer the tree as a symbol of commitment, flowing out of your sense of devotion and love. A vow is really just a symbol. A ritual act to place one's body, heart, and soul toward a vision. A promise to continue that loving.

Spend some time with your tree and listen in your body for what vows you might want to make to the Earth. What commitments would you like to honor as we come close to the end of our journey together? Perhaps look up Joanna Macy's vows, reread mine from this chapter, and then take twenty minutes in silence with your tree and see what might arise in that interstitial, fringe space.

When you have received a sense of what your vows are, consider how you want to mark the moment. Perhaps you'd like to speak them out loud? Write them down? Share them with the tree? Allow your body and intuition to lead you.

When you have shared them in whatever way feels right, trust the mysterious unfolding that occurs when we make public what is in our inner sanctuary.

Growing Deeper

1. How can I extend more compassion and kindness to my body?

2. If queerness is about freedom, what in my body could use more space to feel more free?
3. What does queer ecology evoke in me?
4. What inspires me about the notion of creating a set of vows to honor my relationship with the Earth?
5. What vows do I want to make to the Earth?
6. How and where can I commit to them?
7. If you have shared your vows with the Earth, what did that feel like? How might this set of commitments inform your life?

Conclusion

Death Doula to a Dying World

> *I am not washed and beautiful, in control of a shining world in which everything fits, but instead am wondering awed about on a splintered wreck I've come to care for, whose gnawed trees breathe a delicate air, whose bloodied and scarred creatures are my dearest companions, and whose beauty bats and shines not in its imperfections but overwhelmingly in spite of them.*
> —Annie Dillard

I didn't want to stop. But the little limp body was in the middle of the road. I couldn't leave them like that. I turned around on my bike and circled back. I crouched down low next to the creature. A squirrel. They had been hit by a car. The impulse rose, and I grabbed two sticks and lifted the little one up with some struggle. Maintaining a wobbly balance, I moved them to the grass on the side of the road. *There, now, that's better.* I picked a few flowers and laid them on the body. I said a prayer. I said goodbye.

The very next week, I was on another walk, and another little body appeared in my path. Also a squirrel, but this time, they'd been hit and killed by a bike. Once again, I felt the softness of the body as I gently prodded them. Once again, I found myself balancing the creature on a stick-turned-carrier. I laid this one in a gaggle of daisies. I made a crown out of the yellow flowers and laid it on their body. I said a prayer. I said goodbye.

Both experiences lingered in me. The urge to not let death be lonely. The simple mindful act of moving the body. The ritual of adorning them with something beautiful. The blessing of saying goodbye. These ceremonies took but a few minutes each. I wanted to be a good friend to death by tending to the death of a being from another species. This desire linked me to an ancient intuition about living. We are caretakers of each other's transitions. And we are invited to take such good care.

I've started to expect more little bodies on my meanders. And I've wondered if their spirits could sense what happened between us. Something in us knows; death needs to be witnessed. Companioning the animals' deaths gifted me with the embodied knowing that we are all connected. Even in death. My human hands, their creaturely bodies. My aliveness, their sweet, sad forms. No one saw me do these things. But I did.

What happened in their final moments? Were they scared? Did they see it coming? These two squirrels got me thinking about the broader death march we are on as a planet. Is the Earth scared? Does the Earth see what's coming?

The sixth mass extinction event is already well underway. How do we accompany the Earth in the loss that's happened, in the loss that's happening? What does the Earth need from us? How can we be with a dying planet?

* * *

Our Buddhist eco-chaplaincy cohort had gathered for a biodiversity vigil. With the solemnity of mountains, we gazed at slide after slide of twenty-three now extinct species, pausing with each one. The ivory-billed woodpecker, the Kauaʻi nukupuʻu, the Maui ʻakepa, the flat pigtoe mussel, the Guam bridled white-eye. As the slides slid past, the weightiness swelled. These shapes, colors, and creatures would never be seen again. My spirit slipped through the silence: The disappearance was unfathomable. A preventable global catastrophe that continues to grow in scale and speed flashed before my eyes in a PowerPoint presentation. These deaths were permanent. How can we grasp such an absolute?

Yet the whole Earth is dying. Forty percent of all land has already been converted to food production, one-third of the world's forests are gone, and the species extinction rate is estimated to be between one thousand and ten thousand times higher than natural extinction rates.[1] Since every single species is interconnected, important ecological functions that support human life are threatened, including a stable climate. It's not *if*; it's *now*.

The urgency of this emergency demands swift action. And yet, I wonder if, alongside environmental justice and intersectional, queered activism, there is another, more relational invitation. What if the Earth desires to be witnessed in their dying? What if we could come alongside them in this collapse?

"What is required for us to be with what's occurring?" asked Tayla Shanaye in an interview for my PhD research. "To really say, Yes, this is it. This isn't a place for me to fix. This isn't a planet I need to heal. I need to heal." The urge to save the Earth, while understandable, can also function as a mask of hope rooted in colonial fantasies of progress, warns Bayo Akomolafe.[2] Colonialism was predicated on the notion that there is a better world out there to build and create, no matter the damage in its wake. The environmental movement can often fall into similar philosophical traps: selling hope for the fiction of better worlds.

"But in my tradition, hope is a trickster," says Bayo. "There isn't a binary between hope and hopelessness. To hold hope well is to hold hopelessness, to embrace it, to know that things may not go our way. And that is the beauty of this poetic saga that we call reality."[3] If hope itself is a trickster, perhaps we too should embody that playful uncertainty. Can we be more like sprites than priests? Faeries and nymphs rather than dogmatic preachers? A dryad instead of an evangelist?

Do foster and gently fan the deep yearning and ache for life and love for every living being. Do dream of liberation in community. Do act rightly in justice for all. Do link your body with the trees in this imagining. And do know that this mode of loving is a different kind of ritual from the anxiety-driven rumination, fear, and panic about the state of the world that ripples through the news. The Earth can help us discern the difference. We can ask them directly: How can we be with climate collapse, our desire to take action, and our relationships with our beyond-human kin all at the same time? How can we become such lithe acrobats?

To begin, feel into the grief of climate collapse. Opening our inner forest to this sharp ache is a potent component of our overall trajectory toward connection, and to realizing that, oh yes, reality is not strung on a binary between love and madness. *We are that love in motion.* We can be good medicine for the Earth. Such impossible dearness is a lasting source of resilience. Fear, as its counterpart, is not an enduring fuel for action. Our bodies need consistent regulation to maintain high-load action. Our bodies also need to rest, to lie down in the garden, to be kissed by our kin. This intimate wonder is the salve and the soil. What might grow from such abundant loving?

An enduring courage might alight from the forested places to "hold hopelessness" in the unknown places. A sky of glowing fireflies in midair. Hope not in saving the world, but being so deeply present with the world we are in. To really, deeply, be here, eyes and heart wide open. Belly soft, pressed to the trees. Because this is the impossibly delicate paradox before us.

We are not alone. Our Earth ancestors are here to guide us through the impossible. How to keep loving and living, despite it all. The five-hundred-year-old Oak tree, the long-living river—these beings know more than we do about how to survive, evolve, and reach ever more toward life. The sigh of the trunks hugging each other in the forest, the moaning crack of a Cottonwood adjusting to different temperatures, the ecstasy of the Aspen's leaves spinning like mad as the wind revolves through their branches. Let us sit at their sides and listen, learn, and attend deeply to the health of the influx and outflow of all our relations. Let us wrap our care and witness around their pain.

We are on a razor-thin horizon as a breathing Earth. Death is already here. The question is, *Will we be good companions?*

Poet and author Jacqueline Suskin meditates on these themes in her poem "To Watch the Earth Die":

> *I know that*
> *although I don't want to watch you die,*
> *I am.*
> *I circle around you as you wither*
> *and push light into your skin, saying*
> *while weeping, I wish it weren't so.*
> *Death cannot be wished away.*
> *In this final act, your form trembles*
> *and I won't close my eyes.*[4]

There is a radically compassionate way to mindfully attend to the times we are in. To pair the twin threads of action and contemplation. And it draws on the role of a doula. A doula is a midwife, someone with the capacity, compassion, and care to be a companion to a birthing person. A doula is a loving witness to the miracle of life. Likewise, in death, death doulas (chaplains or caregivers) play a similarly supportive, connective, and calming role. They help people bridge to the other side with as much ease as possible. Doulas, whether at the start or at the end of life, are sacred guardians.

The question I am asking is, *Can we be death doulas to our dying world?*

By being so close to death, we may midwife new life. What wisdom does the Earth have for us in their dying? In order that life can live?

The author Arundhati Roy wrote a beautiful essay about the catalytic opportunity of tragedy, a message that is also fitting for climate change.

> It is a portal, a gateway between one world and the next. We can choose to walk through it, dragging the carcasses of our prejudice and hatred, our avarice, our data banks and dead ideas, our dead rivers and smoky skies behind us. Or we can walk through lightly, with little luggage, ready to imagine another world. And ready to fight for it.[5]

Are we ready? Let us hold the Earth's hand and heart as life crosses these thresholds. Let us be open to the wisdom that arises in the thin places. Unforeseen possibility comes out of the caves, river crossings, and compost heaps. The mess of climate collapse, the disaster of death, might just be the alchemical materials needed for a new arising. Birth follows death. Always. So what is trying to be born?

Perhaps part of the birth pangs is an emerging, wider ecological consciousness that reflects the diversity of life? Perhaps death can teach us to walk into the portal together and midwife this Earth-honoring way of being? Perhaps we can practice diffracted, entangled ways of seeing, living, and communing? Perhaps we are not only to witness the Earth's dying, but to make ourselves available to the interstitial space where wisdom might come through? Perhaps we are bridges, arteries, sensuous passages? I see us tending the garden of collapse—weeding, planting, watering with inexhaustible nurture—the exact conditions for improvisation and surprise. A loving world is possible.

Can we be death doulas to our dying world? Can we harbor hope and hopelessness together? Can we not shrink from pain, but tenderly hold it? Can we press our hearts close to the cave of the unknown? Can we speak the language of trees, become fluent in embodied sensation, and be ecstatically and erotically embedded in the living world? I know this is a big ask, to move closer to death, but we are ready for it.

Beetle kill was here. It's a sweeping and deadly phenomenon. Invasive beetles bore into trees, creating tunnels that cut off their water flow. Drought makes them vulnerable to these infestations. And they've wreaked havoc in Colorado. Blue stain fungi then further clog the trees' water-conducting tissues. And the trees die. We can't escape death, as much as we want to.

I stared at the mountainside to discover to my horror that one-third of the trees, at least, were already dead. Their green needles had been bleached. Muddy brown, opaque trees peppered the mountainside. Death and life coexisted here. Was the forest mourning? Could they heal?

The dead trees gave my heart a shock. But the way I knew the forest was caressing their roots under the soil, sending good care, electrified my heart, too. Can I widen my heart for death and life to also dwell in harmony? Can I refuse to divide these processes and, instead, see it as the continuous, generous loop that it is? It's untenable to comprehend beauty and terror in the same breath.

But this is the invitation the Earth offers, at every moment. This is our task as we live through unprecedented changes to our planet. Nothing is rejected. Nothing is wasted. Even in death, bodies decompose to become nutrients for new life. The cycle is astounding in its complexity and completeness. As I witnessed the collapse of the forest, I reached for the courage to trust the ancient code of life. Trees feed and heal each other. They can do the same for us. Time and space change. Trees die. Mystery begins. Miracle.

We are all up against the myriad deleterious effects of rising temperatures, environmental toxins, political division, and human selfishness. Like the endangered California condor or the red wolf, my little life is also at the mercy of systemic forces so much larger than me. We well know how persistent capitalism, imperialism, and colonialism are. Love, as the counterpart, might be no match for their voracious appetites.

But this book's premise, and my belief, is this: Every single step toward relationship with the Earth grounded in dignity, reciprocity, and love is a tree in the forest of renewal we grow together. We may not nurture the entire forest. But we can certainly tend our roots within the whole of it. We are linked together—we are entangled in love—we are the forest we are growing.

Throughout these pages, you have been invited into a sacred, embodied, erotic relationship with trees, and a queered, justice-centered kinship with the entire living world. All of the creative and necessary actions, like rewilding, planting a garden, volunteering, protesting, voting, participating in nature restoration, reducing your carbon emissions, supporting Indigenous sovereignty, and advocating for businesses and governments to do the same, must be rooted in the relationship you have with the more-than-human world. Keep going. Grow deeper.

Your heart, your right relating with the Earth, your embodied presence with the intimacy of the sensuous world, matters. The forest gets to experience the joy of matter loving matter. You are heart-to-heartwood. And like the tree and its dead interior, you too can wrap your life around what's dying and see what springs from this confabulation. Crescendo of desire. Enjoyment. Neither destination nor origin. An animate circumnavigation of the birth and death process. A worshipful flutter. A death doula to a dying world.

Fall makes death beautiful. On the first of October in the Roaring Fork Valley, the lush soft of summer is fully gone, and what's left behind is the brittle bounty of leaves—dry as bones—crunching underneath my feet. A part of me finally feels at home in death. It's as if the Earth acknowledges, through this seasonal shift, what's been here all along. And as I come closer to the dying, on display in the air, in the leaves, in the wilted flowers and bowed heads of the thistles, is relief.

I passed the little glen, the one where I usually felt so held by the trees. Now, it stood empty. Where there was once providence, now I could see clear through to the mountain below. Fall had come and swept the forest clean.

I wondered, *How does the Earth know when it's time to die? How on Earth did they know?*

Because it was indeed time. Everything had wilted and closed. There was silence. A haunting. A hollow whistle howled through the now empty forest floor. Everyone knew at once. *Now.* Now was the time to die.

I resisted the feeling. I was vulnerable. Naked. Exposed. The architecture of the forest was so empty, in a flash, I felt very alone. Could I join the Earth in their slumber? I wanted to close my wings. I, too, knew that we must prepare for winter. I, too, sensed that this was a very good time to let go.

I spun in a circle and took it all in. This way and that. Every season spilled through my veins finding their own river. I couldn't hold on to it all.

I lay down in the golden dried grass. I turned on my side and surrendered. *Let me die with you, sweet Earth. Show me how.*

Will I decompose alongside these leaves? Will I slide along the spine of the mountain's geological, eternal lifespan? Like them, perhaps I could remember—change is always changing. Life is change. Death is change. As Octavia Butler writes, *God, too, is change.*

But I am not so brave. I cling, I grip, I hold on. I fight change. But fall comes anyway. Winter comes anyway. A partial solar eclipse was about to begin. I felt the tendrils of the sun's tail trailing behind my closed eyes. I wanted to stand up quick to find its source. But I was left in the quiet dark of an Earth blocked by the moon's shadow. I was reminded that even the sun could die.

Nothing lasts. Not even care. The ephemerality of it all whipped my heart awake. And so, lying there on my side in the darkening, or was it a ripening, Earth, all I could do was hold our heartwoods close, cradle them in all my care, *and let go.*

I cannot promise that climate change won't continue to bring the most unfathomable griefs to our shores. I cannot promise that illnesses won't keep appearing in your body, warping your sense of things. But I can guarantee, with all my kinship and kindred relations, that how we meet those crises, and with what love we offer the beings harmed in the process, is a sacred salve. We are the blessing we're praying for.

And so, we face the truth of our changing planet with sobriety and clarity of heart. We don't run from death. We encircle ourselves with the resilience of the river, monarch, and bejeweled trout. We cocoon our beyond-human kin in our love. We ensoil ourselves in the roots of our shared divinity. We stand upright and hold each other tight, arm in bough in arm, and we weather the storm together.

Trees have been our faithful teachers through these pages, and I trust they will carry you now. What will emerge as you plant your heart in soil? What will sprout from the tears we shed to nurture their becoming?

In Mahayana Buddhism, there is a story about a vast cosmic net woven by the god Indra. In the story, the net stretches eternally in every direction. At each node in the net, where the threads intersect, gleams a multifaceted jewel. According to the tale, each one reflects the others in the net, ad infinitum. The part, and the whole, are intrinsically linked. And while the jewels are distinct, they have no inherently individual existence. Everything exists only in relation to everything else.

We cannot fathom the many ecosystems on this planet, or within ourselves, without experiencing that we, too, are jewels in Indra's net. We, also, exist solely in exquisite intimacy with each other. We, too, are ontologically woven together. We each hold the fractal of the entire universe within our beings, and so does every other being, too. We are not separate from the universe. The cosmos is within us.

When I am standing in a forest, I can feel the fractal. It reveals itself. The infinite pattern rolls out from my heart toward their heartwoods and spins from tree to tree. I can inhabit and fill up the tapestry, even for the briefest of moments. This gives my body such an exhale. To know my belonging. To know their belonging to me.

Can we become eco-doulas, attending to these forests, and our world, as the diffracted piece of the fractal we are? Can we nestle up daily to the side of our dying and living kin with ocean-deep care? Can we embody the truth that the flourishing or demise of the bear, the Aspen, the Roaring Fork River, is our own? That their life is our life? Our joy is theirs?

The path of an eco-doula is not one of despair, rather, in that intimate gathering place, is muditā, empathic joy. When we are living in alignment with our original design to be in relationship with the breathing world, we will invariably find that the divine abode of muditā will grow in us. As we give gifts in gratitude to the Earth, muditā will expand. When we rightfully link the teachings of plants and trees with intersectional justice, muditā will rise. When we spend time in mindful presence with our more-than-human kin, muditā will bloom.

Deep joy flows from our understory loving. Our heartwood, taproot, and old-growth bones are reaching toward the Earth just as theirs reach for us. Empathic joy is a geyser from the mineral-dense center of the planet. A link to every molecule, atom, and speck of space. A vein of certitude, a flowing river we can follow. It is a quality sprung from our kinship. Our ecstasy, our enchantment, our wellness, our wholeness, is shared. What if my pleasure feeds the forest? What if a tree's joy is what will seed my own?

The Earth has taught me everything I need to know. Today, I have traveled through the worst of my body's bardo. I am no longer stuck in the despair of the underworld. However, that does not mean I do not experience symptoms, and often. I still have migraine headaches. Some days, I'm tossed back into the well.

But my most recent lab work gave me astonishing news: My autoimmune antibody levels have dropped below the diagnostic threshold. Despite what I was told years ago, they've fallen. I could see it right there in black and white. The illness retreated. I experienced a diminuendo of pain. I did not need a test to tell me that I felt like a different woman. I know. But regardless—if the condition returns, expands, or disappears forever, the enduring gift is already here—I can speak the language of trees. I am awake to the intimacy of the forest. I would not want to return to who I was five years ago, even if I could have avoided so much anguish. There is no going back. The grief in my body led me to the trees. The trees led me to love. And love is the most powerful force in the world.

I now know a mountain can make a woman: spine, hair, teeth. That nature is constantly churning us at the altar of their crucible if we let them. This valley has made and unmade me a million times. It's where I've gone to get lost and reappear in endless loops. After a lifetime of this, I might finally become one of the trees for good. Growing, exploding in color, dying. All over, without end.

For now, I suppose this has been the story of how the trees saved my life. Because they showed me the life I am connected to. I had long sought a spell to cure me, but through the trees, we've become a reverie. The love we share is the incantation. Our companionship is the enchantment. I am no longer alone. I've come home—knit, branch by branch—into the web of life. If an Aspen grove could be a million years old, then I do not have a single origin. What a beautiful thought.

I even saw the bear again—well, heard them. From behind a nearby tree: huffs, puffs, snorts. They were blocking the only trail out of the canyon. Or so I thought. What lay to my left, down toward the river? I didn't know.

But this time, I did not run. I listened to the bear.

And down the hill and over the river and up the opposite ravine, there was another way. There is always another way. We can let the Earth decide. We can let them lead us home.

I watch the theater of change that is fall—hillsides of ombre spectacle exploding beyond compare. Each tree is a torch. A flame whose heart hides the heat. From the trough of the valley to the serpentine edge of the river, I am a student of life. One more yellowing leaf here. Slightly less water smoothing the mountainside there. Knowing the Earth this closely changes me. I, too, am turning color. I, also, am an alpine body flowing.

The breathing world's daily evolutions root me to them. They tell me where I am. *I am filled by place.* I know that now.

I approach my tree family. It is time to say goodbye. But we are in each other now. Our heartwoods have become their own forest. And so goodbye is never forever.

How could I ever thank them? What direction does gratitude go if it is born inside the heart of a tree? If it exists because of it?

I lean in, telling them what they already know. In fall, I will be there when your leaves turn and drop. In winter, I will be there when the snow wraps you in white. In spring, I will be there when your newness unspools like rivers. In summer, I will marvel when you shimmer, whirl, and spin, and flowers jump to a quarter of your height.

How much we have to look forward to. What infinite dearness rolls out before us every which way. I bow. What else can I do? I am kissed all over by trees.

Perhaps they can sense my gratitude.

The cycle goes on.

Perhaps I will spend my life singing thank you.

The cycle continues.

I am at peace with that.

Forever, and ever, without beginning, and without end.

Body Practice: Practicing Equanimity

As we close our time together, in this final body practice, I invite you to try on the sensation of becoming a death doula to a dying world. To do so is to grow the heart to hold death and life together at once. Such a capacity is medicine for the times we are in.

Begin by taking a moment to bring to mind something that hurts about climate collapse. Something not too heavy, so as not to overwhelm your body's sensorial contact with this pain. But do bring something up into your awareness. Perhaps the fact that a third of global trees are at risk of extinction, or perhaps specific environmental changes are affecting where you live.

Now, observe your inner bodily sensations that arise at the truth of this, and notice the impulse to push it away, numb it, or overidentify with it. Breathe with this pain, knowing that the Earth is holding you in that breathing.

Next, orient within your physical space by looking around to find something pleasurable. This could be as simple as the way the light hits the windowsill.

Once you do, place your full awareness on what feels good about it.

Notice that now you are holding both pleasure and pain inside you at the very same time, without diminishing either. With this, you have gone on a journey to "be with" difficulty in a conscious and full-hearted way. You are holding hope and hopelessness together.

After a few minutes, let the practice go. When it feels right, return to it, so as to continue growing your equanimity and brave heart.

Tree Practice: Closing Ceremony

For this final tree practice, I invite you to create a culminating ritual of commitment and dedication to the Earth and the trees based on the vows you made in the last chapter. This is a chance to create your own ceremony around those vows as an extension of the emerging love and care you have developed throughout this book. This does not have to be anything elaborate. This ritual is intended to honor your tree kin and support you to pause this journey in ceremony, so do what feels natural.

When you have completed your ceremony, take some time to integrate the experience. What did it feel like to culminate this experience? How does it feel to know that life is its own ongoing ceremony and that pausing and honoring different stages helps connect us to the vast expanse of life's processes?

We end our time together here with an enduring and new lifelong support system in trees and within your body, coupled with a deep wellspring of commitment to love and protect the Earth we share.

Growing Deeper

1. What was it like to practice equanimity? What did you notice?
2. How do you feel about the invitation to become a death doula to a dying world? What would that look like in your life?
3. Explore your experience around the ceremony you did with the trees. What insights did you gain from doing so?
4. How has your relationship with trees changed from the start of the book to now? How do you want to commune and relate to them moving forward?

5. How has your relationship with your body changed? How do you want to commune and relate to it moving forward?
6. If you could create something expressive to honor and close the journey in *Heartwood*, what might that be (a poem, a drawing, a dance, etc.)?

Epilogue

As winter descended, I received another lesson in death. In the early evening, an iridescent blue hue smoothly covered every surface of white. A river of black obsidian snaked through the forest. The sun slipped to nothing, and every shape, form, and curve became doused in monochromatic black and white.

Each tree yearned outward in frozen sculptures of ecstatic life; each tree coiled inward—collected, cold, and still. Vibrancy was close but separated by the thinnest layer of ice.

Winter, I thought, *is the ultimate nonduality.* The erotic reach and the erotic retreat.

I came across a slew of branches tossed haphazardly into the snow. Aspen leaves from months prior were strewn about, and Pine needles glittered alongside. To my right stood a stump. The surface was lazily lacerated. Evidence of a human cut. I approached.

About three feet up, where the snow gave way, the tree had been torn clear through the heart. I leaned over and counted the rings. Sixteen. Sixteen years of life. Sixteen years of loving. I traced the rings with my fingers along the riven stump. In one wisp of human entitlement, the tree was gone.

An aroma hit me—they pumped sap onto their open wound. Fresh resin, sweet amber, sharp turpentine, deep balsam, and vanilla undertones. The air around me swirled with the aromatic, rich, smoky scent. Was this the tree's language? Was this their dying breath?

Tears fell from my eyes next to the tree's bones. A life had been taken here. I bent down and placed my palm on their heartwood, on their open wound. How, how, can we live together in kincentricity when humans do not see the divinity and spirit of the beings all around us? How, how, can we become enchanted once again?

In time, the tree will offer itself back to the Earth. I knew the forest would not waste this life. I suppose this is what it is, in part, to be an eco-doula. To be open to pain. To pause and press our palms on a dying tree's heart.

In that moment, the sound of the river grew louder all around me. Birds began to sing. The rings of that tree widened my own body, rippling out and out beyond what I thought I could contain.

I could taste their heart on my lips. *I will light a lamp in wait for my lover*, I thought. *I will hold a vigil for this tree.* There is a power in the forest. There is a great possibility for restoration. With my hand on the tree's heart, I could feel the hum of it and the hymn of it. Even still, the song was being sung. Even yet, my body vibrated with its melody. The symphony grew louder, the evening chorus, the obsidian river, my own beating heart. A luminous hope. I gave myself completely. To the tree, to the trees, *to the trees*.

Acknowledgments

I honor the Roaring Fork Valley, the Maroon Creek, and the White River National Forest as my partners, co-conspirators, and originators of this work. I am an apprentice to the forest. To my tree kin: Aspen, Redwood, Cottonwood, Eucalyptus, and Oak, thank you. You are the co-authors of *Heartwood*.

I'd also like to thank a line of human teachers who I have had the pleasure of learning from over many years and who have shaped my heart's participation in the living world. To name a few: Robin Wall Kimmerer, Audre Lorde, Thich Nhat Hanh, Rumi, Alexis Pauline Gumbs, Bayo Akomolafe, Pema Chödron, Alok Vaid-Menon, Terry Tempest Williams, Mirabai Starr, Rev. Jacqui Lewis, Jim Finley, and my Buddhist eco-chaplaincy cohort.

This book is especially inspired by the Lady of Deep Ecology, the great Joanna Macy, who died on my birthday as I finished this book. Thank you infinitely to Father Richard Rohr, who said, "The Earth is the first sacred text," which became a seed that took many years to grow but, indeed, has become a tree now.

Thank you also to my dear friends who nurtured and supported this work along its encircling way. Special thanks to Kerry Docherty, my book sister and anam cara, and to John Newton, who made me perfumes inspired by the language of the trees. Thank you to my agents, Jan Baumer and Lauren Hall, for their unflagging and buoyant support, and to my book doula, Ruby Warrington, a bright champion whose curious and deep mind helped to shape the structure of this book. Thank you to Jacqueline Suskin for admonishing me to find new words to say the same thing. Special thanks to the Hachette family, especially to my remarkable editor, Diana Ventimiglia, for believing so deeply in this book and over so many years. Thank you to Lyric Dodson and Angela Wix for their editorial development. Thank you to my family who made me meals and gave me bouts of uninterrupted time in a perfect writing cave, from which to let this creation gestate.

Thank you to Indigenous peoples the world over, who have practiced sacred relationality with the living world for eons. This animate, relational ecosystem has been systematically suppressed or otherwise sublimated in imperial, capitalist, patriarchal societies. Yet they have guarded, nurtured, and continue to share kin-centricity with the rest of the world. Thank you for holding ancient practices alive that create harmony instead of harm. Thank you for showing us how to love the Earth. May we partner with you in your self-determination and sovereignty.

Lastly, thank you to my Aspen family. Without them, I would never have written this and certainly would not have found my way into relationship with my forest kin. My elders, friends, lovers, and family. Thank you.

The process of writing this book has been an embodied reminder that I am not alone. Not in time, and certainly not in friendship. What is here is because there are beings I am connected to and who have touched me. Thank you to this miraculous heap of life to which we all belong.

Notes

Preface

1. Richard Powers, *The Overstory* (W. W. Norton, 2018).

Introduction

1. The oldest precisely measured single organism living on Earth today remains, for now, a Great Basin Bristlecone Pine tree at about five thousand years. Pando the Quaking Aspen comprises fifty thousand trees and is estimated to be over eighty thousand years old, and the Antarctic glass sponge is estimated to be about fifteen thousand years old, but their ages are assumed from indirect measurements and educated guesswork.
2. David George Haskell, *The Songs of Trees: Stories from Nature's Great Connectors* (Viking, 2017), 82.
3. According to the International Union for Conservation of Nature. Press release, October 28, 2024.
4. C. C. F. Boonman et al., "More Than 17,000 Tree Species Are at Risk from Rapid Global Change," *Nature Communications* 15, no. 166 (2024), https://doi.org/10.1038/s41467-023-44321-9.
5. US Department of Agriculture, Forest Service, *Future of America's Forest and Rangelands: Forest Service 2020 Resources Planning Act Assessment*, General Technical Report WO-102, 2023, https://doi.org/10.2737/WO-GTR-102.
6. Joanna Macy and Chris Johnstone, *Active Hope: How to Face the Mess We're in With Unexpected Resilience and Creative Power* (New World Library, 2022).
7. Robin Wall Kimmerer, "Speaking of Nature," in *The Language of Trees*, ed. Katie Holten (Tin House, 2023), 211–221.
8. A term introduced by Robin Wall Kimmerer in *Braiding Sweetgrass*.
9. Linda Tuhiwai Smith, *Decolonizing Methodologies: Research and Indigenous Peoples*, 2nd ed. (Zed Books, 2012).

1: The Language of Trees

1. In a seminal paper, the authors conclude that spiderweb threads are an integral part of the spiders' intelligence, extending beyond their spider bodies. H. F. Japyassú and K. N. Laland, "Extended Spider Cognition," *Animal Cognition* 20, no. 3 (2017): 375–395.
2. Itzhak Khait et al., "Sounds Emitted by Plants Under Stress Are Airborne and Informative," *Cell* 186, no. 7 (2023): 1328–1336.e10, https://doi.org/10.1016/j.cell.2023.03.009.
3. R. Zweifel and F. Zeugin, "Ultrasonic Acoustic Emissions in Drought-Stressed Trees—More Than Signals from Cavitation?" *New Phytologist* 179, no. 4 (2008): 1070–1079, https://doi.org/10.1111/j.1469-8137.2008.02521.x.
4. Jaycie Fickle et al., "Ring-Specific Vulnerability to Embolism Reveals Damage in the Xylem," *New Phytologist* 246, no. 5 (2025): 2046–2058, https://doi.org/10.1111/nph.70137.
5. Suzanne Simard, *Finding the Mother Tree: Discovering the Wisdom of the Forest* (Vintage, 2022).
6. Paul Kingsnorth, *Savage Gods* (Two Dollar Radio, 2019), 25.
7. Joy Harjo, *A Map to the Next World: Poems and Tales* (W. W. Norton & Company, 2001).
8. Martine Lappé and Robbin Jeffries Hein, "You Are What Your Mother Endured: Intergenerational Epigenetics, Early Caregiving, and the Temporal Embedding of Adversity," *Medical Anthropology Quarterly* 35, no. 4 (2021): 458–475, https://doi.org/10.1111/maq.12683.
9. Sahra Gibbons et al., "Biosocial Medical Anthropology in the Time of Covid-19. New Challenges and Opportunities," Medical Anthropology at UCL, May 1, 2020, https://medanthucl.com/2020/04/29/biosocial-medical-anthropology-in-the-time-of-covid-19-new-challenges-and-opportunities.
10. Jenny Carpenter, "Shared Roots and Survival in the Quaking Aspen," BYU College of Life Sciences, October 17, 2022, https://lifesciences.byu.edu/shared-roots-and-survival-in-the-quaking-aspen.
11. Hugo D. Critchley and Sarah N. Garfinkel, "Interoception and Emotion," *Current Opinion in Psychology* 17 (April 2017): 7–14, https://doi.org/10.1016/j.copsyc.2017.04.020.
12. Lindsay Branham, "Embodied Earth Kinship: Interoceptive Awareness and Relational Attachment Personal Factors Predict Nature Connectedness in a Structural Model of Nature Connection," *Frontiers in Psychology* 15 (2024), https://doi.org/10.3389/fpsyg.2024.1400655.
13. David Abram, *The Spell of the Sensuous: Perception and Language in a More-Than-Human World* (Pantheon, 1996).
14. Gaston Bachelard, *The Poetics of Space* (Penguin Classics, 2014).

2: The Body Is a Place

1. To learn more about Tayla Shanaye and her work, visit https://www.embodytherevolution.com/about.
2. Lawrence Newman et al., "Health Care Utilization and Costs in Patients with Migraine Who Have Failed Previous Preventive Treatments," *Neurology Clinical Practice* 11, no. 3 (2021): 206–215, https://doi.org/10.1212/cpj.0000000000001076.

3. According to the National Institute for Neurological Disorders and Stroke.
4. Katharina Eikermann-Haerter et al., "White Matter Lesions in Migraine," *American Journal of Pathology* 191, no. 11 (2021): 1955–1962.
5. Wahinkpe Topa (Four Arrows) and Darcia Narvaez, *Restoring the Kinship Worldview: Indigenous Voices Introduce 28 Precepts for Rebalancing Life on Planet Earth* (North Atlantic Books, 2022).
6. H. Davis and Z. Todd, "On the Importance of a Date, or, Decolonizing the Anthropocene," *ACME: An International Journal for Critical Geographies* 16, no. 4 (2017): 761–780, https://doi.org/10.14288/acme.v16i4.1539.
7. Miles Richardson, *Reconnection: Fixing Our Broken Relationship with Nature* (Pelagic Publishing, 2023), 14–15.
8. R. A. Wiebe and D. S. Wilcove, "Global Biodiversity Loss from Outsourced Deforestation," *Nature* 639 (2025): 389–394, https://doi.org/10.1038/s41586-024-08569-5.
9. Enrique Salmón, "Kincentric Ecology: Indigenous Perceptions of the Human-Nature Relationship," *Ecological Applications* 10, no. 5 (2000): 1327–1332, https://doi.org/10.2307/2641288.
10. Gregory Cajete, *Look to the Mountain: An Ecology of Indigenous Education* (Kivaki Press, 1994), 113, as cited in Lowan, "Exploring Place from an Aboriginal Perspective: Considerations for Outdoor and Environmental Education," *The Canadian Journal of Environmental Education*, 2009, 47, 37.
11. Gregory Cajete, "Philosophy of Native Science," in *American Indian Thought*, ed. Anne Waters (Wiley, 2004), 45–57.
12. Gregory Cajete, "Philosophy of Native Science," in *American Indian Thought*, ed. Anne Waters (Wiley, 2004), 46.
13. James Hillman, *The Soul's Code: In Search of Character and Calling* (Random House, 1996).
14. Annie DIllard, *Pilgrim at Tinker Creek*. First U.S. edition (Harper's Magazine Press, 1974).

3: Easing Into Consent

1. K. Kealiikanakaoleohaililani and C. P. Giardina, "Embracing the Sacred: An Indigenous Framework for Tomorrow's Sustainability Science," *Sustainability Science* 11, no. 1 (2016): 57–67, https://doi.org/10.1007/s11625-015-0343-3.
2. Fatih Uenal et al., "The Roots of Ecological Dominance Orientation: Assessing Individual Preferences for an Anthropocentric and Hierarchically Organized World," *Journal of Environmental Psychology* 81 (March 2022): 101783, https://doi.org/10.1016/j.jenvp.2022.101783.
3. Robin Wall Kimmerer, *Braiding Sweetgrass: Indigenous Wisdom, Scientific Knowledge, and the Teachings of Plants* (Milkweed Editions, 2013), 183.
4. Henry David Thoreau, *Walden* (Houghton, Mifflin and Co., 1882).
5. Copernicus Climate Change Service, "Warmest January on Record, 12-Month Average over 1.5°C above Preindustrial." Accessed August 9, 2025, https://climate.copernicus.eu/warmest-january-record-12-month-average-over-15degc-above-preindustrial.
6. Roger S. Ulrich et al., "Stress Recovery During Exposure to Natural and Urban Environments," *Journal of Environmental Psychology* 11, no. 3 (1991): 201–230, https://doi.org/10.1016/s0272-4944(05)80184-7.

7. Will Steffen et al., "Planetary Boundaries: Guiding Human Development on a Changing Planet," *Science* 347, no. 6223 (2015), https://doi.org/10.1126/science.1259855.
8. Jason Hickel, "Quantifying National Responsibility for Climate Breakdown: An Equality-Based Attribution Approach for Carbon Dioxide Emissions in Excess of the Planetary Boundary," *Lancet Planetary Health* 4, no. 9 (2020): e399–404, https://doi.org/10.1016/s2542-5196(20)30196-0.
9. Farhana Sultana, "The Unbearable Heaviness of Climate Coloniality," *Political Geography* 99 (March 2022): 102638, https://doi.org/10.1016/j.polgeo.2022.102638.
10. A concept imagined together with and inspired by the shamanic priesthood of the Yoruba healer-trickster, whose vocation goes beyond justice and speaking truth to power to opening up other spaces of power with, and queering fond formulations and configurations of, hope.
11. Bayo Akomolafe, "A Slower Urgency," Bayo Akomolafe [website], n.d. (accessed November 25, 2024), https://www.bayoakomolafe.net/post/a-slower-urgency.
12. Lillian Whiting first noted the phrase *Land of Enchantment* in the title of her book on New Mexico in 1906. This phrase was adopted as the official nickname of the state on June 18, 1999.
13. Fyodor Dostoyevsky, *The Idiot* (Penguin Books, 2004).

4: Erotic Ecology

1. Jalāl al-Dīn Rūmī, *The Essential Rumi*. Translated by Coleman Barks (HarperCollins, 1995).
2. Michael Weiss, "Erotica: On the Prehistory of Greek Desire," *Harvard Studies in Classical Philology* 98 (January 1998): 31, https://doi.org/10.2307/311336.
3. Audre Lorde, *Uses of the Erotic: The Erotic as Power* (Crossing Press, 1978).
4. Jennifer E. Stellar et al., "Positive Affect and Markers of Inflammation: Discrete Positive Emotions Predict Lower Levels of Inflammatory Cytokines," *Emotion* 15, no. 2 (April 2015): 129–133, https://doi.org/10.1037/emo0000033.
5. Maria Monroy et al., "The Influences of Daily Experiences of Awe on Stress, Somatic Health, and Well-Being: A Longitudinal Study During COVID-19," *Scientific Reports* 13, no. 9336 (2023), https://doi.org/10.1038/s41598-023-35200-w.
6. "Immerse Yourself in a Forest for Better Health," New York State Department of Environmental Conservation, n.d. (accessed October 4, 2024), https://dec.ny.gov/nature/forests-trees/immerse-yourself-for-better-health.
7. Q. Li et al., "Effect of Phytoncide from Trees on Human Natural Killer Cell Function," *International Journal of Immunopathology and Pharmacology* 22, no. 4 (2009): 951–959, https://doi.org/10.1177/039463200902200410.
8. Q. Li, "Effect of Forest Bathing Trips on Human Immune Function," *Environmental Health and Preventive Medicine* 15, no. 1 (2010): 9–17, https://doi.org/10.1007/s12199-008-0068-3.
9. Umut C. Kucuksezer, "The Role of Natural Killer Cells in Autoimmune Diseases," *Frontiers in Immunology* 12 (February 25, 2021): 622306, https://doi.org/10.3389/fimmu.2021.622306.
10. J. Lee et al., "Effect of Forest Bathing on Physiological and Psychological Responses in Young Japanese Male Subjects," *Public Health* 125, no. 2 (2011): 93–100, https://doi.org/10.1016/j.puhe.2010.09.005.

11. Murugesan Arumugam and Sunil K. Narayan, "Rethinking of the Concepts: Migraine Is an Autoimmune Disease?" *Neurology, Psychiatry, and Brain Research* 31 (November 2018): 20–26, https://doi.org/10.1016/j.npbr.2018.11.003.
12. L. R. Squires et al., "Psychological Distress, Emotion Dysregulation, and Coping Behaviour: A Theoretical Perspective of Problematic Smartphone Use," *International Journal of Mental Health and Addiction* 19 (2021): 1284–1299, https://doi.org/10.1007/s11469-020-00224-0.
13. adrienne maree brown, *Pleasure Activism* (AK Press, 2019).
14. Audre Lorde, "The Uses of the Erotic: The Erotic as Power." In *Sister Outsider* (Crossing Press, 1984), 53–59.
15. If you are wondering about how eco-eroticism relates to eco-sexuality, look to chapter 13. Eco-sexuality is a radical form of environmentalism developed by queer scholars Annie Sprinkle and Beth Stevens, who literally married the Earth to take a stand against homophobia and xenophobia.
16. T. J. Demos, *Radical Futurisms: Ecologies of Collapse, Chronopolitics, and Justice-to-Come* (Sternberg Press, 2023).
17. John Keats, "Ode on a Grecian Urn," in *Annals of the Fine Arts for 1819, Vol. IV*, ed. James Elmes (Sherwood, Neely, and Jones, 1820).
18. Adapted from a practice in Peter A. Levine, *Waking the Tiger: Healing Trauma* (North Atlantic Books, 1997).

5: Kinship: Secure Attachment to the Earth

1. Mary D. Salter Ainsworth, "The Bowlby-Ainsworth Attachment Theory," *Behavioral and Brain Sciences* 1, no. 3 (1978): 436–438, https://doi.org/10.1017/S0140525X00075828.
2. Mark Schaller, "Is Secure Attachment the Antidote to Everything That Ails Us?" *Psychological Inquiry* 18, no. 3 (2007): 191–193 (at 191), https://doi.org/10.1080/10478400701512802.
3. R. J. Waldinger and M. S. Schulz, *The Good Life: Lessons from the World's Longest Study of Happiness* (Simon and Schuster, 2023).
4. F. Zhang and G. Labouvie-Vief, "Stability and Fluctuation in Adult Attachment Style over a 6-Year Period," *Attachment and Human Development* 6, no. 4 (2004): 419–437, https://doi.org/10.1080/1461673042000303127.
5. V. J. Felitti et al., "Relationship of Childhood Abuse and Household Dysfunction to Many of the Leading Causes of Death in Adults: The Adverse Childhood Experiences (ACE) Study," *American Journal of Preventive Medicine* 14 (1998): 245–258.
6. S. R. Dube et al., "Cumulative Childhood Stress and Autoimmune Diseases in Adults," *Psychosomatic Medicine* 71, no. 2 (2009): 243–250, https://doi.org/10.1097/PSY.0b013e3181907888.
7. To learn more, I recommend Glenn R. Schiraldi, *The Adverse Childhood Experiences Recovery Workbook: Heal the Hidden Wounds from Childhood Affecting Your Adult Mental and Physical Health* (New Harbinger Publications, 2021).
8. K. C. Koenen et al., eds., *A Lifecourse Approach to Mental Disorders* (Oxford University Press, 2013), 291–304; N. L. Sin et al., "Affective Reactivity to Daily Stressors Is Associated with Elevated Inflammation," *Health Psychology* 34 (2015): 1154–1165.

9. Laura D. Kubzansky et al., "Affective States and Health," in *Social Epidemiology*, 2nd ed., ed. Lisa F. Berkman et al. (Oxford Academic, 2014), 320–364.
10. John Bowlby, *Attachment and Loss, Volume 1: Attachment* (Basic Books, 1969); Mary D. Salter Ainsworth et al., *Patterns of Attachment: A Psychological Study of the Strange Situation* (Psychology Press, 1978); Mario Mikulincer et al., "Attachment Theory and Affect Regulation: The Dynamics, Development, and Cognitive Consequences of Attachment-Related Strategies," *Motivation and Emotion* 27, no. 2 (2003): 77–102, https://doi.org/10.1023/a:1024515519160.
11. Susanne Buecker et al., "Is Loneliness in Emerging Adults Increasing over Time? A Preregistered Cross-Temporal Meta-Analysis and Systematic Review," *Psychological Bulletin* 147, no. 8 (2021): 787–805, https://doi.org/10.1037/bul0000332.
12. Sara H. Konrath et al., "Changes in Adult Attachment Styles in American College Students Over Time," *Personality and Social Psychology Review* 18, no. 4 (2014): 326–348, https://doi.org/10.1177/1088868314530516.
13. Miles Richardson, "Modelling Nature Connectedness Within Environmental Systems: Human-Nature Relationships from 1800 to 2020 and Beyond," *Earth* 6, no. 3 (2025): 82, https://doi.org/10.3390/earth6030082.
14. James Hillman and Michael Ventura, *We've Had a Hundred Years of Psychotherapy—and the World's Getting Worse* (HarperSanFrancisco, 1992).
15. Lindsay Branham, "Embodied Earth Kinship: Interoceptive Awareness and Relational Attachment Personal Factors Predict Nature Connectedness in a Structural Model of Nature Connection," *Frontiers in Psychology* 15, no. 1400655 (2024), https://doi.org/10.3389/fpsyg.2024.1400655.
16. A. Wittbecker, "Nature as Self," *The Trumpeter* 6, no. 3 (1989): 80.
17. Daniel E. Baxter and Luc G. Pelletier, "Is Nature Relatedness a Basic Human Psychological Need? A Critical Examination of the Extant Literature," *Canadian Psychology/Psychologie Canadienne* 60, no. 1 (2019): 21–34, https://doi.org/10.1037/cap0000145.
18. Ryan Lumber et al., "Beyond Knowing Nature: Contact, Emotion, Compassion, Meaning, and Beauty Are Pathways to Nature Connection," *PLoS ONE* 12, no. 5 (2017): e0177186, https://doi.org/10.1371/journal.pone.0177186.
19. Although one phenomenological study did explore participants' experiences with the natural world and found that the Earth can be a primary attachment figure and a secure base, more research needs to be done.
20. Alfred North Whitehead, "Nature Alive." Lecture Eight in *Modes of Thought* (Macmillan, 1938), 202–232.
21. Eve Tuck et al., "Land Education: Indigenous, Post-Colonial, and Decolonizing Perspectives on Place and Environmental Education Research," *Environmental Education Research* 20, no. 1 (2014): 1–23, https://doi.org/10.1080/13504622.2013.877708.
22. N. S. Momaday, *The Man Made of Words: Essays, Stories, Passages* (St. Martin's Press, 1997).
23. Eve Tuck et al., "Land Education: Indigenous, Post-Colonial, and Decolonizing Perspectives on Place and Environmental Education Research," *Environmental Education Research* 20, no. 1 (2014): 1–23, https://doi.org/10.1080/13504622.2013.877708.

6: Heart to Heartwood: Listening to the Soul of the Earth

1. Daniel J. Siegel, *The Mindful Brain: Reflection and Attunement in the Cultivation of Well-Being* (W. W. Norton, 2007).
2. Robert D. Schweitzer et al., "The Human–Nature Experience: A Phenomenological-Psychoanalytic Perspective," *Frontiers in Psychology* 9 (June 2018), https://doi.org/10.3389/fpsyg.2018.00969.
3. Cornelia Waldmann-Selsam et al., "Radiofrequency Radiation Injures Trees Around Mobile Phone Base Stations," *Science of the Total Environment* 572 (August 2016): 554–569, https://doi.org/10.1016/j.scitotenv.2016.08.045.
4. M. Barbaresi et al., "Physiological Entrainment: A Key Mind–Body Mechanism for Cognitive, Motor and Affective Functioning, and Well-Being," *Brain Sciences* 15, no. 1 (2025): 3, https://doi.org/10.3390/brainsci15010003.
5. Marc R. Farrow and Kyle Washburn, "A Review of Field Experiments on the Effect of Forest Bathing on Anxiety and Heart Rate Variability," *Global Advances in Health and Medicine* 8 (2019): 2164956119848654.
6. For more on this pain mechanism, see Alan Gordon and Alon Ziv's *The Way Out: The Revolutionary, Scientifically Proven Approach to Heal Chronic Pain* (Random House, 2021).
7. Danielle Ferraro et al., "The Phantom Chorus: Birdsong Boosts Human Well-Being in Protected Areas," *Proceedings of the Royal Society B: Biological Sciences* 287, no. 1941 (2020): 20201811, https://doi.org/10.1098/rspb.2020.1811.
8. Anders Gyllenhaal and Beverly Gyllenhaal, *A Wing and a Prayer: The Race to Save Our Vanishing Birds* (Simon and Schuster, 2023).
9. Elizabeth Weise and Ramon Padilla, "Killer Whales Keep Ramming and Sinking Boats. Scientists Now May Know Why, Report Says," *USA Today*, May 24, 2024, https://www.usatoday.com/story/news/nation/2024/05/24/killer-whales-attacking-sinking-boats-are-bored-scientists-say/73558157007/.
10. See Hempton's *One Square Inch of Silence: One Man's Search for Natural Silence in a Noisy World* (Free Press, 2009), a book that explores his quest to find and record the last remaining natural quiet places on Earth.
11. Bayo Akomolafe, "On Doors and Cracks," Bayo Akomolafe [website], May 16, 2024, https://www.bayoakomolafe.net/post/on-doors-and-cracks.
12. James Hillman and Michael Ventura, *We've Had a Hundred Years of Psychotherapy—and the World's Getting Worse* (HarperSanFrancisco, 1992).

7: Composting Grief

1. Francis Weller, *The Wild Edge of Sorrow: Rituals of Renewal and the Sacred Work of Grief* (North Atlantic Books, 2015).
2. "The Facts of Life" from *Sorry for Your Troubles* by Pádraig Ó Tuama © 2018 by Pádraig Ó Tuama. Published by Canterbury Press. Used with permission of the poet.
3. Alice Walker is the first Black woman in the United States to win the Pulitzer Prize for fiction for *The Color Purple*.
4. According to Francis Weller from *The Wild Edge of Sorrow*, the five gates of grief are: 1) Everything we love we will lose; 2) The places that have not known love; 3) The sorrows of the world; 4) What we expected and did not receive; 5) Ancestral grief.

5. "Earth Just Had Its Warmest July on Record," National Oceanic and Atmospheric Administration, August 12, 2024, https://www.noaa.gov/news/earth-just-had-its-warmest-july-on-record.
6. Copernicus Climate Change Service, "Warmest January on Record, 12-Month Average over 1.5°C above Preindustrial." Accessed August 9, 2025, https://climate.copernicus.eu/warmest-january-record-12-month-average-over-15degc-above-preindustrial.
7. David I. Armstrong McKay et al., "Exceeding 1.5°C Global Warming Could Trigger Multiple Climate Tipping Points," *Science* 377, no. 6611 (2022). DOI:10.1126/science.abn7950.
8. Intergovernmental Panel on Climate Change (IPCC), "Global Warming of 1.5°C: Headline Statements from the Summary for Policymakers," 2019, https://www.ipcc.ch/site/assets/uploads/sites/2/2019/06/SR15_Headline-statements.pdf.
9. National Centers for Environmental Information, "Billion-Dollar Weather and Climate Disasters," NOAA. Accessed August 9, 2025, https://www.ncei.noaa.gov/access/billions/state-summary/US.
10. As seen on the NOAA website, "In alignment with evolving priorities, statutory mandates, and staffing changes, NOAA's National Centers for Environmental Information (NCEI) will no longer be updating the Billion-Dollar Weather and Climate Disasters product. Additional details and the opportunity to submit comments are available at the NESDIS Notice of Changes website. All past reports, spanning 1980–2024, and their underlying data remain authoritative, archived, and available via the Billion-Dollar Disasters dataset landing page." Accessed August 9, 2025.
11. Jason Hickel, "Quantifying National Responsibility for Climate Breakdown: An Equality-Based Attribution Approach for Carbon Dioxide Emissions in Excess of the Planetary Boundary," *Lancet Planetary Health* 4, no. 9 (2020): e399–404, https://doi.org/10.1016/s2542-5196(20)30196-0.
12. Caroline Hickman et al., "Climate Anxiety in Children and Young People and Their Beliefs About Government Responses to Climate Change: A Global Survey," *Lancet Planetary Health* 5, no. 12 (2021): e863–73, https://doi.org/10.1016/s2542-5196(21)00278-3.
13. C. Duvallet et al., "Meta-Analysis of Gut Microbiome Studies Identifies Disease-Specific and Shared Responses," *Nature Communications* 8, no. 1784 (2017), https://doi.org/10.1038/s41467-017-01973-8.
14. Joanna Macy, *World as Lover, World as Self* (Parallax Press, 1991).
15. Linda Hogan, *Dwellings: A Spiritual History of the Living World* (Simon and Schuster, 1996).
16. Joanna Macy, *Widening Circles: A Memoir* (New Society Publishers, 2000). Contains Rainer Maria Rilke's "The Book of Hours," translated by Anita Barrows and Joanna Macy.
17. Mirabai Starr, *Caravan of No Despair: A Memoir of Loss and Transformation* (Sounds True, 2015).

8: Spirals of Belonging

1. To go deeper on this subject, I recommend Resmaa Menakem's *My Grandmother's Hands: Racialized Trauma and the Pathway to Mending Our Hearts and Bodies* (Central Recovery Press, 2017).
2. See the Oscar-nominated documentary *Sugarcane*, directed by Julien Brave NoiseCat and Emily Kassie (National Geographic, 2024), for a harrowing and heartfelt exploration of this topic.
3. For more on this, read Robert Macfarlane's *Is a River Alive?* (Hamish Hamilton, 2024).
4. J. J. Wiens, "How Many Species Are There on Earth? Progress and Problems," *PLoS Biology* 21, no. 11 (2023): e3002388, https://doi.org/10.1371/journal.pbio.3002388.
5. Raphael Ranola, "Opinion: Unpacking the Environmental Cost of Your Amazon Prime Purchases," *Daily Illini*, November 6, 2023, https://dailyillini.com/opinions-stories/2023/10/27/opinion-amazon-prime-environment.
6. S. Schöngart, Z. Nicholls, R. Hoffmann, et al., "High-Income Groups Disproportionately Contribute to Climate Extremes Worldwide," *Nature Climate Change* 15, no. 6 (2025): 627–633, https://doi.org/10.1038/s41558-025-02325-x.
7. As cited in Vendana Shiva's *Earth Democracy* (South End Press, 2005), 1.
8. Richard Powers, *The Overstory* (W. W. Norton, 2018).
9. E. Brondizio et al., *Global Assessment Report on Biodiversity and Ecosystem Services*, Intergovernmental Science-Policy Platform on Biodiversity and Ecosystem Services, 2019, https://doi.org/10.5281/zenodo.3831673.
10. Donna Haraway, "Animal Sociology and a Natural Economy of the Body Politic, Part I: A Political Physiology of Dominance," *Signs: Journal of Women in Culture and Society* 4, no. 1 (1978): 57–72, https://doi.org/10.1093/oso/9780198751458.003.0005.
11. Donna Haraway, "Anthropocene, Capitalocene, Plantationocene, Chthulucene: Making Kin," *Environmental Humanities* 6, no. 1 (2015): 159–165.
12. Vanessa Watts, "Indigenous Place-Thought and Agency Amongst Humans and Non-Humans (First Woman and Sky Woman Go on a European World Tour!)," *Decolonization: Indigeneity, Education, and Society* 2, no. 1 (2013): 21.
13. The trek goes from Winnemem Waywaket (McCloud River) to the Bay-Delta Estuary at the Ohlone site, Sogorea Te (Glen Cove, Vallejo, California). Support their efforts at http://run4salmon.org.
14. Roberto Cazzolla Gatti et al., "The Number of Tree Species on Earth," *Proceedings of the National Academy of Sciences* 119, no. 6 (2022), https://doi.org/10.1073/pnas.2115329119.
15. According to the UN Environmental Programme.
16. Bo Zheng et al., "Record-High CO_2 Emissions from Boreal Fires in 2021," *Science* 379, no. 6635 (2023): 912–917, https://doi.org/10.1126/science.ade0805.

9: Sacred Reciprocity

1. Wahinkpe Topa (Four Arrows) and Darcia Narvaez, *Restoring the Kinship Worldview: Indigenous Visions for a Sustainable Future* (North Atlantic Books, 2022), 149.
2. Wahinkpe Topa (Four Arrows) and Darcia Narvaez, *Restoring the Kinship Worldview*, 147.

3. Wahinkpe Topa (Four Arrows) and Darcia Narvaez, *Restoring the Kinship Worldview*, 187–188.
4. "Aspen Trees," Colorado Encyclopedia, n.d., accessed November 25, 2024, https://coloradoencyclopedia.org/article/aspen-trees.
5. Oren Rabinowitz, "The Mystery of Aspen Powder," Ecology and Evolutionary Biology, College of Arts and Sciences, University of Colorado Boulder, October 20, 2015, https://www.colorado.edu/ebio/2015/10/20/mystery-aspen-powder.
6. James Baldwin, *Notes of a Native Son* (Dial Press, 1963).
7. Emilee Speck, "California Firefighters Already Battled 1,500 Wildfires as Searing Heat, Dry Grass Give Ample Fuel," Fox Weather, June 5, 2024, https://www.foxweather.com/extreme-weather/2024-california-wildfire-season-starts-above-average.
8. Eric C. Schneider et al., *Mirror, Mirror 2021—Reflecting Poorly: Health Care in the U.S. Compared to Other High-Income Countries*, Commonwealth Fund, August 2021, https://doi.org/10.26099/01dv-h208.
9. Georgina Kenyon Mosaic, "'If the Land Is Sick, You Are Sick': An Aboriginal Approach to Mental Health in Times of Drought," *Scroll.In*, April 28, 2019, https://scroll.in/pulse/921558/if-the-land-is-sick-you-are-sick-an-aboriginal-approach-to-mental-health-in-times-of-drought.
10. Suzanne W. Simard et al., "Net Transfer of Carbon Between Ectomycorrhizal Tree Species in the Field," *Nature* 388, no. 6642 (1997): 579–582, https://doi.org/10.1038/41557.
11. Suzanne W. Simard, "Mycorrhizal Networks Facilitate Tree Communication, Learning, and Memory," in *Memory and Learning in Plants*, ed. F. Baluska et al. (Springer, 2018), 191–213.
12. Suzanne W. Simard, *The Mother Tree: Discovering the Wisdom of the Forest* (Alfred A. Knopf, 2021).
13. Merlin Sheldrake, *Entangled Life: How Fungi Make Our Worlds, Change Our Minds, and Shape Our Futures* (Random House, 2020).
14. Sheldrake, *Entangled Life*, 52.
15. Scott F. Gilbert et al., "A Symbiotic View of Life: We Have Never Been Individuals," *Quarterly Review of Biology* 87, no. 4 (2012): 325–341.
16. Florencio F. Portocarrero et al., "A Meta-Analytic Review of the Relationship Between Dispositional Gratitude and Well-Being," *Personality and Individual Differences* 164 (October 1, 2020), https://doi.org/10.1016/j.paid.2020.110101.
17. Sara B. Algoe et al., "Beyond Reciprocity: Gratitude and Relationships in Everyday Life," *Emotion* 8, no. 3 (2008): 425–429, https://doi.org/10.1037/1528-3542.8.3.425; S. B. Algoe, "Find, Remind, and Bind: The Functions of Gratitude in Everyday Relationships," *Social and Personality Psychology Compass* 6, no. 6 (2012): 455–469, https://doi.org/10.1111/j.1751-9004.2012.00439.x; S. B. Algoe, "Positive Interpersonal Processes," *Current Directions in Psychological Science* 28, no. 2 (2019): 183–188, https://doi.org/10.1177/0963721419827272.
18. Kim-Pong Tam, "Gratitude to Nature: Presenting a Theory of Its Conceptualization, Measurement, and Effects on Pro-Environmental Behavior," *Journal of Environmental Psychology* 79, no. 101754 (February 2022), https://doi.org/10.1016/j.jenvp.2021.101754.
19. Tam, "Gratitude to Nature," 11.

20. K. Whyte, "Too Late for Indigenous Climate Justice: Ecological and Relational Tipping Points," *WIREs Climate Change* 11, no. 1 (2020): e603, https://doi.org/10.1002/wcc.603.
21. This idea was shared with me in an interview I conducted with Bayo Akomolafe, September 5, 2022.

10: Cosmic Entanglement

1. William Bateson, "Notes for 'Gamete and Zygote' Lecture," December 1, 1917 (B 3320).
2. Donna J. Haraway, *Staying with the Trouble: Making Kin in the Chthulucene* (Duke University Press, 2016), 4.
3. Haraway, *Staying with the Trouble*, 2.
4. *Parks and an Equitable Recovery*, Trust for Public Land, 2021, https://e7jecw7o93n.exactdn.com/wp-content/uploads/2024/02/Parks-and-an-equitable-recovery-The-Trust-for-Public-Land.pdf.
5. *Lynching in America: Confronting the Legacy of Racial Terror*, 3rd ed., Equal Justice Initiative, 2020, https://eji.org/wp-content/uploads/2020/09/lynching-in-america-3d-ed-091620.pdf.
6. Karen Barad, *Meeting the Universe Halfway: Quantum Physics and the Entanglement of Matter and Meaning* (Duke University Press, 2007).
7. Suzanne W. Simard, "Mycorrhizal Networks Facilitate Tree Communication, Learning, and Memory," in *Memory and Learning in Plants*, ed. F. Baluzka et al., Signaling and Communication in Plants (Springer, 2018), 191–192, https://boomwachtersgroningen.nl/wp-content/uploads/2019/04/Simard2018_Chapter_MycorrhizalNetworksFacilitateT-1.pdf.
8. Thich Nhat Hanh, *Love Letter to the Earth* (Parallax Press, 2013).
9. Donna J. Haraway, *Staying with the Trouble*, 37.

11: Spirit, Magic, and Ceremony

1. Wahinkpe Topa (Four Arrows) and Darcia Narvaez, *Restoring the Kinship Worldview: Indigenous Voices Introduce 28 Precepts for Rebalancing Life on Planet Earth* (North Atlantic Books, 2022), 14.
2. Kim-Pong Tam, "Anthropomorphism of Nature, Environmental Guilt, and Pro-Environmental Behavior," *Sustainability* 11, no. 19 (2019): 5430, https://doi.org/10.3390/su11195430.
3. James Hillman, *The Thought of the Heart and the Soul of the World* (Spring Publications, 1998), 48.
4. Christopher D. Stone, "Should Trees Have Standing? Toward Legal Rights for Natural Objects," *Southern California Law Review* 45 (1972): 450–501.
5. David Abram, *Becoming Animal: An Earthly Cosmology* (National Geographic Books, 2011).
6. Walter D. Mignolo and Catherine E. Walsh, *On Decoloniality: Concepts, Analytics, Praxis* (Duke University Press, 2018).
7. Aleksandar Janca and Clothilde Bullen, "The Aboriginal Concept of Time and Its Mental Health Implications," *Australasian Psychiatry* 11, no. 1 suppl. (2003): S40–44, https://doi.org/10.1046/j.1038-5282.2003.02009.x.

8. Tyson Yunkaporta, *Sand Talk: How Indigenous Thinking Can Save the World* (HarperCollins, 2020), 18, 41.
9. William Edward Hanley Stanner, *White Man Got No Dreaming* (Australian National University, 1979).
10. Leo Killsback, "Indigenous Perceptions of Time: Decolonizing Theory, World History, and the Fates of Human Societies," *American Indian Culture and Research Journal* 37, no. 4 (2013): 85–114.
11. Sumana Roy, *How I Became a Tree* (Yale University Press, 2021), 62.
12. Tricia Hersey, *Rest Is Resistance: A Manifesto* (Little, Brown Spark, 2022).
13. William A. Richards, *Sacred Knowledge: Psychedelics and Religious Experience* (Columbia University Press, 2015).
14. Jalāl al-Dīn Rūmī, *The Essential Rumi*. Translated by Coleman Barks (HarperCollins, 1995).
15. Hannes Kettner et al., "From Egoism to Ecoism: Psychedelics Increase Nature Relatedness in a State-Mediated and Context-Dependent Manner," *International Journal of Environmental Research and Public Health* 16, no. 24 (December 16, 2019): 5147, https://doi.org/10.3390/ijerph16245147.
16. Quoted in Warwick Fox, "The Intuition of Deep Ecology," *The Ecologist* 14 (1984).
17. N. Scott Momaday, *Earth Keeper: Reflections on the American Land* (HarperCollins, 2020), 54.
18. Adapted from the Sati Centre for Buddhist Studies and School of Lost Borders.

12: Intersectional Wild Weave of Justice

1. A term used by Indigenous peoples to refer to North America.
2. Alexander Koch et al., "Earth System Impacts of the European Arrival and Great Dying in the Americas After 1492," *Quaternary Science Reviews* 207 (January 2019): 13–36, https://doi.org/10.1016/j.quascirev.2018.12.004.
3. The majority of Indigenous peoples living in the Americas were lost from the impacts of European colonization.
4. *U.S. Forest Resource Facts and Historical Trends*, August 2014, US Forest Service, https://www.fs.usda.gov/sites/default/files/legacy_files/media/types/publication/field_pdf/forestfacts-2014aug-fs1035-508complete.pdf.
5. Jean-Francois Bastin et al., "The Global Tree Restoration Potential," *Science* 365, no. 6448 (2019): 76–79, DOI:10.1126/science.aax0848.
6. Justin Farrell et al., "Effects of Land Dispossession and Forced Migration on Indigenous Peoples in North America," *Science* 374, no. 6567 (2021), https://doi.org/10.1126/science.abe4943.
7. World Resources Institute (WRI): Indigenous Forests Are Some of the Amazon's Last Carbon Sinks. 2023; Rights and Resources Initiative (RRI). A Global Baseline of Carbon Storage in Collective Lands. Indigenous And Local Community Contributions To Climate Change Mitigation. 2023.
8. Calculated based on US forests currently absorbing 11 percent of US carbon emissions, or 150 million metric tons of carbon a year, equivalent to the combined emissions from forty coal power plants, according to the US Department of Agriculture.

9. US Department of Agriculture, Forest Service, *Future of America's Forest and Rangelands: Forest Service 2020 Resources Planning Act Assessment*, General Technical Report WO-102, 2023, https://doi.org/10.2737/WO-GTR-102.
10. Inspired by C. Cipolla et al., eds., *Queer Feminist Science Studies: A Reader* (University of Washington Press, 2017).
11. Terry Tempest Williams, *Red: Passion and Patience in the Desert* (First Vintage Books, 2002), 147.
12. "History—Southern Ute Indian Tribe," n.d., https://www.southernute-nsn.gov/history.
13. "Bear Dance—Southern Ute Indian Tribe," n.d., https://www.southernute-nsn.gov/culture/bear-dance.
14. Resmaa Menakem, *My Grandmother's Hands: Racialized Trauma and the Pathway to Mending Our Hearts and Bodies* (Central Recovery Press, 2017).
15. Robert Macfarlane, *Is a River Alive?* (W. W. Norton & Company, 2025).
16. Audre Lorde, "The Master's Tools Will Never Dismantle the Master's House," in *Sister Outsider: Essays and Speeches* (Crossing Press, 2007), 110–114.
17. Adrienne Rich, "Blood, Bread, and Poetry: The Location of the Poet," *The Massachusetts Review* 4, no. 3 (1983): 521–540.
18. I highly recommend taking up other books and resources including the masterful works by Resmaa Menakem, Kimberlé Crenshaw, Audre Lorde, Karen Barad, and many more to navigate this challenging terrain together in the spirit of justice.
19. Linda Tuhiwai Smith, *Decolonizing Methodologies: Research and Indigenous Peoples* (Bloomsbury Publishing, 2016).
20. As quoted in Robin Wall Kimmerer, *Braiding Sweetgrass: Indigenous Wisdom, Scientific Knowledge, and the Teachings of Plants* (Milkweed Editions, 2013), 340.
21. To learn more about Ekua's work, visit ekuaadisa.com.
22. Vandana Shiva, "The Tree Saviors of Chipko Andolan: A Woman-Led Movement in India," *Kosmos Journal* 20, no. 3, https://www.kosmosjournal.org/kj_article/99176.
23. For example, I have been deeply impacted by the ceremonial praxis of the ritual arts collective BAKINÉ, which is self-described as "guided by the alchemy of atonement." I honor the influence of their example as they weave praxis, justice, and art into a prayer with spiritual and ecological implications. Formerly called Lead to Life, this arts collective held public ceremonies where they would melt guns into shovels to plant trees, "to repair the ancestral memory of funerary traditions African peoples were denied to practice under the trauma of enslavement."

13: Queer Ecology and Making Vows

1. Donna J. Haraway is currently professor emerita in the History of Consciousness Department at the University of California, Santa Cruz.
2. Donna J. Haraway, *Staying with the Trouble: Making Kin in the Chthulucene* (Duke University Press, 2016), 24.
3. Sophie Strand, *The Flowering Wand: Rewilding the Sacred Masculine* (Simon and Schuster, 2022), 113.

4. As quoted in Nadia Nooreyezdan, "Talking With Alok Vaid-Menon About Art, Activism, and the Transfeminine Movement," *The Swaddle* (January 14, 2019), https://www.theswaddle.com/talking-with-alok-vaid-menon-about-art-activism-and-the-transfeminine-movement.
5. Chela Sandoval, *Methodology of the Oppressed* (University of Minnesota Press, 2000).
6. *Reverie* means to dream in French. I use the word *reverie* here in the tradition of the French philosopher Gaston Bachelard, who wrote extensively about it as an entire cosmogony and philosophy of life. *The Poetics of Reverie: Childhood, Language, and the Cosmos* (Beacon Press, 1971), published in English seven years after Bachelard's death, is an exploration of reverie as a special kind of imagination. He writes, "Instead of looking for the dream in reverie, people should look for reverie in the dream." I believe that to reverie is an essential aspect of kinship with the living world.

Conclusion: Death Doula to a Dying World

1. *The Global Land Outlook*, 2nd ed. United Nations Convention to Combat Desertification, 2022.
2. This idea was shared with me in an interview I conducted with Bayo Akomolafe, September 5, 2022.
3. From a lecture at the Othering and Belonging Institute, University of California, Berkeley, May 4, 2023.
4. Jacqueline Suskin, "To Watch the Earth Die," from *The Verse for Now*. Used with permission from the poet.
5. Arundhati Roy, "The Pandemic Is a Portal," *Financial Times*, April 3, 2020, https://www.ft.com/content/10d8f5e8-74eb-11ea-95fe-fcd274e920ca.

Index

Abram, David, 13, 92, 201
Adisa, Ekua, 41–42, 237–239
Adverse Childhood Experiences (ACEs) study, 86
adversity, childhood, 85–86
Ainsworth, Mary, 83
Akomolafe, Bayo, 48–49, 112, 262–263
Albrecht, Glenn, 63
aliveness
    capacity for, 67
    as code of life, xix, 145
    as a language, 6
    with the living, 199
    shared, 201–202
    in touch with one's, 74
Amanita muscaria mushroom, 197, 201–202
Amazon, 146
ancestral history, 242–243
anger, 163–164
Anglo-Saxons, 6
animacy and individualism, 145
animal mourning, 127
animal nature, 72–73
animism, 199–202
anxious attachment, 84
Apalech Clan, 204
Aspen trees
    author's vision with an elder, 198–199, 201

catkins, 95–96
Cottonwoods collaborating with, 151–152
embody community, 11–12
graveyard of, 33
heart attacks in, 7
heat stress, 7
homecoming song from, 59–60
language of, 11
lifespan of, 11
in mud season, 95–96
in Roaring Fork Valley, xv–xvi
sound of, 11–12
taking advantage of disasters, 33–34
therapeutic properties of, 162
attachment injuries, 88
attachment security, 83
attachment styles
    anxious, 84
    avoidant, 84
    behavior profiles and, 83–84
    disorganized, 84, 85–86
    as fluid, 83–84
    secure, 82–86, 92, 97–98
attachment wounds, 88–89
attention regulation, 102–103
attentiveness, 70, 171
attunement, 103–104
Australian Aboriginal peoples, 205

Index

autoimmune disorders
  frequency of, 67
  general prognosis for, 67–68
autoimmunity, disembodiment
  contributing to, 70
autumn, 268–269
avoidant attachment, 84
awareness, focused, 111
Ayahuasca, 212–213

Bachelard, Gaston, 13
Baldwin, James, 164
Barad, Karen, 183, 186, 249
Bateson, William, 180
Bear Dance, 233
beauty, as nature's attraction spell, 61
Becoming Animal (Abram), 201
Beech trees, 6
beetle kill, 266
belonging
  author's struggle with, 155
  Bob's search for, 139–140
  celebrating diversity, 151
  ceremony as vehicle for, 215
  origin stories and (See origin stories)
  in the Roaring Fork Valley, 152
  through toning, 156–157
Betty Joyce (author's grandmother),
  81–82, 113–114, 140–142
binaries, 247
biodiversity vigil, 262
biophonies, 109–110, 115–116
black bears, xxv–xxvi
Black communities, inequitable access to
  greenspace, 185
Bob (author's grandfather), 139–140,
  155–156
Boc, 6
body awareness, 12, 49, 54–55, 66, 69,
  219–220. *See also* human body
body intelligence, 46
body practice
  body scan, 37–38
  devotion to the body, 256–258
  Earth to Sun breath, 192–193
  entanglement with the living world,
    192–193
  gratitude, 173–174
  heartbeat awareness, 98–99
  honoring our ancestors, 242–243
  inner belonging through toning,
    156–157
  inner yes, inner no, 53–54
  mindful awareness to sound, 114–115
  noticing sensation, 15–16, 219–220
  practicing equanimity, 273–274
  rhythmic tapping, 134–135
  trusting the body, 219–220
  welcoming back embodiment, 77–78
body scan practice, 37–38
boreal fires, 153–154
Bowlby, John, 83
Braiding Sweetgrass (Kimmerer), 43, 215
Branham, Lindsay (author)
  Aspen elder, vision with, 198–199, 201
  at Buddhist eco-chaplaincy training
    retreat, 36, 177–178
  chronic health journey, 3–6, 8–9, 14,
    64–65, 168, 271
  colonics therapy, 87–88
  during COVID pandemic, 20, 50–51
  erotic and embodied ecology with
    trees, 75
  face-to-face with her own nature,
    71–72
  finding her yes, 50–51
  grandfather of (See Bob)
  grandmother of (See Betty Joyce)
  gratitude to the trees, 272–273
  as humanitarian filmmaker, 26–27
  language of trees, speaking the,
    271–272
  lesson in death, 277–278
  LiYan and, 177–179
  migraine headaches, 24–26
  in New Mexico, 19–20
  Plum Village visit, 188–189
  at psilocybin ceremony, 209–210

psychedelic facilitator training, 211–212
at Roaring Fork Valley, xv–xvi
saving a treetop, 128–129
sleep paralysis experience, 19
tinnitus and, 106–108
yoga teacher training, 106
brown, adrienne maree, 70
Buddha, xxi–xxii
Butler, Octavia, 269

Cajete, Gregory, 30, 31
capitalism
acts of defiance against, 255–256
challenging, 73–74
ecosystem out of balance with, 165
globalized extractive, 48, 165
linear time and, 203, 207
oppression from, 126
severing people from the Earth, 28–29, 31
turning greed into a virtue, 165
Capra, Fritjof, 212
carbon emissions. *See also* global warming
Amazon and, 146
from boreal fires, 154
critical juncture of, 45
Global North as largest exploiters of, 125
mass deforestation and, 229–230
nations responsible for, 47–48, 125
Cartesian dualism (Descartes), 27
catkins, 95–96
Cedar grove, 252
Cedar trees, 255
ceremony
giving thanks to the Earth in, 215–216
healing wounded lands through, 238
opening ways of knowing, 216
as reconnecting with the living world, 208–210
tree practice, 221–224, 274–275
as vehicle for belonging, 215
childhood adversity, 85–86

Chinook salmon, 149–150
Chipko movement, 239–240
Christian values, mind-body split ideology, 27–29
chronic health crisis, 165
circular time, 203–207. *See also* time
climate anxiety, 126
climate change
entangled with health disparities, xviii–xix
global rate of nature's decline, 148
Global South, effects on, 125
global warming, 44, 124–125
impacts of, 126
individualism and, 90
planetary boundaries from, 47–49
rhythms of life and, 96
solving, 188
climate collapse, feeling grief of, 263–264
climate crisis, colonization of the US and, 228–229
climate justice, relationships in, 172
collective memory, 147
colonialism, 23, 28–29, 143–144, 250–251
colonics, 87–88
colonization of the US
as beginning of climate crisis, 228–229
Indigenous land loss from, 229
invisible carnage of, 229–230
Colorado River, 21–22, 231–232
commercial logging, 239–240
Commonwealth Fund, 165
compost, 132–133
consent
from the Earth, 41–42
experiment with, 54–55
as foundational to kincentricity, 42
seeking, 52, 54–55
in tree practice, 78
from wild mountain rose, example, 43–44
Copernicus Climate Change Service, 124
corporealgia, 63
cosmogonic oblivion, 117

Cottonwood trees, 76, 151–152, 191, 231, 251
Council of All Beings, 253–254
COVID pandemic, 20, 50–51
cracks, as portal of new realities, 112–113
Crete, Greece, 202–203
cytokine interleuken-6 (IL-6), 66–67

death
    author's lesson in, 277–278
    eco-doula, 270–271, 278
    fall and, 268–269
    in harmony with life, 266–267
    nature's knowing of, 268–269
    tending to, 260–261
death doulas, 265–266, 273–274
decolonization, 237
deep time. *See* time
deer, sacredness of, 44–45
deforestation, 228–230
degradation of place, 29
Demos, T. J., 76
dendrites, 46
Descartes's Cartesian dualism, 27
desire, 60–61, 73, 93–94
devotion, as art of loving, 257–258
diffraction, 249
disconnection with nature, xix, 9–10, 27, 89, 112, 147, 204
disembodiment, 27–29, 35, 70, 85
disorganized attachment, 84, 85–86
dissociation, 219
Dostoyevsky, Fyodor, 53
doulas
    death, 265–266, 273–274
    description of, 264–265
    eco-, 270–271, 278
Dreaming, the, 205
drought, causing heart attacks in trees, 7
dualism, 27

Earth. *See also* nature
    acoustics of, 108–109
    aliveness of, 199–202
    apex predators of, xxvi
    attentiveness to relationship with, 172
    communicating its limits, 44
    consent to relationship with, 41–43
    creating secure relationships with, 94–95
    exploitation of, 29–30
    facing truth of changing, 269–271
    as first sacred text, 51–52
    fluidity, 247
    generosity as life-blood of, 161
    as greatest teacher of intersectional environmental justice, 239–240
    human beings attuning to, 103
    infinite creative expression of, 246–247
    kinship with, xvii–xviii
    as partner in grief, 119
    as polymorphous, xxiii
    reciprocity of, 253–254
    right relationship with, 234–236, 267–268
    as a safe haven, 93–94
    seduction from, 60
    shifting human attachment to secure relationships, 93
    speaking through sensation, 10
    window of tolerance, 47–49
Earth Keeper (Momaday), 217
Earth-relationship privilege, 235–236
eco-anxiety, 126
ecocide, 29
ecodelia, 212
eco-doulas, 270–271, 278
eco-eroticism, intersectional justice intertwined with, 75–76
eco-grief, 126
eco-justice, 145, 183
ecological attachments, individualism and, 241
ecological breakdown, 165
ecological consciousness, 255, 265–266
ecological destruction, 225–226, 230–231
ecological dominance, 43
ecological wisdom, 201–202, 216–217

Index

ecotones, 148
emancipatory horizon, 76
embodied experiences, 32–33, 77–78
embodied listening, 8–9
emotional awareness, 69
emotional dysregulation, 68–69
emotions
   anger, 163–164
   ecological loss and, 164
   impact on physical health, 88
   regulated, 47
   sensations as, 66
Engaged Buddhism, 188, 227
entangled futures, 181
Entangled Life (Sheldrake), 167
entanglement with the living world
   body practice, 192–193
   dissolving boundaries, 180
   as ecological reality, 179–180
   examples of, 186–187
   of forests, 166–167
   lost sense of, 182–183
   nature-culture dualism, 183–184, 186
   new life from, 190
   as ongoing act of co-creation, 180–181
   as process in action, 187
   reimagining, 144
   tree practice, 193–194
entrainment, 104–106
epigenetics, 10
epistemicide, 29
Equal Justice Initiative, 185
equanimity, 273–274
eros, 62, 71, 74, 76
erotic
   as akin to life force, 73–74
   as capacity to find a yes, 65–66
   in communion with, 74
erotic ecology, 62, 76
Estés, Clarissa Pinkola, 9–10
extinct species, 262

Fairy Slippers, 62
fall (autumn), 268–269
Fanon, Frantz, 31, 233
fireweed, 120
Flowering Wand, The (Strand), 248
fluidity between humans and nature, 247
focused awareness, 111
forests. *See* nature; trees
forgiveness, 87–88
Four Arrows, 215–216
Fronsdal, Gil, 179
fungi, 167–168, 249

Garcia, Niria Alicia, 149
Garden of Eden, 147
Garhwal Himalayan region, 239–240
generosity, 161, 170
genetics, 180
Global North, 47–48, 125
Global South, 47–48, 125
Global Tree Assessment, xx
global warming, 44, 124–125. *See also* climate change
globalized extractive capitalism, 48, 165
gratitude, 131, 170–171, 272–273
Greece, 202–203
greenspaces. *See also* nature
   in Black communities, 185
   Equal Justice Initiative, 185
   inequitable access to, 184–185
grief
   bearing witness to, 126
   as complicated, 120
   Earth as partner in, 119
   ecologically conscious practices, 130–132
   five gates of, 118–119, 120–121
   as food for growth, 118
   infinite expressions of, 118
   like a seed, 121
   of trees, 127
   unwitnessed, 120
   writing a letter to your, 135–136
grief alchemy, 132–133
Griffith Park, 252–253, 255

Grizzly Reservoir, creating ecological
    destruction, 225–226

Haraway, Donna, 32, 148, 181–182,
    189, 247
Harjo, Joy, 9
Harvard Study of Adult Development, 83
Harvey, Samantha, 187
Haskell, David, xix
head pain. *See* migraine headaches
healing
    acoustic universe of the Earth as,
        108–109
    definition of, xxiv, 52
    as emergent collective process, 238
    as ongoing process of loving, 189
    psychology's limited views of, 113
    wounded lands, 237–239
heartbeat awareness, 98–99
heart-to-heartwood connections, 105
Hempton, Gordon, 111
Hersey, Tricia "the Nap Bishop", 207
Hill, Julia Butterfly, 190
Hillman, James, 33, 89–90, 113, 199
Hogan, Linda, 131
homogeny, 151
Honorable Harvest, 43–44
hope, xxiii, 263–264
hopelessness, 263–264
human beings
    attuning to Earth, 103
    becoming curious about embodied
        experiences, 32–33
    as Earth's apex predators, xxvi
    fluidity between nature and, 247
human body
    ancestral history and, 242–243
    devotion to, 256–258
    as landscape, 22
    language of the land resides within,
        23–24
    as nature, 22–24
    as a place, 21–22
    relationship with yours, 256–258

resonating with Earth's frequencies,
    60–61
sharing same elements with nature, 154
trust in, 219–220
hyphae, 167

imperial growth paradigm, 48
Indigenous peoples
    cosmogonic myths of, 149
    decimation of, 228
    definition of, xxiii–xxiv
    forced removal of, 184
    on importance of interspecies
        communications, 12–13
    kincentric ecology of, 30
    land loss from colonization, 229
    Northwest First Coast Nations, 187
    origin story of, 31
    as protectors of planet's biodiversity,
        229–230
    on rebalancing life on Earth, 160–161
    relationships as foundation for being
        in the world, 97
    right to self-determination, 31
    settler colonialism and, 143–144
    Suquamish tribe, 146
    Ute people, 232–233
    Winnemem Wintu peoples, 149–150
individualism
    animacy and, 145
    destroying relationships, 89–90
    ecological attachments and, 241
    healing, 76, 113
    myth of, 90, 143
Indra's net, 270
intention, 221
interbeing, 188–189, 191
Intergovernmental Panel on Climate
    Change (IPCC), 125
interoceptive awareness, xxii, 12, 99,
    114–115. *See also* body awareness;
    open awareness
intersectional environmental justice
    in action, 236

eco-eroticism intertwined with, 75–76
Engaged Buddhism and, 227
participation in, 239–241
interspecies communications, 12–13
Is a River Alive? (Macfarlane), 234
isotope tracing, 103
IUCN Red List, xx

James, William, 66
Johnston, Basil, 161
Judeo-Christian origin story, 147
Judeo-Christian values, 27–29
Juniper, 51

Kaishian, Patricia, 249
Keats, John, 77
Kennedy, Liz, 76
Killsbak, Leo, 206–207
Kimmerer, Robin Wall, xxiii, 43, 172, 215
kincentricity, 30–31, 42, 97–98
Kingsnorth, Paul, 8
kinship with nature, xx–xxi, 91–92, 98, 145, 170–171. *See also* making kin
Klamath River, 150
knowledge, control of resources through, 236–237

language of sensation, 22, 69, 84–85, 92, 172, 230, 255
language of the land, 23–24
language of the senses, 9–10, 12–13
language of trees
  communication, 6–8
  to help us repair, 31–32
  interoceptive awareness and, 12
  as language of the senses, 12–13
  resensitizing our bodies to, 69
  speaking the, 12–14, 271–272
  trembling Aspens and, 11
Lee fire, 230–231
LGBTQIA+ people, 248–252
linear time, 203–207
listening, 223
living beings, objectifying, 29

LiYan, 177–179, 192
logging, commercial, 239–240
loneliness, 89. *See also* disconnection with nature
Lorde, Audre, 65, 73–74, 75, 234
Los Angeles
  fires, 133, 153–154
  Griffith Park, 252–253, 255
  secret forest, 252–253
love
  devotion as art of, 257–258
  as radical acceptance, 251
  as revolutionary political force, 251–252
  unconditional, 82

Macfarlane, Robert, 234
Macy, Joanna, xxiii, 129, 131–132, 237, 252
magic, as witnessing life, 218–219
Mahayana Buddhism, 270
Majjhima Nikāya of the Pali Canon, xxi–xxii
making kin. *See also* kinship with nature
  importance of, 181–182
  with other species, 181–182
  process of, 32–33
Māori tribe, 200
Maroon Creek canyon, 8, 71–72
Maroon Creek river valley, 241–242
mass deforestation, 228–230
mass extinction event, 261, 262
mast seeding, 191
Menakem, Resmaa, 233
Mendocino coast, 61–62
migraine headaches, 24–26, 251
mind-body split ideology, 27–29
Mindful Brain, The (Siegel), 103
mindfulness
  attunement as skill of, 103–104
  body practice, 114–115
  open awareness and, 107
  types of, 103
Momaday, N. Scott, 97, 217
monarch butterflies, 159–160

more-than-human, 92
Mother Tree, The (Simard), 166
mountain bluebird, 101
Mourning Dove, 199
mud seasons, 95–96
muditā, 170, 271
music of the spheres, 105
My Grandmother's Hands (Menakem), 233
mycelium, 167–168

Narvaez, Darcia, 160–161
National Oceanic and Atmospheric Administration (NOAA), 124, 125
Native people. *See* Indigenous peoples
natural killer cells, 67
natural silence, 111–112
nature. *See also* trees
    entanglement with (See entanglement with the living world)
    fluidity between humans and, 247
    fungi, 167
    interconnective system within, 166
    kinship with, 52
    knowing when time to die, 268–269
    monarch butterflies, 159–160
    receiving legal standing, 200
    regenerating itself, 190
    therapeutic properties of, 162
nature-culture dualism, 183–184, 186
New Mexico, 19–20, 50–51
New York COVID support hotline, 20
New Zealand, 200
Nhat Hanh, Thich, 165, 188
nonlinear time, 203–208
Norse mythology, 147
Northwest First Coast Nations, 187
Notes of a Native Son (Baldwin), 164
Nuche, 233

Ó Tuama, Pádraig, 119
Oak trees, 133–134
O'Donohue, John, 61
open awareness, 107–108, 113–114
oppression, 126. *See also* colonialism

oral storytelling, 144
orca whales, 109–110
orchids, wild, 62
origin stories
    in the collective memories of trees, 147
    as essential, 143
    helping with belonging, 142–143
    Judeo-Christian, 147
    Norse mythology, 147
    as symbolic narratives, 142
    tree practice, 157
    Western, 145–146
    of Winnemem Wintu peoples, 149–150
overculture, 9–10, 73, 77, 199
Overstory, The (Powers), 147

Pacific Lumber Company, 190
pain, sound of, 27, 108
parasympathetic nervous system, 46
permission. *See* consent
Persephone, myth of, 63–64
Piaget, Jean, 88
place-based rooting and living, 35–36
place-thought, 148–149
planetary sound, 105, 108–109
pleasure
    attentiveness to, 70
    experiences of, 66–67
    as medicine, 67
    stillness and quietude as, 68–69
Pleasure Activism (brown), 70
Plum Village, 188–189
pollinators, 160
pollution, 242
polycrisis, symptoms of, xix
polymorphous relations, 250–251
pothos, 62–63
Powers, Richard, 147
privilege, settler colonialists, 234–235
progress, myth of, 29–30, 145–146
psilocybin ceremony
    author's experience, 208–210
    as eco-erotic connection to Earth, 211

psychedelics
    Ayahuasca, 212–213
    commercialization of, 213–214
    facilitator training, 211–212
    misuse and harm from, 214
    potential efficacy of, 214
    psilocybin ceremony, 208–210
    renaissance of, 213
purity, 28
Pyramid Peak, 246

Queen Anne's lace, 61
queer ecology, 248–252
queered love technology, 252
queerness
    as affirmation of holiness of the fringe, 249–250
    as integral to nature, 249
quiet places, 111–112

radiofrequency electromagnetic fields, 104–105
rainbow trout, 218–219
reciprocity
    among trees, 166–167
    brings balance, 170
    climate justice and, 172
    communicating desire to embody, 175
    of the Earth, 253–254
    engagement in, as way of life, 173
    interconnective system within forests and, 166–168
    kinship symbiosis through, 170–171
    modeled after laws of nature, 161–162
    monarch butterflies and, 160
    origins of, 160–161
    relational tipping point and, 172
Red (Williams), 232
red clover tea, 162
Redwood tree elders, 74–75, 153–156, 190, 253
refractions, 249
refuge, definition of, 129–130
relational attachment theory, 83–84

relational tipping point, 171–172
relationships
    attentiveness to, 171
    with the Earth, 93, 94–95
    between humans, 42
    individualism destroying, 89–90
    interpersonal attunement in, 103
respect, movement toward, 45
Rest Is Resistance (Hersey), 207
Restoring the Kinship Worldview (Wahinkpe Topa and Narvaez), 160–161, 199
Rich, Adrienne, 235
Richards, William, 208
right action, 227, 234–236, 267–268
right effort, 227
right seeing, 227
Rilke, Rainer Maria, 132, 133
ritual. *See* ceremony
rivers, as easily wounded, 234
Roaring Fork River, 225–226, 242
Roaring Fork Valley
    author's experience in, xv–xvi, xviii, 35
    in autumn, 248–249
    belonging and, 151–152
Rocky Mountains, 8, 241
Rohr, Richard, 51, 168
rootlessness, feelings of, 143
Roy, Arundhati, 265
Rūmī, Jalāl al-Dīn, 62
Run4Salmon ceremony, 149–150

Sabina, Maria, 208
Sacred Knowledge (Richards), 208
sacred reciprocity. *See* reciprocity
safe havens, 92–93, 96–97
salmon, Chinook, 149–150
Salmón, Enrique, 42
sanctuary, finding, 129–130
Sandoval, Chela, 251
Seattle, Chief, 146
secure attachment, 82–86, 92, 97–98
secure base, 92–93

self-determination, Indigenous peoples' right to, 31
sensations. *See also* language of sensation
　of aliveness, 6
　body practice, 15–16, 219–220
　as body's way of communicating barriers, 42
　Earth speaking through, 10
　as emotions, 66
　healing and harm in, 34
　of inner belonging, 156
　inner language, 12–13
　learning the language of, 15–16
senses, language of. *See* language of sensation
settler colonialism, 28–29, 143, 234–237
Shanaye, Tayla, 22, 262
Shasta Dam, 149
Sheldrake, Merlin, 167
Sheldrake, Rupert, 147
Siegel, Dan, 103
Simard, Suzanne, 7, 166
Simpson, Leanne Betasamosake, 234
Sisk, Caleen, 149
sleep deprivation, 107
sleep paralysis, 19
slowing down, 13, 45, 48–49, 162, 207, 221, 255
Smith, Linda Tuhiwai, 237
snowy bluebell wildflowers, 102
solastalgia, 63
Solnit, Rebecca, 49
sound, 104–105, 114–116, 159
soundscape ecology, 108–110
spiders, extended cognition of, 4
spiritual insight, sacredness of, 201
Stanner, W. E. H., 205
Staying with the Trouble (Haraway), 181–182, 189
Stone, Christopher, 200
stories. *See also* origin stories
　helping with belonging, 142–143
　oral storytelling, 144
Strand, Sophie, 248

Strange Situation experiment, 83
sun, luminosity of, 20–21
Suquamish tribe, 146
Suskin, Jacqueline, 264
symbiosis, 170

thankfulness, 44
thimbleberries, 241
Thoreau, Henry, 44
Three Jewels of Buddhism, 130
three refuges, 130
time
　as ascending spiral, 254–255
　to Australian Aboriginal peoples, 205
　circularity of, 203–206
　linear, 203–207
tinnitus, 106–108, 111
toning, practice of, 156–157
Topanga State Park
　adopt a baby Oak tree program, 162–164
　author camping at, 168–170
tragedy, as opportunity, 265
trauma-informed somatic care, 87–88
tree hugging, 239–240
tree practice
　ceremony walk, 221–224
　closing ceremony, 274–275
　communicating desire to embody reciprocity, 175
　entanglement with the living world, 193–194
　family system of the Earth, 99–100
　kinship origin stories, 157
　knowing place, 38
　letter to grief, 135–136
　listening to biophonies, 115–116
　listening to tree's history, 243–244
　relationship with a tree, 16–17
　seeking permission, 54–55
　taking a vow, 258
　touching the tree, 78
tree topping, 121–124

trees
  Aspen (See Aspen trees)
  attunement among, 103
  bereavement ritual, 128–129
  collective responsibility to each other, 7
  communication among (See language of trees)
  in constant collaboration, 7
  Cottonwood (See Cottonwood trees)
  digestive system of, 127
  embodying reciprocal kinship, 166–167
  extinction risk for, xx
  as fire-resistant guardians, 133–134
  grief of, 127
  heartwood of, xxi–xxii
  as intelligent, 5
  life of, tied to human life, xx
  listening to story and history of, 243–244
  listening to the forest exercise, 36
  mortality rates, 127
  nervous system of, 46
  Oak, 133–134
  as oldest living organisms, xix–xx
  as pure beingness, 5
  Redwood tree elders, 74–75, 153–154, 155–156
  rhythms of, 105
  as a sanctuary, 92
  as secure family system, 91–93
  sensitive to certain frequencies, 104–105
  as symbol of racial terror, 185–186
  trimming technique, 121–124
Triple Gem, 130

UCLA rheumatology department, 64
unconditional love, 82
US Department of Agriculture, 230
"Uses of the Erotic" (Lorde), 65
Ute people, 232–233

vagal toning, 46
vagus nerve, 46, 156

Vaid-Menon, Alok, 250
Ventura, Michael, 89–90
Vishnu Schist, 231
Vouves Olive Tree, 202–203
vows, 252–255, 258

Wahinkpe Topa (Four Arrows), 27, 160–161
walking, 49
wandering, 222–223
Wasson, Robert, 208
Watts, Vanessa, 148
wealth disparities, climate impacts and, 146
Weil, Simone, 69
Weller, Francis, 118, 128, 132
Whanganui River, personhood status to, 200
White River, 24
White River National Forest, 232–233
Whitehead, Alfred North, 97
white-rot fungus, 102
Whyte, Kyle Powys, 171–172
Wilber, Ken, 213
Wild Edge of Sorrow (Weller), 132
wild mountain rose, 40–41, 43–44
wild mountain rose tincture, 44, 53
wild orchids, 198
wildflower season, as teacher of open awareness, 113–114
Williams, Terry Tempest, 232
window of tolerance, 47
Winnemem Wintu peoples, 149–150
winter, as ultimate nonduality, 277
Wittbecker, Alan, 93–94
Work That Recommends (Macy), 131
worlding, 186–187

yes
  author finding her, 50–51
  capacity to find your, 65–66
  getting in touch with your, 73
Yunkaporta, Tyson, 204

About the Author

Lindsay Branham, PhD, is an environmental psychologist, Emmy-nominated film director, and eco-doula exploring embodied and erotic ecology. For two decades, she has directed collaborative film-based interventions to improve human rights and ecological crises. She holds a PhD in psychology from the University of Cambridge and has been featured by *The New York Times*, BBC, CNN, and National Geographic. She is a regular columnist for *The Aspen Times*. She lives in Los Angeles, California, and Colorado. For more, visit lindsaybranham.com.